Women and Work in Indonesia

This book examines the meaning of work for women in contemporary Indonesia. In focusing on women's life experiences, we assume a broad definition for the word 'work', including not only those activities that bring in income but also home duties, child care, healing and civic work that fulfils obligations for maintaining social and community networks. This in turn impels interrogation of assumptions about economic activity, remunerable activity, divisions of labour, state and other formal definitions of work, and ultimately about the public and private spheres. The contributions to this book discuss women's work in a range of different settings, both rural and urban, and in different locations in Sumatra, Lombok, Java, Sulawesi and Kalimantan, and in Singapore and Malaysia. A wide range of types of employment are considered, including agricultural and domestic labour, industrial work, and new forms of work in the tertiary sector such as media and tourism, demonstrating how capitalism, globalization and local culture together produce gendered patterns of work with particular statuses and identities.

Michele Ford chairs the Department of Indonesian Studies at the University of Sydney, Australia, where she teaches Indonesian language and Asian Studies. Her research focuses on the Indonesian labour movement, labour migration in Southeast Asia, and women and work.

Lyn Parker is Associate Professor in Asian Studies at the University of Western Australia. She teaches Asian Studies and Anthropology, Indonesian and Women's Studies. Her main research interests are gender relations in Indonesia and Asia, the anthropology of women and the nation-state, education and health.

Asian Studies Association of Australia
Women in Asia series

Mukkuvar Women
Gender, hegemony and capitalist transformation in a South Indian fishing community
Kalpana Ram

A World of Difference
Islam and gender hierarchy in Turkey
Julie Marcus

Purity and Communal Boundaries
Women and social change in a Bangladeshi village
Santi Rozario

Madonnas and Martyrs
Militarism and violence in the Philippines
Anne-Marie Hilsdon

Masters and Managers
A study of gender relations in urban Java
Norma Sullivan

Matriliny and Modernity
Sexual politics and social change in rural Malaysia
Maila Stivens

Intimate Knowledge
Women and their health in north-east Thailand
Andrea Whittaker

Women in Asia
Tradition, modernity and globalisation
Louise Edwards and Mina Roces (eds)

Violence against Women in Asian Societies
Gender inequality and technologies of violence
Lenore Manderson and Linda Rae Bennett (eds)

Women's Employment in Japan
The experience of part-time workers
Kaye Broadbent

Chinese Women Living and Working
Anne McLaren (ed.)

Abortion, Sin and the State in Thailand
Andrea Whittaker

Sexual Violence and the Law in Japan
Catherine Burns

Women's Movement in Postcolonial Indonesia
Gender and nation in a new democracy
Elizabeth Martyn

Women, Islam and Modernity
Single women, sexuality and reproductive health in contemporary Indonesia
Linda Rae Bennett

Women and Labour Organizing in Asia
Diversity, autonomy and activism
Kaye Broadbent and Michele Ford (eds)

Women and Work in Indonesia
Michele Ford and Lyn Parker (eds)

Women and Work in Indonesia

Edited by Michele Ford and Lyn Parker

Routledge
Taylor & Francis Group

LONDON AND NEW YORK

First published 2008
by Routledge
2 Park Square, Milton Park, Abingdon, Oxon OX14 4RN

Simultaneously published in the USA and Canada
by Routledge
270 Madison Ave, New York, NY 10016

*Routledge is an imprint of the Taylor & Francis Group,
an informa business*

Transferred to Digital Printing 2009

Typeset in Times New Roman
by Jayvee, Trivandrum, India

British Library Cataloguing in Publication Data
A catalogue record for this book is available
from the British Library

Library of Congress Cataloging in Publication Data
Women and work in Indonesia / edited by Michele Ford and Lyn Parker.
p. cm.—(ASAA women in Asia series)
Includes bibliographical references and index.
ISBN 978–0–415–40288–0 (hardback : alk. paper)—ISBN
978–0–203–93236–0 (ebook) 1. Women—Employment—Indonesia.
2. Women—Indonesia—Social conditions. I. Ford, Michele. II. Parker, Lyn.
HD6194.W66 2008
331.409598—dc22
2007030653

ISBN10: 0–415–40288–3 (hbk)
ISBN10: 0–415–54640–0 (pbk)
ISBN10: 0–203–93236–6 (ebk)

ISBN13: 978–0–415–40288–0 (hbk)
ISBN13: 978–0–415–54640–9 (pbk)
ISBN13: 978–0–203–93236–0 (ebk)

Contents

Contributors

Simone Alesich completed her PhD in the Department of Anthropology, Research School of Pacific and Asian Studies, at the Australian National University in 2006. Her thesis considered how ideas of development are expressed through health and childbirth practice in Indonesia. She conducted a year of fieldwork in 2004, in two villages in Southeast Sulawesi, examining the interaction of an Australian maternal and child health project with rural communities, and its impact on rural health and childbirth practice. Her research built on her Honours thesis, which examined the impact of Australian aid in rural Indonesia in the context of a water and sanitation project in Lombok. Her research interests include development, aid projects, medical anthropology, gender, politics and Southeast Asia (particularly Indonesia).

Linda Rae Bennett is a medical anthropologist whose key research interests include reproductive and sexual health and human rights among youth and different Muslim populations in Southeast Asia and Australia. She is a VicHealth Public Health Research Fellow at the Australian Research Centre in Sex Health and Society at LaTrobe University. At present her research is focused on how sexuality and gender shape, and are shaped by, young women's participation in paid employment and Islamic education both in Indonesia and Australia. Dr Bennett's most recent books are *Women, Islam and Modernity* (Routledge, 2005), and *Violence against Women in Asian Societies* (Routledge, 2003, co-edited with L. Manderson).

Evelyn Blackwood is Associate Professor in Anthropology and Women's Studies at Purdue University, USA. She has published a number of works in areas ranging from Native American female two-spirits, *tomboys* in Indonesia, gender and power, matrilineal kinship and theories of sexualities. She wrote a monograph on the Minangkabau of West Sumatra entitled *Webs of Power: Women, Kin and Community in a Sumatran Village* (Rowman and Littlefield, 2000). She co-edited the award-winning book *Female Desires: Same-sex Relations and Transgender Practices across Cultures* (Columbia University Press, 1999, with Saskia Wieringa) and *Women's Sexualities and Masculinities in a Globalizing Asia* (Palgrave Macmillan, 2007, with Saskia Wieringa and Abha Bhaiya).

Gaynor Dawson received her doctorate in Women's Studies and Asian Studies from Murdoch University, Western Australia. Her fieldwork on women's work in a transmigration settlement was undertaken in Riau, Sumatra. Her doctorate followed a Masters degree in Asian Studies which analysed development policy and planning for women in the transmigration programme. Currently she works as a gender and community development consultant on international aid projects. She has worked mainly in Indonesia and also in Timor Leste, India, Vietnam, Laos and Cambodia. Her publications include a monograph *Development Planning for Women in the Indonesian Transmigration Program* (Monash University Press, 1992) and 'The History of Women's Participation in the Economy' (with Carol Warren) in the *International Encyclopedia of Women's Studies* (Routledge, 2001).

Michele Ford chairs the Department of Indonesian Studies at the University of Sydney, where she coordinates the Indonesian language programme and teaches about social activism and human rights in Southeast Asia. Her research is focused on the Indonesian labour movement, labour NGOs, labour migration, women and work, and transnationalism. She has published on these topics in a range of journals including *Asian Journal of Women's Studies*, *Signs*, *Review of Indonesian and Malayan Affairs* and *International Migration*, and is editor, with Kaye Broadbent, of *Women and Labour Organizing in Asia: Diversity, autonomy and activism* (Routledge, 2007).

Nurul Ilmi Idrus is a lecturer in the Department of Anthropology, Faculty of Social and Political Sciences and the Graduate Program of Hasanuddin University, South Sulawesi, Indonesia. Her research interests and major publications are on gender, sexuality, marriage, women's rights, violence against women, and Bugis *adat* (custom) in South Sulawesi. Her recent research has focused on lesbians in South Sulawesi and Bugis migrant workers. Among her publications are 'Behind the Notion of *Siala*: Marriage, *Adat* and Islam among the Bugis in South Sulawesi', *Intersections: Gender, History & Culture in the Asian Context* (Vol. 10, August 2004), and '"It's the Matter of One's Feeling": Gender, Desire and Sexuality among Female Same-Sex Relations in Globalised South Sulawesi, Indonesia', *Antropologi Indonesia* (No. 30, Vol. 1, 2006).

Kuntala Lahiri-Dutt is a Fellow in the Research School of Pacific and Asian Studies, the Australian National University. Kuntala's publications on the gendered impacts of mining have reformulated conceptions of the relationship between extractive industry, gender equity, poverty alleviation and 'community development'. One such work, *Pit Women and Others: Women Miners in Developing Countries* (jointly edited with Martha Macintyre), was published in 2006 by Ashgate. Kuntala has worked with mine-displaced indigenous people in Jharkhand (India) in an Oral Testimony Project in 2002, and has organised International Workshops and Roundtables on gender issues in mining. She has also been an active participant in the gender mainstreaming processes in the extractive industries sector and a member of the Steering Committee of Gender Water Alliance. Kuntala is the Chief Investigator of an Australian Research Council funded Linkage project 'Creating Empowered Communities: Gender and Sustainable Development in a Coal Mining Region in Indonesia'. She is the editor of *Fluid Bonds: Views on Gender and Water* (Kolkata: Stree, 2006), the author of *In Search of a Homeland: McCluskiegunge and the Anglo-Indians* (Calcutta: Minerva, 1990) and co-editor of *Water First: Issues and Challenges for Nations and Communities* (forthcoming in late 2007 from SAGE).

Lenore Lyons is Director of the Centre for Asia-Pacific Social Transformation Studies (CAPSTRANS) at the University of Wollongong, Australia. She has recently completed an ARC Discovery project with Michele Ford on transnational encounters between Singaporeans and people living in Insular Riau. Lenore is currently working on an ARC funded project on migrant worker activism in Singapore and Malaysia, and an ARC Linkage Grant on skilled migrant women in NSWA. She has published widely on the women's movement in Singapore, trans/national activism in support of migrant domestic workers, and cross-cultural feminist methodology. Her most recent book is *A State of Ambivalence: The Feminist Movement in Singapore* (Brill Academic Publishers, 2004).

Pam Nilan is an Associate Professor in Sociology at the University of Newcastle, Australia. She is co-author of *Global Youth? Hybrid identities, plural worlds* (Routledge, 2006), and has just finished writing a book on Australian youth. Her research interests are youth, popular culture, gender and education in Indonesia and Fiji. She has published widely in journals, including recent articles in *Review of Indonesian and Malaysian Affairs* (2003 and 2004) and the *International Review of Education* (2003), and in edited books such as *Medi@sia* (Oxford University Press, forthcoming), *Internationalising Education: Critical Explorations of Pedagogy and Policy* (University of Hong Kong and Springer Press, 2004) and *Globalization, Culture and Inequality in Asia* (Trans Pacific Press, 2003).

Lyn Parker is an Associate Professor and former Head of Asian Studies at the University of Western Australia in Perth. She teaches Asian Studies and Anthropology, Indonesian and Women's Studies. She is an anthropologist and has conducted fieldwork intermittently over 20 years in Indonesia, mainly in Bali. Her main research interests are gender relations in Indonesia and Asia generally, the anthropology of women and the nation-state, education and health. She wrote *From Subjects to Citizens: A Balinese Village Within the Indonesian Nation-State* (NIAS, 2003) and edited *The Agency of Women in Asia* (Marshall Cavendish, 2005). She has published articles in journals such as *Journal of the Royal Anthropological Institute* (formerly *Man*), *Women's Studies International Forum* and *Asian Studies Review*, and chapters in edited books such as *Borders of Being: State, Fertility and Sexuality in Asia and the Pacific* (edited by Margaret Jolly and Kalpana Ram, University of Michigan Press, 2001). Recently she co-edited a special issue of the journal *Antropologi Indonesia* on Bali and she was guest editor of the electronic journal *Intersections: Gender, History & Culture in the Asian Context* for a special issue on 'Indonesian Women: Histories and Life Stories' (2004).

Kathryn Robinson is a Senior Fellow in Anthropology, Research School of Pacific and Asian Studies, the Australian National University. Her main research interests are in Indonesia and Southeast Asia, development, gender and medical anthropology. She has published *Stepchildren of Progress: The Political Economy of Development in an Indonesian Mining Town* (State University of New York Press, 1986) and co-edited *Women in Indonesia: Gender Equity and Development* (with Sharon Bessell; ISEAS, 2002), *Youth, Gender and Sexuality in Indonesia* (with Iwu Utomo; Special Issue of *Review of Indonesian and Malaysian Affairs*, 2002) and *Living Through Histories: Culture, History and Social Life in South Sulawesi* (with Mukhlis Paeni; Anthropology, ANU in collaboration with the Indonesian National Archives, 1998). In addition she has contributed papers to a wide variety of journals and edited books and worked as a consultant with organizations such as AusAID and the Asian Development Bank.

Prahastiwi Utari holds a Masters degree in Communications from the University of Indonesia, and a PhD from the University of Newcastle, Australia. She is a lecturer in Communications at Sebelas Maret University in Solo, Central Java, Indonesia. Her research interests are journalism practice and learning, and women in media industries. She has published *Media and Communications Work in Indonesia: Transformations and Challenges* (in J. Burgess and J. Connell [eds] *Globalisation and Work in Asia*, Oxford: Chandos Publishing, 2007; with Pam Nilan) and 'The Lucky Few: Female Graduates of Communication Studies in the Indonesian Media Industry' (*Asia-Pacific Media Educator*, Issue 15, pp. 63–80 with Pam Nilan). She is currently working on a project with Pam Nilan on young people's school to work transitions in Central Java.

Rossi von der Borch was appointed to Flinders University in 2007 after completing a doctoral thesis on the relationships between Indonesian migrant domestic workers and expatriate employers in Singapore, where she resided from 2000 to 2006. Her interest in labour migration has grown from her experience living and working among refugees in the late 1980s, when she was employed by the Bangkok-based Jesuit Refugee Service Asia-Pacific. Her current research is on the sexual identities of migrant domestic workers in Singapore and the politics of commensality in households employing migrant domestic workers.

Nicolaas Warouw teaches in the Department of Anthropology and the Graduate Programme of Cultural and Media Studies at Gadjah Mada University, Indonesia. He is also deputy of the university's Centre of Southeast Asian Studies. His interest in labour issues began in the early 1990s as a student activist involved in organizing work and living amongst the industrial workers in central and western Java. His research interests include modernity and modern identity, the problems of industrialization and globalization, and new social movements. His publications include 'Community-based Agencies as the Entrepreneur's Instruments of Control in Post-Soeharto Indonesia' (*Asia Pacific Business Review*, 12(2), 2006).

Series Editor's Foreword

The contributions of women to the social, political and economic transformations occurring in the Asian region are legion. Women have served as leaders of nations, communities, workplaces, activist groups and families. Asian women have joined with others to participate in fomenting change at micro and macro levels. They have been both agents and targets of national and international interventions in social policy. In the performance of these myriad roles, women have forged new and modern gendered identities that are recognisably global and local. Their experiences are rich, diverse and instructive. The books in this series testify to the central role women play in creating the new Asia and recreating Asian womanhood. Moreover, these books reveal the resilience and inventiveness of women around the Asian region in the face of entrenched and evolving patriarchal social norms.

Scholars publishing in this series demonstrate a commitment to promoting the productive conversation between Women's Studies and Asian Studies. The need to understand the diversity of experiences of femininity and womanhood around the world increases inexorably as globalisation proceeds apace. Lessons from the experiences of Asian women present us with fresh opportunities for building new possibilities for women's progress the world over.

The Asian Studies Association of Australia (ASAA) sponsors this publication series as part of its on-going commitment to promoting knowledge about women in Asia. In particular, the ASAA women's caucus provides the intellectual vigour and enthusiasm that maintains the Women in Asia Series (WIAS). The aim of the series, since its inception in 1992, is to promote knowledge about women in Asia to both the academic and general audiences. To this end, WIAS books draw on a wide range of disciplines including anthropology, sociology, political science, cultural studies and history. The series could not function without the generous professional advice provided by many anonymous readers. Moreover, the wise counsel provided by Peter Sowden at Routledge is invaluable. WIAS, its authors and the ASAA are very grateful to these people for their expert work.

Louise Edwards (University of Technology Sydney)
Series Editor

Introduction

Thinking about Indonesian women and work

Michele Ford and Lyn Parker

Women and Work in Indonesia is an edited collection of papers that aims to examine the meaning of work for women in contemporary Indonesia. The chapters interrogate some of the formerly clear-cut divisions that even the rhetoric of advanced capitalism is now questioning: the splits between work and life, work and family, between paid work and housework, paid work and child care, and between production and reproduction. In focusing on women's life experiences, we assume a broad meaning for the word 'work', including not only those activities that bring in income but also home duties, child care, healing and civic work that fulfils obligations for maintaining social and community networks. This in turn impels interrogation of assumptions about economic activity, remunerable activity, divisions of labour, state and other formal definitions of work, and ultimately about the public and private spheres. The book thus seeks to make a significant contribution both to empirical studies of the lived experience and meaning of women's work in Indonesia and to feminist thinking about women's work in the non-Western world.

Work as economics

Dichotomies between paid and unpaid work and between work and other aspects of life are largely unchallenged in the scholarship about women's work in Southeast Asia. In this body of literature, 'work' largely remains the province of economists and political scientists. Neo-classical economics is based on the assumption that rational, economic 'man', *homo economicus*, maximizes his own interest. The question of what constitutes rationality in this model is highly contested: does non-market decision-making – based, for instance, on perceptions of morality or social acceptability – constitute irrational behaviour? The presumption that *homo economicus* makes his decisions based on the urge to maximize individual self-interest reveals not only a utilitarian philosophy but also a secular and particular worldview. Although feminist economics has made great ground in the last 20 years, particularly through critical development studies – by scholars such as Agarwal (1997), Beneriá (2001), Jackson and Pearson (1998) and Sen (2001) – and in publications such as the journal *Feminist Economics*, conventional conceptions of work continue to thrive untroubled by the postmodern turn or by profound gender analysis. For instance, neo-classical feminist economists, who concentrate on female participation in the workforce, the wage gap and occupational segregation, leave unexamined the assumption that participation in the paid workforce is the route to emancipation and empowerment for women (Barker 2005: 2192). Their attention to the otherwise invisible women in the workforce; the recognition of women's reproductive labour (such as housework); and discrimination regarding wages and conditions is well-intentioned and, to an extent, effective. However, it does not interrogate the fundamental assumptions which underpin mainstream economic studies of work.

To anthropologists and others who study non-Western cultures, the economist's world-view seems ethnocentric and, as the basis of a major social theory, to lack explanatory power.[1] Descriptive economics, even gender disaggregated, is of limited use because it leaves the concepts and analytical tools, and therefore the structures and the power relations of our objects of study, intact. As many feminists have noted in relation to the ways language constructs gender, classifications create and naturalize difference. There is very little deconstruction of received categories in economics, almost no discourse analysis and an almost total absence of self-reflexivity. Of all the social sciences, economics seems to have been the most impervious to the postmodern turn of the last quarter-century (Beneriá 2001, vol. I: xiii). Standpoint theory, positionality, attention to muted voices – these are all foreign lands to conventional analyses of work. Even where well-intentioned economists include gender as a variable, the resulting statistics usually fail to consider 'how gender is symbolized and produced', contributing to 'the belief that differences between men and women are essential, universal and ahistorical' (Cosgrove 2003: 91). The challenge for feminist scholars is then to acknowledge gender difference yet not to essentialize and eternalize it.[2]

'Rational choice' theory has continued to prevail in political science as well as economics, but anthropologists and other social scientists have tended towards more culturally sensitive frameworks, shifting through the decades from structural functional approaches, through structural analyses and culture theory to post-structural and practice theory. The current paradigm, which stresses attention to the discursive formation of practising subjects, is indeed a long way from mainstream neo-liberal economics. However, while the postmodern approach has contributed much to the study of identity politics, the inter-relationships between knowledge and power and to intersections of race/ethnicity and gender, it has in many cases de-emphasized the material aspects of life. In Indonesia and many developing countries (not to mention pockets within the 'First World'), survival and the provision of basic needs are still the main concern of many women.[3] This is where feminist concern with the experience of female subjects – particularly marginalized or subordinated female subjects – can correct a tendency for neglect. We argue that there is a need to re-examine understandings of work in Indonesia – the work of production, but also the work of domesticity, of social reproduction and care – in light of these kinds of feminist scholarship.

Many feminist ethnographic studies have shown that, in practice, resources are allocated differentially within communities and within households and families according to differentiated obligations and interests. These allocations and strategies are not necessarily 'rational' in the sense of being obviously instrumental in maximizing the well-being of the individual. Sometimes they are communal or collective decisions taken in order to maximize group or social status or to comply with notions of social acceptability. Sometimes they are 'moral' decisions, based on gender ideologies of what makes a good woman or man, on positions within the family and extended family, on world-views associated with large social stratificatory systems such as caste hierarchies, on relationships based on patron–client ties, or on concepts of reciprocity. When we come to study real women working in Indonesia, we come to understand that we are dealing with single women, daughters, mothers and wives who are not free to make market-based decisions about what will provide the most income or best career for them as individuals. Rather, they make choices about work – or sometimes have their decisions made for them – and in the process they constitute their own identities as full, gendered human beings: as good mothers, capable wives, virtuous daughters or reputable, marriageable young women. We would argue, then, that 'work' decisions always occur within cultural domains, such that economic decisions and work practices are inseparable from other ideological and symbolic systems, the material demands of living and the multiple everyday roles that women play.

Feminist analyses of work

As noted earlier, feminist scholars have made a significant contribution to the documentation of women's work in an effort to make women's work 'count' – and be counted – in countries like Indonesia. Ester Boserup's landmark work, *Women's Role in Economic Development* (1970), was the first to examine how development differently affected women and men, and prompted a wide-ranging and abundant literature, and prolific development/aid practice, known as the women in development (WID) approach. This body of work assumed that women were marginalized by their unequal access to development-derived, new sources of employment and economic growth in the modern sector. Purpose-built, WID-inspired development programmes aimed to help integrate women into the development process and into the labour force, through better education and training. Through the 1980s, the WID approach was largely superseded by the gender and development (GAD) approach, which better recognized that 'woman' was part of the social construction of gender systems. Despite this, to this day the term 'gender' is often taken to mean 'women', such that terms like 'gender studies', 'gender-sensitive' and 'gender mainstreaming' often mean making women the topic, or including women as a category, rather than actually making the relations between men and women, or the complexity of gendered differentials, clear.

Much of the work done under the umbrella of WID and GAD has been on the feminization of the international labour force under policies of export production by multinational corporations. Scholars have concluded that 'female labor has been crucial for labor intensive and export-oriented industries in developing countries and very significant for economic development (at least in many cases)' (Benería

2001: xvii). However they have disagreed in answering questions about the benefit of the feminization of the labour force for women workers. Some of the most interesting work done on women's work in Indonesia has been a contribution in this field. Scholars such as Robinson and Wolf have shown that variations not only pertain by country but also by segmentation of and within industries (such as mining – see Robinson 1988, also Lahiri-Dutt and Robinson ch. 6 of this volume), and indeed within households (Wolf 1992). Wolf, in her important study of 'factory daughters' in rural Java, is one of a number of feminist fieldworkers who have challenged conventional understandings of the household as a homogeneous unit of production and consumption (see also Blackwood ch. 1 of this volume). Meanwhile, scholars such as Agarwal (1997) and Kabeer (1998) have made a real contribution to empirical knowledge of the on-the-ground practice of household economics. In fact, this has been one of the most fruitful areas of feminist intervention in economics. Several chapters in this collection develop this line of research, notably Dawson's analysis of transmigration households in Riau (ch. 2) and Blackwood's chapter on Minangkabau farmers (ch. 1).

An important contribution from recent feminist scholarship – mainly from postmodern scholarship but also from the GAD literature – is the realization that we must explore the instability and potentials of 'women' as a category. Some feminists have resisted the insistent call to deconstruct the idea of 'woman', seeing in this move a threat to the classic feminist agenda of opposing patriarchy. In this line of thinking, if there is no single, common or universal cause, what can be the rationale and the agenda for feminism? However, postmodernists have successfully argued that diverse female positions and identities mean that female interests and agendas must also be diverse, and indeed, that women may simultaneously be positioned within several different discourses and social systems (e.g. Mohanty 2003). This theorizing of female diversity precludes the presumption of perpetual female subordination, and of universal and eternal patriarchy. Its anti-essentialism also militates against the automatic feminizing of any subaltern grouping, without denying the probability of female disadvantage within most social systems. For instance, using a postmodern feminist approach it would not be tenable to characterize a wealthy, powerful, minority Chinese Indonesian identity as masculine vis-à-vis the poor, helpless, feminine *pribumi* – 'native' Indonesian – nor vice versa, except in particular cases where the gender of individuals was relevant.

While it is now commonplace to assert that gender intersects with cleavages and interests of class, religion, and race/ethnicity (e.g. Bottomley *et al.* 1991) or with disciplines and other highly abstract notions (e.g. the electronic journal *Intersections: Gender, History and Culture in the Asian Context*), it seems difficult to get beyond this assertion other than by way of description of particular cases. Sometimes gender interests are internally contradictory, such as when middle-class and wealthy women employ poor women as domestic workers in exploitative conditions (see von der Borch ch. 10 of this volume). Sometimes the powerlessness of female gender reinforces ethnic/race subordination, but wealthy women exploit poor women, acting in class interest against their own gender. What can we say about these intersections, apart from pointing them out in their specificity? Are any patterns discernible? Are comparisons possible? Are there any lessons to be drawn? In Blackwood's chapter, the category of rural Minangkabau 'women' is divided not by ethnicity but by class and kinship. Likewise, it is class and national-ity – not simply gender – that determine the experiences of the Indonesian foreign domestic workers in Singapore about whom von der Borch writes in her contribu-tion (ch. 10).

Another feature of feminist scholarship on women's work has been its generally inclusive approach to women's reproductive work. (A possible exception is some early Marxist feminist scholarship which saw that, under capitalism and the capi-talist division of labour, women were always identified with the subordinate in the classic dualisms of paid versus unpaid, productive versus reproductive, waged labour versus domestic labour.) In conventional economics, and in much work done in labour studies, women's work in domestic maintenance (for example, housework, cooking and washing, supply of household resources such as firewood and water), family reproduction and caring labour (for example, childbearing, child care, kin maintenance and care of the elderly, disabled and sick), and community development (for example, maintenance of neighbourhood networks and commu-nal labour) has been consistently neglected, if not denigrated. It is almost as if, 'Over time, the household came to be seen as a site of consumption rather than pro-duction, and the activities performed in the household, what we now call reproduc-tive labor, were classified as economically unproductive' (Folbre 1991 cited in Barker 2005: 2197). When these tasks become paid work, they remain feminized, and therefore poorly regarded and poorly recompensed (Barker 2005: 2199). Again we see the feminist challenge: on the one hand, we seek to attend to, if not valorize, this work, and on the other, to change the role that this labour, especially domestic labour, plays in creating and maintaining women's subordinate status. The latter could involve redefining such tasks so that they are not seen as 'women's work' – for instance, having men share responsibility for the cooking and associated shop-ping, or not automatically assuming that 'mother' will attend to all the family birth-days or community ritual occasions. Another approach is to commodify women's reproductive and care work, in the belief that attaching an economic value to it will raise its status and hence public appreciation.[4]

A feminist analysis of work requires more than the 'add women and stir' recipe, more than just enhancing the visibility of women's work and more than simply the disaggregation of data by gender (although even that is missing in most statistics on Indonesia).[5] We would argue that an adequate feminist understanding of women's work requires a much more holistic approach than that taken by economists or political scientists – one that entails understanding of the nature of the individual, of social relations and of relationships of unequal power in any given cultural and historical context; understanding of intra-household relations and cultural scripts of gender roles and norms; sensitivity to the ways gender intersects with other iden-tities and ideologies; knowledge of nation-state ideologies, media discourses, as well as international discourses of development and globalization; understanding of the ideological construction of the division of labour, of remuneration for labour and of working conditions. More broadly still, we consider that a feminist understanding of women's work involves the deconstruction of many binary analytical tools such as formal and informal employment, production and reproduction, production and consumption, and the public and private domains.

Barker advocates what she calls an 'interpretive approach' to women's work; an approach that aims to illuminate the relationship between the conceptual (ideological and symbolic) aspects of gender and the empirical (matters such as relative access to and control of resources), though these are not necessarily separated in practice. For instance, there is no sense collecting statistical data on female participation in the workforce if women do not count their work as maids or traders as 'work'. (This is particularly relevant in Indonesia, as several of the chapters in this collection point out, e.g. Idrus ch. 8 of this volume.) We contend that work cannot be meaningfully measured if we do not first understand how work is constituted and defined by the people answering the census or survey questions. Barker's interpretive approach is based on the assumption that 'analyses of identity and representation, knowledge and power, and authenticity and culture are crucial to understanding economic and political structures' (2005: 2193). We have adopted this approach in our book, because we believe that 'the material and discursive are not radically separate' (Barker 2005: 2194). Scholars such as Escobar (1994) and Bergeron (2004) have shown that economic and social processes such as 'development' are constituted through discourse. They require not only top-down government policy but also a public discourse that naturalizes and valorizes 'development', makes subjects compliant and induces them to work productively towards development goals. Similarly, an understanding of women's work in the domestic sphere must be cognizant of the subtle constructions of gender that can mean, for instance, that a husband's absence from home can actually decrease a wife's workload (Dawson ch. 2 of this volume). As Alesich observes in her study of labour around birthing (ch. 3 of this volume), hegemonic norms of the gendered division of labour mean that, while women are expected to substitute for men when men are sick, men are not expected to do women's work when women are incapacitated.

Women and work in Southeast Asia

As well as contributing to the theory and ethnography of women and work in Indonesia, this study has an explicitly feminist objective. It aims to shift the discourse on women and work in Southeast Asia from the study of discursive effects on women to the study of experience and meaning. Many of the studies of women's work in other countries of the region – studies of women as factory workers, domestic workers and sex workers – suggest that women are relegated to the lowest-paid, most exploited and most marginal positions within these rapidly modernizing economies. Our intention in making this shift is to avoid assumptions of victimization that often underlie studies of women as workers, and the silencing of women as human beings that seems to accompany this discourse.

A focus on experience forces the voices of women to be heard – voices that describe the satisfactions and empowerment of 'work' just as often as its frustrations and difficulties. Attention to the meaning of work for women draws attention to the everyday complexity of working in particular cultural environments. For instance, women working in a hotel in Lombok are not gender-neutral workers: their identity as hotel workers is inseparable from a discourse that constructs hotels as places of illicit sexual activity and a gendered double standard that turns a blind eye to extra-marital sex for men while condemning such relationships for women (Bennett ch. 4 of this volume). If women hotel workers want to maintain a respectable self-image they have to devise strategies to dispel that aura of immorality. Thus, attention to the meaning and experience of work forces the researcher to attend to the ways women exert agency. This is evidenced in Ford and Lyon's study (ch. 9 of this volume) of how some sex workers in the Riau Islands succeed in using their commercial interactions with foreign men as a basis not only on which to move out of sex work, but also to alter their class position. These women achieve this by deploying the resources provided by their cultural environment. It is important to note that 'culture produces and enables agency, as well as, in the more conventional mode, constrains agency' (Parker 2005: 218).

At the same time, however, we seek to avoid painting an overly rosy picture of women's experiences of work. There is now a significant body of literature on gender relations, and particularly on the contribution and status of women, in Southeast Asia. Until recently, this literature propounded an image of Southeast Asian women as relatively autonomous beings, certainly less subject to male power than their sisters in South and East Asia. Claims for the relative autonomy and high status of women in Southeast Asia, and especially in Indonesia, have focused on the economic activity of women; their operation in the public sphere; and the absence of the strict gender segregation commonly found in the Muslim countries of the Middle East and South Asia. Historians such as Reid (1988, 1989) and anthropologists such as Firth (1966) traced women's comparatively high status in Southeast Asia to pre-existing local religious and cultural systems – animistic and ancestor-worshipping traditions, *adat* (customs, traditions) that valorized cooperation, reciprocity and sharing, bilateral and even matrilineal kinship systems, and systems of social hierarchy based on criteria such as precedence, age and class. In this body of literature, female rulers, female soldiers and female traders were presented as evidence of women's real power and independence in the public sphere historically, and women's economic activity, dominance of markets and responsibility for household economic management as evidence of their economic autonomy.

Over the last two decades, these claims have been subject to scrutiny and ever more sophisticated analysis. Recent studies have examined the historical and academic conditions behind the production of the image of the autonomous, economically independent Southeast Asian woman (e.g. Stivens 1992 for Malay women; Ong and Peletz 1995 for Southeast Asia generally). For Indonesia, amazingly, these claims have rarely been examined from the point of view of women's work and the meaning of that work, both to the women involved and to their families, communities and nation-state. A few scholars have argued, using Anderson's seminal work on local understandings of power in Java (1972), that precisely because work and 'doing' is low status compared with 'being' and ruling, working women have little status or power (e.g. Djajadiningrat-Nieuwenhuis 1987). The New Order

regime of President Soeharto (1966–98) had a particular ideology of gender relations, with women as submissive, docile appendages of their husbands (e.g. see
Suryakusuma 1996). This state ideology fits this rather monolithic and static view
of Javanese culture like a glove. One could also take the more pessimistic radical
feminist view of patriarchy: that if women do the work, automatically the status of
the work is low.

More recently, scholars such as Brenner (1998) and Bain (2005) have suggested
ways to work 'against the grain' of this earlier work. Following such suggestions,
and in order to evaluate these claims, we focus on the meaning and status of
women's work for the women themselves, taking the experience of women as the
starting-point. The chapters in this collection do not historically deconstruct the
image of 'the autonomous Southeast Asian woman', nor do they trace its evolution
in academia. We have, however, attempted to elicit studies of a wide range of types
of employment over the last three decades in Indonesia – agricultural labour
(Blackwood ch.1; Dawson ch. 2) as well as industrial work (Warouw ch. 5; Lahiri-
Dutt and Robinson ch. 6) and some of the new forms of work in the tertiary sector
such as in the media and tourism (as described in the papers by Nilan and Utari ch.
7 and by Bennett ch. 4), alongside commodified forms of intimacy, household and
reproductive labour (Alesich ch. 3, Ford and Lyons ch. 9, Idrus ch. 8, von der Borch
ch. 10) in rural and in urban areas, and in different locations throughout Indonesia
and beyond – in an effort to examine how capitalism, globalization and local
culture together produce gendered patterns of work with particular statuses and
identities.

Women and work in Indonesia

When we come to look at the meaning of work for women in Indonesia, we need to
examine not only economic structures, but also how gender ideologies of the
nation-state, organized religion and the community shape public perceptions of
women as workers. Our aim here is to examine how cultural notions of gender –
religious sensibilities, *adat* and ethnic identities – inform, constrain and enable
women's work. How do state policies and programmes intervene in women's
working lives? How does working help Indonesian women construct their selves?
How does working define Indonesian women within the family and community?
How are the worlds of home and work articulated? Does women's work straddle,
separate or conflate the public and private domains, if we can talk of such?

In Indonesia, concepts drawn from Western industrialized contexts converge
with state, cultural and religious discourses about gender roles to exclude not only
reproductive labour, but also a significant proportion of economic activity, from
official and popular definitions of 'work'. As Indonesia became integrated into the
modern global system of capitalism, it absorbed the assumptions about public and
private spheres, and about the gap between productive and reproductive work, that
have prevailed in the West. Western concepts of work developed at a time when a
large proportion of the labour force was employed in formal sector occupations,
and where sharp divisions had emerged (at least in theory) between work and

leisure and between productive and reproductive tasks. These divisions make little sense in countries like Indonesia, where even after an extended period of rapid industrialization only 30–40 per cent of working men and 20–30 per cent of working women are employed in waged or salaried positions – and over half of all working women and over 40 per cent of working men are in the informal sector. As Pinches (1987) has argued, in relation to the Philippines, they also ignore the fluid boundaries between formal and informal kinds of work, as circular rural–urban migrants and the urban poor slip in and out of formal sector employment.

Yet while many Western societies are now being forced to re-evaluate these distinctions – as patterns of employment change; as the boundaries between work and leisure become blurred; and as reproductive tasks become increasingly commodified – narrow definitions of work continue to dominate discussions about the Indonesian labour market. This failure to recognize the full breadth of economic activity affects both men and women, but leaves women particularly vulnerable because of the way their productive and reproductive labour is framed by the state, organized religion and local cultures. According to official statistics, in 2005 almost half of all employed women continued to work in agriculture, while a quarter were involved in trade. A further 14 per cent were categorized as being employed in services (Depnakertrans 2005). However, of a total working-age female population of over 77 million in 2004, only 43 per cent were considered to be 'employed', while another 39 per cent 'kept house' (*mengurus rumah tangga*) (Depnakertrans 2004).

One of the main reasons women are under-represented in the labour statistics is because women's status as workers is subordinated to their status as housewives. The utterly non-feminist Indonesian state has long acknowledged that women have both productive and reproductive roles to play, as suggested by the term '*peran ganda*', or double role, adopted by the New Order government to prescribe women's proper function in society. This role is described extensively in Blackwood's chapter (ch. 1) in this volume, and alluded to in many of the other contributions. A Department of Information publication entitled 'The Women of Indonesia' explains the New Order's official development ideology as follows:

> [D]evelopment requires the maximum participation of men and women in all fields. Therefore women have the same rights, responsibilities, and opportunities as men to fully participate in all development activities. [But] the role of women does not mitigate their role in fostering a happy family in general and guiding the young generation in particular, in the development of the Indonesian people in all aspects of life.
>
> (Murdiati *et al.* 1987: vii, quoted in Wright 1997: 8)

However, as this statement demonstrates, the New Order saw women's primary duty as being to their husband and children rather than to their (income-earning) work. As a result, women working in a whole range of occupations – from teaching to trading – have focused on their identity as wives and mothers rather than on their status as workers. In particular, economic activities conducted in and around the domestic domain became invisible. This collection both explores the implications of this construction of female identity and challenges it by showing not only how work feeds into the self-perceptions of women employed in the formal sector, but also its importance for women who may not derive their primary identity from their income-earning activities.

Although the gender discourse of the New Order has been shifted from centre stage since the fall of Suharto, many of the assumptions about women and work that prevailed during that time remain strong. Some of the chapters in this book address the question of the meaning and valuing of women's 'traditional' work, whether that be agricultural labour, domestic work or other kinds of reproductive labour, both during and after the New Order period. These forms of work are often not counted as work in conventional economic studies, and correspond to state constructions of female identity and responsibility. Several chapters in this volume challenge state constructions of women as 'only' mothers and housewives, and demonstrate how women accommodate their 'real' work and externally imposed constructions of ideal women. Meanwhile, Blackwood's chapter on Minangkabau rice farmers in West Sumatra (ch. 1), for example, shows how during the New Order women thought of themselves as farmers and negotiated new definitions of 'housewife'. Their mobilization of kinship and village relations confuses conventional categories such as wage labour and the domestic sphere. One of the themes of these chapters is that the separation of productive and reproductive labour is not meaningful. Where responsibility for maintaining the family and allocating household resources rests with women, a gendered division between the domestic reproductive and public productive spheres is untenable, as argued in Dawson's chapter on women's work in transmigrant communities in Riau (ch. 2).

At the same time that many forms of women's labour became invisible, other forms of work traditionally undertaken by women as part of their familial and community obligations became commodified. These 'new' forms of 'old' work are important sites of contestation between local cultural systems and the market economy, which challenge boundaries between the public and private spheres. The third chapter in this collection juxtaposes new and traditional forms of the work of midwives. The delivery of babies and care of new mothers has traditionally been the preserve of senior mothers, but trained midwives are increasingly employed now in Indonesia, transforming this ancient female domain. Alesich shows how the 'new' and the 'old' have come to recognize their differences in effectiveness and source of authority along the way, such that now in Southeast Sulawesi there are parallel midwifery services. Her chapter argues that the shift in personnel has wrought other dramatic changes in the gendered division of labour in healing and in relationships between the midwife and the community. Another sphere in which 'traditional' women's work associated with housework and cultural values of hospitality and community has been transformed into waged work is tourism. Bennett's chapter addresses the ways tourism impacts upon young women and how young women make use of the opportunities it offers. In her study of young women who work in hotels along the beaches of west Lombok (ch. 4), she contrasts the romantic appeal of working in the international tourism industry with the reality of life for young women as they search for marriage partners, manage child care, and seek to maintain respectability with regard to local cultural and religious norms. In particular, Bennett attends to how women working in such occupations attempt to conform to dominant gender ideals and traditional roles, and negotiate the often difficult terrains of respectability and acceptable social status jeopardized by perceptions of the sexual impropriety of their work.

Although women are still widely represented as 'housewives', over the last four decades there has been a dramatic shift in women's employment in Indonesia towards waged work. This shift has brought very different ways of working for women (Ford 2003; K. Sen 1998). This is nowhere more evident than in the extensive development of light manufacturing industries from the mid-1980s, which brought many rural and urban women into waged employment for the first time (Manning 1998: 254). As demonstrated by Warouw's contribution (ch. 5) about young women from rural areas who work in the factories of Tangerang, near Jakarta, industrial work brings dramatic shifts in the life experience of these young Indonesian women. Warouw argues that young factory women experience the regimentation of factory work as an entry-point to modernity which represents hopes for a better life rather than an end in itself. Factory work provides these young women with the financial certainty to sustain their urban existence and with the self-respect and dignity that enables them to construct a modern, urban identity, and separates them from their rural past.

As Warouw's article also attests, women's readiness to work 'outside the home' is strongly affected by local culture. In Tangerang, local women rarely choose to work in the heavily feminized factories in their neighbourhood, which are instead staffed by rural migrants. This supports Manning's (1998: 240) findings that historically poor provinces with a traditionally high level of female labour market participation maintained those levels throughout the New Order period (1966–98). The historically low participation rates of Sundanese and Betawi women in non-domestic work are reflected in the low contemporary female labour participation rates in the Greater Jakarta area, despite the strong presence of female-dominated export-oriented industries in that region.

Women have also found employment in traditionally male-dominated areas. Chapters 6 and 7, by Lahiri-Dutt and Robinson and Nilan and Utari respectively, show the significance of gender transgression in the workplace to the women who work in coal mining and the media industry respectively. In turn this highlights the underlying structural strength of the gendered division of labour. Chapter 6 focuses on the issue of menstruation leave, an allowance payable to many women workers in Indonesia as a gender right. Through this lens, the authors explore how the differences between the formal and informal sectors feed into constructions of femininity, and the tensions between gender 'equality' and 'difference' in feminist practice. Chapter 7, by Nilan and Utari, deals with another highly masculinized work sphere, the Indonesian media. Despite high numbers of female graduates in media studies, this new and burgeoning industry is dominated by men. The authors find reasons for this male domination, at least partly, in understandings of gender. This chapter focuses on how work is constructed 'male' or 'female', a theme that runs through several other chapters as well. For instance there is a common perception that most kinds of media work are too tough for women. But gender constructions of work include not only the working conditions of those in the industry but also the expectations about division of labour at home: the expectation that media work involves irregular hours, and often night work, conflicts with expectations that women will be at home with their families at night. These chapters raise another issue that is implicit throughout much of this book – the role of organized religion, particularly Islam, in Indonesian constructions of women's work. Nilan and Utari analyse the impact of the Islamic construction of *kodrat wanita*, or biological destiny of women, noting that even professional middle-class women are challenged by the expectations of the media industry. In contrast, Lahiri-Dutt and Robinson contextualize Muslim concerns about women's health and moral wellbeing in international debates around the protection of women workers.

The final three chapters deal with two forms of women's work that present perhaps the greatest challenge to cultural, religious and state expectations about women's work: sex work and overseas labour migration. Idrus' chapter on Bugis women who seek their fortune in Malaysia (ch. 8) clearly forefronts the importance of religion in shaping women's experiences abroad. Idrus writes about the ways in which women negotiate religious and cultural restrictions in order to maintain their honour while working overseas, specifically by broadening the concept of *muhrim* (close male relatives with whom a Muslim woman may travel) to permit them to leave with female family members or others in the community. She also discusses how women's expectations of finding a marriage partner overseas provide an important measure of their success. Ford and Lyons (ch. 9) describe the very different path to foreign marriage travelled by some sex workers in the Riau Islands, which are located on Indonesia's border with Singapore and Peninsular Malaysia. Their chapter argues that sex work in the transnational space of the borderlands offers some migrant women a chance to develop their social capital and access a lower middle-class lifestyle that has very little in common with their experiences in their home villages. The Indonesian domestic workers in Singapore described by von der Borch (ch. 10) also have very different migration experiences from Idrus' undocumented labour migrants, who leave from Sulawesi to trade or work in Malaysian factories and homes. However, all three chapters tell stories of personal transformation achieved through labour migration. Like Idrus, von der Borch describes the fundamental change in the sense of self of women migrants as a result of their time abroad, which leaves them 'straddling different worlds'. Her chapter, the final contribution in this volume, examines the complex constellation of losses and gains foreign domestic workers experience as they shift between home and the country in which they work, concluding that, overall, women are enriched not only financially, but personally, by their experience.

Conclusion

This book is the first systematic attempt to analyse the claims for the relative autonomy and high status of women in Indonesia in terms of their work and economic activity. While it is premature to make a definitive assessment, there is enough material in this collection to call such claims into question in the contemporary era. The compromises, strategic negotiations and frustrations women experience as they try to satisfy social and religious constructions of ideal womanhood – while feeding their families and finding self-fulfilment in work – show that the idea of women working is still contested in Indonesia. Indeed many of the case studies suggest that status still accrues to those women who do not work in the public sphere or whose work can be constructed as being close to the domestic sphere (e.g. Lahiri-Dutt and Robinson ch. 6; Nilan and Utami ch. 7; Idrus ch. 8). Similarly, following Barker (2005), the chapters show how the ideological and symbolic aspects of gender constitute interpretations, and indeed the definition of 'work'. They show that it is meaningless to count female participation in the workforce if we do not first attend to what kinds of 'work' count.

The idea that there are class inflections in the idea of women working is nothing new. However, the continuing strength of the gender ideologies that place women in the home, as carers of husbands and children, is perhaps surprising. In rural settings, such as the Minangkabau highlands and the transmigration settlements of Riau, women's work remains disguised by wifely duties. Likewise, the image of the working woman in some modern, formal workplaces, such as those associated with the media industry, is one of radical transgression rather than positive autonomy. Women who move long distances for work are even more suspect: migrant factory workers and domestic workers – and especially sex workers – have little if any place in national imaginings of who women are and the work they should do.

This does not imply, however, that work is not important to Indonesian women. The chapters in this volume suggest that women in Indonesia are generally proud of their achievements in providing for their families and see much meaning and value in their work. Sometimes the content of the work (as in the Tangerang factories) is of little moment to women workers, but symbolically it can be very meaningful – in that case, as a means of providing the wherewithal to 'become modern'. Similarly, those women who work in 'male' jobs seem to derive immense satisfaction not only from the content of the work (driving big machines, travelling all around the country in search of a good story) but also in overcoming the stereotypes of women as weak and 'at home'.

Most importantly, as this collection demonstrates, a meaningful study of women's work cannot be made in isolation. Overwhelmingly the chapters in this volume show how work and family, work and life, are inextricably meshed. Women's working lives – as farmers, traders, journalists, hotel workers, truck drivers, midwives, factory workers, domestic workers and sex workers – are shaped by their everyday lives as members of families and communities. The 'rationality' that underpins their decisions about work is not dictated by economic considerations nor, indeed, by state ideology. It is a product of the entirety of their lived experience, and of their aspirations for themselves and for those close to them.

Notes

1 Duncan and Edwards (1997) provide a useful critique of the assumption of the 'rational economic man'. Their critique is applied in a Western setting to the economic decision-making of lone mothers, suggesting that the charge of ethnocentrism could be extended to nuclear-familism and sexism.
2 Barker (2005) describes this as a contradiction, but we disagree.
3 We acknowledge the many problems associated with terms such as 'the West' and 'First World'. The reduction of large numbers of heterogeneous societies into homogeneous and essentialized masses is indeed problematic, not least because of the eradication of difference, geographical confusion and the encouragement to create static binary oppositions which are too easily stratified into superordinate and subordinate. However, such terms also have their utility as shorthand that can highlight commonalities, such as ideological position, economic disparity and asymmetrical power relations.
4 For instance, breastfeeding is a significant sex/gender-based activity that marks women's labour as different from men's. Feminist economists have calculated the empirical costs (and benefits) of breastfeeding – not only in terms of labour costs but also in terms of opportunity cost to lactating working women, and the class and race/ethnic dimensions of this (e.g. Galtry 1997).
5 For example, the main government institution for producing national statistics, Badan Pusat Statistik (BPS), has produced a leaflet of macrostatistics for Indonesia in which there is no gender breakdown, but in which national macro-indicators are provided by province. See http://www.bps.go.id/leaflet/leaflet-sep-05-ind.pdf (accessed 9 January 2005). The website for BPS includes statistics on employment in which the population is divided by age (under or over 15 years) and educational attainment, but not by gender. See http://www.bps.go.id/sector/employ/index.html (accessed 9 January 2005). For more on gender mainstreaming in the statistical representation of women in Indonesia see Surbakti (2002).

References

Agarwal, B. (1997) '"Bargaining" and gender relations: within and beyond the household', *Feminist Economics*, 3 (1): 653–64.

Anderson, B. R. O'G. (1972) 'The idea of power in Javanese culture', in C. Holt (ed.) *Culture and Politics in Indonesia*, Ithaca, NY: Cornell University Press.

Bain, L. (2005) 'Women's agency in contemporary Indonesian theatre', in L. Parker (ed.) *The Agency of Women in Asia*, Singapore: Marshall Cavendish Academic.

Barker, D. K. (2005) 'Beyond women and economics: rereading "women's work"', *Signs: Journal of Women in Culture and Society*, 30 (4): 2190–209.

Benería, L. (2001) 'Introduction', in L. Benería and S. Bisnath (eds) *Gender and Development: theoretical, empirical and practical approaches*, vol. 1, Cheltenham, UK: Edward Elgar Publishing Ltd.

Bergeron, S. (2004) *Fragments of Development: nation, gender and the space of modernity*, Ann Arbor: University of Michigan Press.

Boserup, E. (1970) *Women's Role in Economic Development*, New York: St Martin's Press.

Bottomley, G., Lepervanche, M. and Martin, J. (eds) (1991) *Intersexions: gender, class, culture, ethnicity*, Sydney: Allen and Unwin.

Brenner, S. (1998) *The Domestication of Desire: women, wealth, and modernity in Java*, Princeton, NJ: Princeton University Press.

Cosgrove, L. (2003) 'Feminism, postmodernism, and psychological research', *Hypatia*, 18 (3): 85–104.

Depnakertrans (Departemen Ketenagakerjaan dan Transmigrasi) (2004) 'Penduduk berumur 15 tahun ke atas menurut kegiatan dan jenis kelamin, tahun 2004'. Online: http://www.nakertrans.go.id/pusdatinnaker/BPS/PUK/puk_kegiatan_jekel_2004.php (accessed 26 August 2006).

——(2005) 'Penduduk yang bekerja menurut lapangan pekerjaan utama dan jenis kelamin, tahun 2005'. Online: http://www.nakertrans.go.id/pusdatinnaker/BPS/Bekerja/bekerja_lapkerutama_jekel_2005.php (accessed 11 August 2006).

Djajadiningrat-Nieuwenhuis, M. (1987) 'Ibuism and Priyayization: path to power?', in E. Locher-Scholten and A. Niehof (eds) *Indonesian Women in Focus*, Dordrecht: KITLV, Foris Publications.

Duncan, S. and Edwards, R. (1997) 'Lone mothers and paid work – rational economic man or gendered moral rationalities?', *Feminist Economics*, 3 (2): 29–61.

Escobar, A. (1994) *Encountering Development: The Making and Unmaking of the Third World*, Princeton, NJ: Princeton University Press.

Firth, R. (1966) *Housekeeping among Malay Peasants*, London: University of London and Athlone Press.

Ford, M. (2003) 'Beyond the *Femina* fantasy: the working-class woman in Indonesian discourses of women's work', *Review of Indonesian and Malaysian Affairs*, 37 (2): 83–113.

Galtry, J. (1997) 'Suckling and silence in the USA: the costs and benefits of breastfeeding', *Feminist Economics*, 3 (3): 1–24.

Jackson, C. and Pearson, R. (eds) (1998) *Feminist Visions of Development: gender analysis and policy*, London: Routledge.

Kabeer, N. (1998) 'Jumping to conclusions? Struggles over meaning and method in the study of household economics', in C. Jackson and R. Pearson (eds) *Feminist Visions of Development: gender, analysis and policy*, London: Routledge.

Manning, C. (1998) *Indonesian Labour in Transition: an East Asian story?*, Cambridge: Cambridge University Press.

Mohanty, C. T. (2003) '"Under Western Eyes" revisited: feminist solidarity through anti-capitalist struggles', *Signs: Journal of Women in Culture and Society*, 28 (2): 499–535.

Ong, A. and Peletz, M. (eds) (1995) *Bewitching Women, Pious Men: gender and body politics in Southeast Asia*, Berkeley: University of California Press.

Parker, L. (2005) 'Conclusion', in L. Parker (ed.) *The Agency of Women in Asia*, Singapore: Marshall Cavendish Academic.

Pinches, M. (1987) ' "All that we have is our muscle and sweat": the rise of wage labour in a Manila squatter community', in M. Pinches and S. Lakha (eds) *Wage Labour and Social Change: the proletariat in Asia and the Pacific*, Clayton, Vic.: Centre for Southeast Asian Studies, Monash University.

Reid, A. (1988) and (1989) *Southeast Asia in the Age of Commerce, 1450–1680*, vols 1 and 2, New Haven, CT: Yale University Press.

Robinson, K. (1988) 'What kind of freedom is cutting your hair?', in G. Chandler, N. Sullivan and J. Branson (eds) *Development and Displacement: women in Southeast Asia*, Monash Papers on Southeast Asia No. 18, Clayton, Vic.: Centre of Southeast Asian Studies, Monash University.

Sen, A. (2001) [1983] 'Economics and the family', *Asian Development Review*, 1 (2): 14–26, reprinted in L. Beneriá and S. Bisnath (eds) *Gender and Development: theoretical, empirical and practical approaches*, vol. 1, Cheltenham, UK: Edward Elgar Publishing Ltd.

Sen, K. (1998) 'Indonesian women at work: reframing the subject', in K. Sen and M. Stivens (eds) *Gender and Power in Affluent Asia*, London and New York: Routledge.

Stivens, M. (1992) 'Perspectives in gender: problems on writing about women in Malaysia', in J. S. Kahn and F. Loh (eds) *Fragmented Vision: culture and politics in contemporary Malaysia*, Sydney: Allen and Unwin.

Surbakti, S. (2002) 'Gender mainstreaming and sex-disaggregated data', in K. Robinson and S. Bessell (eds) *Women in Indonesia: gender, equity and development*, Singapore: Institute of Southeast Asian Studies.

Suryakusuma, J. (1996) 'The state and sexuality in New Order Indonesia', in L. J. Seares (ed.) *Fantasizing the Feminine in Indonesia*, Durham, NC and London: Duke University Press.

Wolf, D. L. (1992) *Factory Daughters: gender, household dynamics, and rural industrialization in Java*, Berkeley: University of California Press.

Wright, J. (1997) *In Their Own Words: working women of Yogyakarta*, Clayton, Vic.: Monash Asia Institute.

1 Not your average housewife

Minangkabau women rice farmers in West Sumatra

Evelyn Blackwood

Farming and farm labour are contested domains for women in Indonesia. In state assessments of labour, women landowners are frequently subsumed under the category of housewife. When women perform farm labour, they are usually considered to be part of 'family labour', or an extra hand in the field, due to state assumptions about families and 'nuclear' households. State representations of women as mothers encourage them to direct their labour toward their husbands and children; other work, even farming, is considered secondary. The women-in-development literature tends to represent Indonesian women farm labourers as poor, down-trodden workers in need of liberation from their wearying toil. West Sumatra is an area where women participate in a wide range of labour relations, including farming one's own land, agricultural wage labour, collective labour and sharecropping. By examining women's farm work and, more broadly, their labour practices, in West Sumatra, this chapter explores the contestations over the definition of women's 'work', asking how women's 'farm work' in West Sumatra is both integrated into and resists notions of 'work'.

Defining women and work

A brief analysis of the way women's work is understood in Indonesia reveals a number of inconsistencies. Labour force statistics and studies show increasing numbers of women in the industrial labour force and a displacement of women from agricultural labour (Robinson 2000). But these statistics tend to exclude paid work that is seasonal, home-based or domestic-oriented, such as sewing, cooking and cleaning, thereby ignoring large numbers of women engaged in money-making activities in their homes (Sullivan 1994). During Suharto's New Order era, 'work' came to be seen as something done outside the house (and by men), leading many married women to describe themselves as housewives, despite being engaged in a range of income-producing activities (Blackwood 2000; Sullivan 1994). Sen notes that during the early New Order, state officials claimed that only men 'work', despite the fact that women have always worked to support their families, either by providing for subsistence needs or producing income (Sen 1998; see also Brenner 1998). Consequently, the range of women's income-producing activities in

Indonesia is under-represented (Sullivan 1994). The definition of 'work' as paid labour outside the home excludes not only some of women's income-producing activities but any productive and reproductive activities oriented to subsistence needs.

Within the development literature, Indonesia's women workers were synonymous with working-class women, the under-paid, highly exploited factory workers and maids of global development (Sen 1998). These women were viewed primarily as victims, the reasons for their labour charged to neglectful or absent husbands or to poverty. The suggestion by even some feminist scholars that women work because of material dictates, although intended to show the difficulties women face in earning a sufficient income, helped to solidify a view that women as paid workers are primarily victims of economic conditions rather than historical agents shaping their productive labour (see, for example, Papanek and Schwede 1988; Wolf 2000).

Many of the problems associated with women and work in Indonesia arise from state constructions of the domestic domain. The New Order state represented the ideal woman as a mother devoted to her husband and her children, as a number of feminist scholars have attested (for example, Robinson 1998; Tiwon 1996). During this period most of the attention given to women's issues by the state centred on women's 'domestic' role in child care, nutrition and health. The New Order insistence that women's primary duty was to husband and children marked women as domestic denizens first, workers second. 'Work' for women was redefined as non-essential, only something to be taken up in time of need, while the more important duties were their domestic responsibilities, which were broadly defined as non-productive. Work done by 'housewives' within the realm of family and home disappeared into a newly defined domestic domain, making productive labour and a domestic domain mutually exclusive. For instance, Weix (2000) suggests that elite women's entrepreneurial practices in Java are hidden from view because they are home-based. Further, the association of the term 'housewife' with middle-class status, which was encouraged by the state, led women engaged in home-based income-earning to deny that they worked (Blackwood 2000; Sullivan 1994). This redefinition of work as something separate from households gave rise to a sharp distinction between housewives and working women.

Although women are still popularly represented as 'housewives first' in Indonesia, Sen (1998) argues that a new 'working woman' is replacing the housewife as the paradigmatic female subject. This working woman, however, is not a labourer but a professional woman, *wanita karier*, exemplified by affluent middle-class women who work in professional, white-collar jobs as teachers, civil servants, managers and administrators (see Brenner 1998; Nilan and Utari ch. 7 of this volume). According to Sen (1998), the Indonesian state is promoting the professional woman as a new symbol of Indonesia's modernity. With the new visibility of the career woman, Robinson (2000) suggests that women's work is fracturing into professional and proletarian classes, the proletariat represented by the growing numbers of women in Indonesia's industrial labour force – in clothing, footwear, textile and electronics factories – and by women wage labourers in agriculture. The division between professional and proletariat establishes important class distinctions for women's work but it too creates a binary distinction that tends to conceal the complexities of women's work, particularly in reference to women's farm work.

Much of the literature on women's farm work comes from peasant studies, which, as Stivens (1994, 1996) has pointed out, ignores women and considers the farm household, like other households, to be a black box. Not only was the head of household assumed to be a man, he was synonymous with farmer. Women have been invisible in peasant households, their labour categorized as unpaid 'family labour' and therefore not counted or examined (see also Saptari 2000b). Even the category 'peasant' helps to disguise the multiple forms of productive labour and income-earning activities in which most farm households engage (Stivens 1994). Use of the term 'peasant' has come under increasing criticism because of its association with a homogeneous form of supposedly 'traditional' production in which 'peasants' control their own means of production and produce for themselves (see Kearney 1996). Kearney argues that the category 'peasant' has essentially disappeared in this global era. I prefer to use the term 'farmer' or 'farm household' to avoid the assumptions associated with the term 'peasant' and to allow room for thinking about the multiple relations that are present in Minangkabau households studied here (see also Hart 1992).

Several studies focused on Indonesian and Malaysian farm women have been instrumental in furthering analysis of women's farm labour, associated landholding rights, and the conditions of labour for poor women farmers.[1] I expand on those analyses to examine the complex 'work' relations among women within one village in West Sumatra. Women in rural agricultural areas are not just 'wage labourers': they often occupy multiple positions, for instance working simultaneously as labourer, sharecropper and owner. Because this 'work' does not fit neatly within categories of paid or unpaid labour, professional or proletariat, I use the Marxist-inflected term 'production relations' to represent the multiple, intersecting and dynamic relations that occur in farm work. Three aspects of women's farm work are discussed: first, the intersections of landowning, sharecropping and wage labour for individual women; second, the tensions between well-off farmers, sharecroppers and workers; third, women's views of farming and householding in light of the Indonesian state's models of women as housewives and career women. This chapter examines the way women's productive activities converge with household, kin and labour relations to make categories of home and work, owner and labourer problematic. It brings into view not just individual women landholders and their decision-making processes but also inter-relations among wealthy women farmers, medium- and small-landholders, and those women farmers without land. As farmers, these women complicate any simple boundaries between working woman and housewife, or professional and proletariat.

History and setting in West Sumatra

The Minangkabau of West Sumatra are citizens of a post-colonial state that since the late 1960s has consistently emphasized 'development' based upon integration into the world capitalist economy. To hasten its progress toward this goal, the state formulated an ideology of modernization aimed at creating a citizenry in step with the 'modern' world. At the same time it instituted a concerted drive toward agricultural development. However, the penetration of capitalism has not resulted in a peasant proletariat dispossessed of their land and living off wage labour. Numerous case studies reveal the continued presence of smallholder farming and sharecropping in Southeast Asia (e.g. Bray 1983; Hart *et al.* 1989). In West Sumatra, despite the transition to double-cropping and the use of new technologies, smallholders and sharecroppers continue to dominate the landscape. The adoption of Green Revolution technologies by most farmers has meant that farming ancestral rice fields continues to be a viable economic strategy.

Since 1965, agricultural development has transformed the way the land is worked. Most farmers have switched to high-yielding varieties of rice that they sell as a cash crop to local rice millers. In the early 1980s, walk-behind motor-driven tractors became available for ploughing. Large equipment such as the combine harvester has not been adopted because rice plots are divided by bunds, making access to the fields nearly impossible for large machinery.[2] Rice farmers in the central highland district of Lima Puluh Kota produce many tons of rice for regional and international markets every year. The technological requirements of the new strains of rice make access to cash essential to farming. Although farmers now produce two crops per year, with a resulting increase in income, cash requirements have increased the difficulties of farming for smallholders. Several women complained to me that now they have to pay for everything, the seed, the fertilizer and all the labour, whereas under the old system, they did not need cash for farming. Cash requirements mean that many more farmers operate on a credit basis than in the past, borrowing cash from rice merchants at the beginning of the growing season to pay for seed and fertilizer, as well as labour, and repaying the loan at harvest by selling the harvested *padi* (unhusked rice) directly to the lender.

Rural Minangkabau villagers participate in and are shaped by the strategies and technologies of agricultural development and global capitalism. As such, they typify many rural communities in Indonesia, yet at the same time they contain intriguing contrasts. While kinship in Southeast Asia tends to be bilateral (cognatic) or patrilineal (Hüsken and Kemp 1991), the Minangkabau are one of the few ethnic groups that practise matrilineal kinship. In Minangkabau villages, matrilineal practices form the basis of social, land and labour relations. Women landholders dominate the landscape as heads of households, which are built around matrilineal ties, and holders of ancestral land.[3] They actively farm their own lands (with the help of husbands, if they are also farmers) and comprise most of the labour for tasks such as planting, weeding and harvesting, while men prepare the rice fields for planting and assist with harvesting. The changes in technology have meant that more men are involved at harvest-time cutting and threshing than in the past, a trend common throughout Southeast Asia (Hart 1986; Robinson 2000; Wolf 2000), but the expected displacement of women from farming due to the switch in technologies is inconsistent at best in West Sumatra, where women continue to work in (and oversee) all phases of rice production.

The following discussion of women farmers is based on research in a rice-producing village in West Sumatra located in a fertile valley between volcanic Mount Sago and the mountains that form a barrier between east and west Sumatra.[4] Taram has a long history as a rice-producing community, a centre of Islam and a stronghold of matrilineal practices (see Blackwood 2000). In 1989, Taram had a population of 6,800; over 75 per cent of all households in Taram were farm households; and the total number of farmers and farm labourers exceeded 85 per cent of the adult population. My research focuses on the 125 households in the hamlet of Tanjung Batang; 106 are farm households, defined as those that depend on income from farming for some or most of their household expenses.[5] Of these households, 83 per cent hold rights to some rice land, either as landholders or through use rights to land owned by kin.[6] Only 17 per cent of farm households in the hamlet are landless, their income deriving primarily from sharecropping or agricultural wage labour.[7] Of the 188 adult women in the hamlet, 72 per cent are involved in farming in a range of capacities, another 14 per cent have businesses that provide their main source of income, and the rest are civil servants, non-agricultural labourers, unemployed or unable to work due to age.[8]

Terms such as proletarian or semi-proletarian do not adequately convey a sense of the economic relations within the village. Proletarianization suggests a linear movement from peasant production, in which peasants own the means of production, to wage labour, in which households have only their labour to sell. Farm households in Tanjung Batang rely on farm income from rice sold on the market, but also draw on additional sources of income, including agricultural and non-agricultural wage labour, civil service, petty trade, sale of petty commodities, and remittances from family members who have migrated to jobs in other areas. Both women and men migrate from the village to find wage labour opportunities elsewhere, but the labour lost to farm households by migration is replaced by labour from landless households.[9] Many individuals migrate on a temporary basis; others return to the village permanently only after they have retired from jobs or careers elsewhere. Nearly one in four daughters (usually elder daughters) temporarily migrated from the village at the time of my research, compared to only 7 per cent of women in the 1920s and 1930s, reflecting the greater availability of jobs for women outside the village than in the past.[10]

Due to differences in access to land among farm households, Taram households evince some variation in wealth. Villagers speak of households as *kaya* (rich), *biasa* (ordinary or common; also *sederhana*, of modest means), or *miskin* (poor). Roughly following these designations, I developed three class divisions to distinguish among the 106 farm households in Taram: well-off (26 per cent), average (32 per cent) and poor (42 per cent). I call the middle group of households 'average' rather than 'middle' class to avoid the common associations with the term 'middle class'. 'Ordinary' is a better translation of the colloquial term '*biasa*' but that term too has certain connotations that speak to people's own ideas about what is normal or acceptable in their community. My choice of the term 'average' is meant simply to signify those in the middle in terms of resources and income. These divisions are based on the amount of rice households produce per harvest;

rice production is a good predictor of how much land they control. The three divisions align with other research on Southeast Asia that suggests that access to land is an important indicator of class status (see Hart 1986; Wolf 1992). In terms of resources and income, poor householders do not control sufficient land to meet subsistence needs; average householders have sufficient land for subsistence needs and daily expenses, including school fees; well-off householders have large land-holdings that produce a profit. The differences across these three classes are not large, particularly when compared to Indonesia's urban upper class (see White 1989), and tend to correlate closely with kinship rank. The kinship ranks are composed of elites (*orang asli*), who are members of the original founding lineages (*suku*); commoners or client kin (*orang datang*), newcomers or outsiders who arrived later and were adopted into the original lineages; and descendants of slaves, who were bought by and became subordinate members of the original lineages (see also Bachtiar 1967: 373).[11] Access to land in connection with lineal rank bears important implications for political and economic relations in the village.

Redefining work in light of women's farm work

In the Minangkabau literature many scholars agree that women control economic production in West Sumatra, by which they usually mean that women manage their rice fields on a day-to-day basis and use the produce for household needs.[12] This economic framing inscribes women's work within a supposed domestic domain; although working in the rice fields is productive activity that creates income, it is seen as activity for the household. Such an interpretation is reinforced by state agricultural planners, educated in the West, who play out the Western binary division between domestic and public domains in their development policies. During the early years of agricultural development, state agricultural officers in West Sumatra worked predominantly with men farmers, who were considered the landowners and household heads, although these men were usually working with their wives on their wives' land or working for their mothers. Extension programmes that assisted farmers in applying new farming techniques were introduced to Minangkabau farmers through meetings between agricultural extension officers and male village elders and religious leaders (*ulama*) (Esmara 1974; see also Dawson ch. 2 of this volume, for the same gender model extended to transmigrant farmers). Programmes geared toward rural women's needs focused solely on women's domestic responsibilities (see Blackwood 1995). Women were not considered farmers in their own right but were seen, incorrectly, as household members who assisted with farm labour.

Feminist critics have long noted that rural women's work combines both productive and reproductive tasks (Deere 1995). In farm households, work and home, domestic and productive tasks cannot easily be separated. In West Sumatra child care and household chores occur alongside agricultural and husbandry tasks, such as husking corn, drying rice, shelling coconuts, collecting eggs, grazing goats or catching fish in the family pond. The product of these activities may be for family use or for sale, depending on the need for cash. Young children may go with their mothers to the rice fields and spend the day there in the shade of a small shelter while their mothers weed or plant rice. All family members provide some form of (unpaid) labour or contribute cash to the household from outside jobs. Even young children run errands. By their teen years, daughters help the family by weeding the rice fields, while adult daughters living at home plant, weed and harvest rice on the family land. Unmarried sons carry bags of fertilizer from home to the field and help with the harvest, usually by carrying the sacks of unhusked rice to the miller and clearing the stalks from harvested fields. They also tend the family cows, chickens and goats, or help in the family garden. If husbands do not have salaried jobs, they are expected to prepare and plough the rice fields and help at harvest time with cutting, threshing and transporting of rice. At other times they find temporary work in construction or building trades. Minangkabau farm households effectively blur any neat divisions of work and home for women and men, while at the same time revealing the multiple income-producing activities of their members.

According to van Reenen (2000), looking at farm production in West Sumatra from the view of the household is problematic (see also Hart 1992) because households are not dependent solely on family members for labour. Yet such a perspective helps to reveal the intersections of kinship groups, located in households, and community. Farm work is not carried out solely by individual women farmers and their families; they rely on additional labour beyond their own households during critical phases in the agricultural cycle. Although it is especially true of large landowners, in Taram even smallholders call on kinswomen and neighbours to provide additional help during planting and harvesting. Women farmers exchange labour so that tasks can be finished more quickly. If one woman takes a week to plant her field, the plants will not ripen all at the same time. With several women working together, the field can be planted in a day, ensuring that the plants will mature at the same time (Syahrizal 1989). Smallholders form exchange groups of between five and seven members who work together from year to year.[13] Exchange groups of women work in each other's rice fields during the growing season without getting paid. As one farmer stated, 'We pay with our bodies.' The story of one farm household demonstrates the intersections of kin and labour relations. Fitriani, a smallholder, manages her rice fields with the assistance of family members and close kin. Fitriani has retired from farming, retaining a supervisory role only. Her daughter Lina works their one plot of rice land with the assistance of one or two other kinswomen. To help with planting and weeding, Lina works on an exchange labour basis with other smallholders. Lina complains that she is very busy because of these exchange arrangements; sometimes her own rice field has to wait while she goes off to help another woman with her planting or weeding. She said they just ask each other, can you do such-and-such tomorrow at my rice field, and if they can (*boleh*), then the next day they go there.

Labour exchange groups extend household- and kin-based productive activities beyond individual households to incorporate women from other households. Through these exchange practices, women farmers create cooperative labour networks. These labour networks, which are based on ties of kinship and friendship, are key to understanding the complex transformations that have occurred in women's farm work in West Sumatra. Hart (1992) demonstrates the importance of women-organized labour gangs in Malaysia in allowing poor women continued access to agricultural labour. In West Sumatra these groups have implications for the average landholders as well. Taking into account these labour groups, I provide an analysis of farm households and women's farm work that incorporates individual households as well as labour relations that extend beyond those households (see also Koning *et al.* 2000).

Women's farm labour and access to land

For rural Minangkabau farmers in Taram, land, its use and its ownership are intimately tied to matrilineal inheritance practices – practices in which land is controlled by and moves from mother to daughters – and to considerations of rank. Elite kin groups and their senior women hold all rights to ancestral land in the village; in this context, elite women are the landowners, not their kinsmen, although major decisions to pawn land cannot be made without the agreement of the kin group.[14] Within this framework of land rights, almost all women farmers, elites and non-elites, have access to some land. It may be their own land or have come through their (elite) husbands or fathers in the form of use rights, or come from a sharecropping arrangement or in pawn from the landowners. Although in the village people speak of those who have rice fields and those who do not, even some of those whose only access to rice fields is through sharecropping or use rights, not permanent rights, do fairly well if the land is large enough. Households that rely solely on

Figure 1 Female farmers planting rice.

Figure 2 Minang farmer measuring the harvest.

Figure 3 Minang farmers planting rice.

sharecropping arrangements for access to land and/or have members who hire out as agricultural labourers comprise only 17 per cent of the total in Taram; 44 per cent of all farm households do some sharecropping and 40 per cent of all farm households engage in some agricultural wage labour (these are overlapping percentages) in addition to farming their own land. Very few have no land and no access to land (5 per cent); these are considered the unfortunate poor, usually newcomers to the village who lack established ties to long-time residents and must depend on agricultural wage labour or other forms of labour to survive.

In the typical sharecropping arrangement, the landholder supplies the seed and pays for half the fertilizer, while the sharecropper handles all other inputs and keeps the owner informed of the progress of the crop. The sharecropper shares the produce with the owner 50/50 (*paduoan*, Minangkabau, meaning to split in half). Sharecroppers are usually husband and wife teams who split the work along customary gender lines. Sharecroppers use the same labour strategies as owner-operators, relying on the assistance of kin, exchanging labour, or paying for additional labourers. On the final day of the harvest, the owner goes to her field to oversee as the sharecropper measures and bags the *padi* for transport to the mill and pays off the labourers. Many sharecroppers are close relatives of the landowner – in some cases daughters, but more likely sons because they do not have rights of inheritance – or they may be kin within the same lineage (*sasuku*) or members of the husband's or father's lineage. Married daughters are usually given land by their mothers as a form of early inheritance; the produce from this land does not have to be split with the mother. If a daughter does have a sharecropping arrangement with her mother, usually in cases in which mother and daughter live separately, she will typically inherit that land from her mother when her mother passes away. A son who is given access to land by his mother is obliged to return half of the harvest to his mother in the same way a sharecropper would. Those landowners who arrange to have close kin sharecrop their land tend to be small or elderly landowners who no longer work their own fields. In some cases landowners find a sharecropper from close neighbours or people who live near the field. Over time, however, even non-kin sharecroppers come to be seen as related (*famili*) to the landowner.

Agricultural development has transformed the types of labour relationships in farm work. Prior to the adoption of the new high-yielding varieties of rice, farmers usually worked their own land or set up a sharecropping arrangement. The switch to high-yielding varieties of rice and the shift from production for use to production for sale on the market was accompanied by an increase in the use of agricultural wage labourers, both women and men, particularly for ploughing, planting and weeding. Sharecropping has continued to be a predominant form of access to land, while other practices, such as exchange labour, are employed to a lesser extent than before. In West Sumatra individually hired labourers (*buruh*) are paid for a day's labour. For transplanting and weeding, women earned Rp. 1,250 a day in 1990 for 6 hours' work.[15] Men were paid Rp. 2,500 a day for ploughing with an animal they provided. The daily wage for transplanting or weeding is less than a subsistence wage – barely enough to meet the basic daily food requirements of the worker and her family.[16] One farmer, who has no land of her own, showed me just how far a day's wages go:

She brought out a small litre can filled with husked rice [*beras*] to show me how much they eat each day. She said she cooks 4 litres of rice a day to feed her family of five, which costs Rp. 800 a day just for rice. That doesn't figure in anything else, such as condiments [*sambal*], shopping or cooking oil. She said it's hard, if you only earn Rp. 1,000 a day, there just isn't enough for anything, and she has two children already in school with their school fees to pay.

(Field notes)

Daily wage work does not cover subsistence for most families. It is a less reliable source of income than sharecropping due to widely fluctuating seasonal demand, potential loss of income due to illness, ceremonial obligations that take time away from work and other problems. The vagaries of agricultural wage work are evidenced in landless households that depend solely on wage labour. These households are poor primarily because wages are simply too low to support a family. Another poor farmer, Yeni, and her family only have access to low-paying wage work and no land of their own from which to build up some income. When I asked Yeni if she had any land, she held out her hand palm up and said, 'This, this is my rice field.' Yeni, who has no children, uses some of her income to help her mother and sisters, who live nearby, so there is never extra money even in her own small household. For Yeni and other poor farmers, the prospect of depending solely on wage labour is not a happy one.

The difference between wage labour and a sharecropping relationship is significant. Whereas sharecropping is the basis for a long-term stable relationship between the landowner and the sharecropper, wage labour cannot guarantee anything past one day's pay. Because agricultural wages are so low, a labourer is hard put to earn a subsistence income. Consequently, wage labour alone is not an adequate replacement for sharecropping rights or smallholding. Rather than hiring out their labour on an individual basis, women have created or joined labour groups that provide more consistent access to work. Contract labour groups (*borongan*) work for a specified number of days doing transplanting or weeding for a set wage that is slightly higher than the wage for day labourers, approximately Rp. 1,500 in 1990. Contract work is arranged between a landowner and a woman who has several other workers whom she can call on to work with her. Some of these groups were originally exchange groups whose members worked in each other's fields but now hire themselves out to work for landowners who are not members of the group. At harvest time these groups cut and thresh the *padi* and are paid in-kind based on how much the group harvests.

A second type of work group, the collective farming group (*kelompok tani*), also developed out of exchange labour groups but in this case arose through the initiative of a state development programme for farmers (Koperasi Unit Desa) during the 1960s. Tanjung Batang boasted a large farm group of 100 women at one time. The farm programme no longer assists in organizing and funding these groups, but smaller farm groups remain in operation. The collective in Tanjung Batang now numbers approximately 30 women who usually work twice a week planting or weeding. Owners who need labourers for planting or weeding contact the group head, who then contacts group members to work the next day. Large landowners, owner/operators and other group members hire the group to work for them. Most of the women in the collective are small landholders or sharecroppers in the village. Members of the group and the head refer to each other as *kawan*, which can be translated as friend or partner, suggesting the equal status of all members of the group and their relationship to each other. Similar to labour gangs in Malaysia (Hart 1992), these groups and the landholders they work for are based on women's social and kin networks and function to diminish class differences among women landowners and labourers.

Women of average households and their farming strategies

While the preceding section looked at farm work from the point of view of the labourer with or without access to land, this section focuses on women landholders of the average class (*biasa*) – those of ordinary means – and the types of farm work in which they engage. These women, who as a group constitute 32 per cent of all households and stand between the well-off and poor households, are involved in complex production activities that cross-cut owner/labourer relations. Much of the literature on 'peasant' villages in Southeast Asia has focused on the growing divide between rich and poor, owners and labourers, particularly in Java, where, according to some figures, an increase in landlessness since 1970 has left a small proportion of households in control of 70 to 80 per cent of all farmland (see Hart 1986; Hart *et al.* 1989; Scott 1985; Wolf 1992). A middle group of average landholders, who work on their own land but also hire out their labour to other landowners, has received very little attention in the literature. Wolf (2000) notes that researchers have yet to fully explore the dynamics between agricultural workers and landowners where family and kin ties intermingle (but see Blackwood 1997), even less so the dynamics of shifting owner/worker relations.

In Taram this block of average women farmers with small to medium landholdings also pawn in land or have use rights to family land, as well as working as sharecroppers and agricultural wage labourers in the collective labour and contract labour groups.[17] For example, one woman farmer, who has no land from her own mother, holds some land in pawn, which gives her full rights to the harvest; she has access to another piece of land through her husband, from which she keeps 100 per cent of the harvest; and she works a third piece of land as a sharecropper, keeping 50 per cent of the harvest. In addition she works as a day labourer with a collective labour group. Most of the 30 or so women in this collective labour group own or have access to small or medium plots of land for rice production, but two are well-off women with large landholdings. The labour networks in which these women participate both as landholders and labourers are based on ties of kinship and friendship that have cemented social relations within the village for years and, as noted earlier, arose out of women's exchange labour practices.

Because of these labour networks, this group of average landholders is able to operate within multiple owner and worker relations. When they work with the farm collective to earn cash planting or weeding other women's rice fields, their status is subordinate to that of the landowner, yet that landowner is often related by ties of kinship or community. A few average landholders have sharecroppers who work their land for them, thereby standing in a superior position to their sharecroppers, while also sharecropping for other women. When they work as sharecroppers, these women hire their own exchange groups to work at planting and harvest time for wages. As landholders, most of these women hire labourers at harvest time, who may be members of the same labour group in which they work. Consequently, on one day a woman farmer may be standing on the side of her rice field overseeing the workers who are planting or harvesting her field, while on another day, she may be knee-deep in mud in someone else's rice field, working alongside the same women who worked for her the day before. Thus, this group of average landholders works the land alternately as landowners and as labourers, blurring the divisions between workers and owners.

This class of average women landholders represents an intriguing phenomenon for farm studies. They are neither simply landholders nor farm labourers, neither owners nor proletariat. Their multiple positions bridge both categories, working to undercut binary divisions of subordinate workers and dominant owners. While it is the case that many of these women and their families are just able to make ends meet with their small landholdings and thus find it necessary to work as labourers as well, this complex multiple positioning is more than simply a survival strategy. For instance, average landholders who work with the collective regard that labour system as a form of savings because they are not paid until harvest. 'Each day worked is like money in the bank', I was told. The lump sum payment at harvest is used for things other than daily expenses, such as purchasing livestock, paying for house repairs, renovations or additions, or hosting lifecycle ceremonies. The willingness of average landholders to cross class lines of owner/worker to take advantage of cash-earning opportunities helps to blur class differences in the village.

The average farmers lessen the divisions between dominant and subordinate, rich and poor, as well as the attendant tensions created by differences in wealth and status. Wolf noted that 'changes caused by the Green Revolution and the New Order have tipped the balance in favour of the rich and the landed' (1992: 49), particularly in Java, but for average landholders in West Sumatra the changes are not so stark. Studies of women's informal and formal networks in Java have shown that inter-household ties work to strengthen women's position in the workplace and household (Saptari 2000a; Weix 2000). In West Sumatra, labour networks allow women to shift between their positions as landholders and labourers to earn sufficient income for their households. These average landholders act as a buffer against the development of a large class of rich landowners and the potentially exploitative labour relations it might create.

Working for the boss woman: wealthy landowners, their workers and sharecroppers

In contrast to the group of average landholders stands another group of landowners who own land but do not work it themselves. Some of these women have other businesses, both farm and non-farm, such as petty trade, food stalls, gardens, buying/selling rice and construction supply stores, while others are retired from farming. All of them supervise the work that is done on their rice fields by working closely with a sharecropper, or hiring and paying for labour and overseeing the harvest. These women have often been confused with 'housewives' (*ibu rumah tangga*) by census agents and often add to the confusion by identifying themselves as such to state officials. As landowners and overseers of their farm land, however, they are farmers, not housewives.

These women constitute a different category of farmer from the average land-holders because they do not engage in farm labour. Women who oversee their fields are found across all categories of households from poor to wealthy. Of interest here, however, are the large landowners (18 per cent of all farm households) in the well-off group, primarily from the elite rank, who do not work their own land.[18] This group has the largest number of workers dependent on them for access to land through sharecropping or wage labour arrangements. Over the course of the agricultural cycle, large landowners employ a considerable number of workers. One woman, who arranged for sharecroppers to manage her fields, had over 30 people working at harvest. They were organized into nine work groups, each group containing anywhere from one to eight people. The workers were primarily women, but included four or five men and older boys who were cutting and threshing, and several teenage girls threshing and winnowing. In addition to those working the harvest, the sharecropper had brought in 20 women for planting, ten women for weeding two times, plus two or three men (including the sharecropper's husband) to plough, fertilize, and fix the canal, and several men to help haul the sacks to the miller. Because the same workers were usually called upon by the sharecropper for different tasks, the total number of individual workers was approximately 35 to 40. This landowner has another large field that is worked by a different sharecropper who employs a completely different set of workers. Thus, with those two fields alone the landowner has approximately 70 to 80 workers who are dependent on her for their income.

Despite the control that large landowners have over their sharecroppers, share-cropping in Taram is not just an agrarian relationship but a relationship embedded in kin ties. For landless or near landless farmers, access to land comes through elite members of lineages (*suku*) to which they belong. The sharecropping relationship, often based on kinship ties or residential proximity, has been described in Southeast Asia in general and Java more particularly as a benevolent or moral relation that advantages small landholding peasants who can claim such ties (Hefner 1990; Hüsken 1989). Jay noted that the Javanese landholder becomes a patron to the sharecropper, giving material aid in emergencies, as well as advice and gifts, in return for labour and social gestures that acknowledge his 'quasi-paternal role and superior rank' (1969: 230). Patron–client ties in Java are similar to elite–client ties in West Sumatra in terms of the perceived advantage and moral obligations of the relationship. The broader social and economic conditions in West Sumatra, however, differ from Java. The elite–client relationship involves landowners and client kin in a wide range of social and ceremonial obligations and duties, situating the client within an idiom of kin relations that surpasses the economic relationship.

One well-off landowner explained the importance of client kin as her sharecroppers in the following way:

> [Client kin] can get rice land if there is an agreement between us. They can work our rice land, but they divide the produce in half with us. It's better if it's our relatives [*kamanakan*] who work our rice land rather than other people, if they're good workers. We're already related [*famili*], we help each other. Client kin help the elite family and that help is returned; it's an exchange of help [*tolong-menolong*].

For this woman and other wealthy landowners, it is better if the person working the land is a client because they have a kin bond (*hubungan famili*) with their elite kin. Of client families in Tanjung Batang who sharecrop (and who identified the landowner), 90 per cent of the landowners were their elite kin. Some client families have sharecropped the same land for their elite kin for more than a generation.

The embeddedness of sharecropper relations in a kinship idiom is evident in the interactions between clients and elites. Even though owners have higher status than their workers, status differences are muted. Terms of address remain the same, dependent on age differences, although sometimes workers joke about the woman landowner being the boss (*tuan*, usually associated with a man). Sharecroppers address the owners in the usual manner based on relative age: a slightly older owner is *kak* (older sister) and a younger one is called by her first name. Muted public acknowledgement does not obviate the fact, however, that sharecropper and workers depend on the owner for their income. The ability to provide access to land to subordinate kin secures the bond between elite women landowners and their client kin. Their control over others' livelihood is a great incentive for loyalty. Not only does elite women's ability to hire workers or sharecroppers give them higher status than those who work for them, it also strengthens their authority and influence over large numbers of families in the village, a situation quite similar to elite Javanese women managing family firms in Weix's (2000) study. Such client kin generally fall in line with the opinions of their superiors and support their decisions, maintaining the political power of senior women and their families within the village.

Back talk and other levelling mechanisms

The complexities of labour and landowner practices found in this village are not without some tensions across rank and class, despite the levelling mechanisms of kin bonds and cross-cutting owner/worker practices. Scott (1985) addresses these tensions primarily as a binary between rich landowners and poor farmers, who find ways to resist the influence of and exploitation by the rich. The tensions in Taram do not coincide neatly with class or rank, as Scott's analysis would suggest, because wealth and influence crisscross class and rank, creating complex dynamics among villagers. Most of the tensions arise between well-off women landowners and those medium- and smallholder women of average means who work their own fields and work as labourers as well. Poor women, who are dependent on all these women for access to land or for day wages, voiced few complaints, partly because they cannot afford to antagonize landholders by seeming ungrateful for the work they are given. Their pragmatic attitude was reflected by one older landless woman, who with her husband, now deceased, raised four sons, and continues to do farm work although she is in her 60s. She said, 'I work in the rice fields or I don't eat. If I have no rice left at home, then I have to work for wages to buy rice.' Her attitude earns the great respect not only of her elite kin but also of her neighbours, who all came to mourn with her and provide her with food when one of her sons suddenly died.

The tensions between well-off and average landholders are never directly voiced but come in the form of 'back talk' (Scott 1985), disparaging comments made about the well-off, that attempts to keep them in line with community values of mutual support (*tolong-menolong*) and generosity. One of the symbols of wealth is 'staying home', that is, not having to work in your own or others' rice fields. 'Staying home' is acceptable for older women who have retired from farming; however, a few women who are well-off and choose to stay home even though they could work in the fields are spoken about with some resentment and envy. One average landholder woman stated it this way: 'I have to search for money continuously (*harus cari uang terus*), while the rich (*orang kaya*) sit around and just wait for the harvest to come in.' The ability to just collect profits while others work hard in the rice fields marks a grating disparity for these women farmers. Their resentment at this disparity is further reflected in comments that some large landowners were short-changing their workers by under-calculating the amount of harvested rice produced. Well-off landowners were also accused at times of being 'ungenerous' or 'stingy' toward their neighbours and client kin and guilty of not helping out sufficiently during life-cycle events or in times of illness. These 'weapons' are not so much acts of resistance, as in Scott's (1985) study, but levelling mechanisms that work to keep wealthy women from acting too proudly or from deviating too far from community norms of mutual help. One of the well-off farmers in fact makes an effort to deflect criticism by winnowing *padi* during harvest along with her women workers, a task that is not as rigorous as cutting or threshing rice but that reflects her desire to be seen as the same as other women.

The tensions in this village occur primarily among women landholders of the average and well-off classes, rather than between the landless and the well-off. Sharecropping arrangements between the landless and well-off work to mute antipathies and provide mutual bonds of loyalty and generosity. The people who are said to be poor are those without any rice fields. Landownership is a marker of rank and status in the village, one which women feel should make them equal to other landholders. The tensions thus reflect the attitudes of a class of women who, as landholders and elite or 'near' elite, feel they should be equal to other landholders, but do not have the same privileges and access to wealth as the well-off.

Contradictory housewives

Minangkabau women farmers contend with state images of womanhood that encourage them to think of themselves primarily as housewives. A number of discourses promoted through education, state programming for women, media, and Islamic fundamentalism create a hegemonic ideology of domesticity for Minangkabau women.[19] The images familiar to rural Minangkabau women in the 1990s underscore the values of domesticity, motherhood and the nuclear family. Rural Minangkabau women understand that in the 'modern' world, staying home and taking care of their children represents the good life and accords with state philosophy about women's position. Even the 1990s professional career woman with her salaried white-collar job is far from the working lives of rural Minangkabau women. These career women are seen as having 'real' jobs, while farm work is viewed as something that only backward women do (see also Idrus ch. 8 of this volume). Consequently, Minangkabau women do not see their work nor its value reflected in national media or state policies. State-sponsored programmes available to women in the village of Taram in 1989 included mother/child health initiatives, inoculations, family planning and diarrhoea control. Mothers were expected to bring their young children to the village nurse for monthly check-ups. The nurse complained to me that mothers who worked in the rice fields did not cooperate. Her words conveyed the predominant attitude that women farmers were backward, uneducated women who needed to become better mothers. Work was seen as interfering in their ability to properly care for their children. Women as farmers have rarely been a focus of state policy-making. Rather, state initiatives to raise women's income centre on teaching women 'modern' (feminine) skills, such as sewing and cooking (Blackwood 1995; Sullivan 1994).

State views of farming as a backward sector in need of modernization have contributed to the negative attitudes toward women farmers. As noted earlier, state agricultural initiatives were directly primarily toward men, who were thought to be the landowners and farmers. The neglect of women farmers meant that men took early advantage of cooperative farm programmes begun in the 1960s. One such programme – *Koperasi Unit Desa* (KUD) – set up in 1967 in Taram, started with 57 members, of whom only one-quarter were women. Of those women who registered with the programme, half were identified as housewives, although they were most likely women who managed their rice fields; only four were listed as farmers. Through their own efforts, women farmers learned of the benefits this programme provided in gaining access to agricultural inputs necessary to sell rice on the market. In the ensuing years, more and more women became involved so that by 1972 nearly as many women as men were registered in the programme; most of the officers of the local KUD branch remained titled men of elite families.

In this context, how do women farmers understand their work? The power of media images and state policies in women's lives sometimes brought surprising (to me) answers to my questions about their work as rural farmers. Women defined 'work' as something that is done for a regular salary, like office work or civil service jobs. When I asked one young unmarried woman what kind of work a recently married man was doing, she said, 'He doesn't have work, he's a farmer.' Women farmers sometimes described their own occupation as 'just farmers' (*petani aja*), the 'just' signifying a negative connotation of farm work as something that is not modern or valued. One woman told me that farming is '*hasil keringat*', the result of sweat (hard labour), not like real jobs that are gained through education. Villagers further distinguished between 'just farmers', who were seen as 'traditional', and respected 'modern farmers', who use advanced agricultural technology or have farm-related businesses, such as rice milling or tractor rental. In this comparison, 'just farmers' only make enough to get by, but 'modern farmers' are educated and smart enough to be successful and make money through the use of Green Revolution technology. However, people in the village used these labels for different purposes. The one woman who by all accounts was recognized as a 'modern' farmer, called herself a plain farmer because she did not want to appear better than others and because she did not like some aspects of modernity. Further, most farmers are in reality 'modern' farmers in the sense that they use high-yielding rice technology and its associated inputs, which are required in order to sell rice on the market. In practice, the term 'modern' distinguishes between poor and average farmers and those farmers who are able to become well-off from farming. All these distinctions reflect the impact of state modernization efforts to 'develop' the farm sector by encouraging farmers to adopt Green Revolution technology.

Given the devaluation of farming in general and women as farmers in particular, along with the emphasis on women's domestic role, it is not surprising that women farmers with adequate to large landholdings declare that they are housewives. In part their assertions reflect a desire to be seen as middle class, which is often associated in Indonesia with a working husband and stay-at-home wife. Many women admire the image of the middle-class housewife found in cosmopolitan magazines and advertisements; her life seems preferable to work in the mud of the rice fields. One of the larger landowners, who works her own fields and sometimes works as a labourer, told me, 'Farming is hard. People don't want to do it any more. You can't get ahead that way.' Another hard-working elite woman said, 'It's a pity if your daughter has to work in the rice fields. It's difficult.' Their dreams for their daughters were that they would find salaried jobs rather than remain in what they conveyed to me was dead-end, low-status work in the rice fields. In fact, many of the daughters of elite women were encouraged to find jobs in urban areas or to join work programmes for overseas factory work, which were seen as good sources of income. At least two elite women went into debt or pawned their rice fields to collect enough money to enrol their daughters in these programmes. While overseeing one's landholdings seemed the ideal for an older generation of elite women, the younger generation imagines their daughters gaining a good education and well-paying job far from the rice fields of home.

Farming remains a contested category of work for women in the village. Despite elite desires for a different future for their daughters, farming is not being abandoned across the board but its meaning and value have shifted over time as education and desires for middle-class status reorient perceptions of village life. At the same time that some say farming is devalued, others acknowledge that if a person works, even as a farmer, it is respected. Owning and farming one's own land is valued because land ownership secures independence and status. The difficulty for women in the era of state modernity and globalization is how to integrate the state category of 'housewife' with their work as farmers. Women farmers of lower rank and poorer households generally identify themselves as farmers without apology or recourse to claims about being housewives. One such woman, who runs a small shop by her house with her husband but also works her own rice fields, said without hesitation that she was a farmer. The issue of whether a woman was a farmer or housewife came up primarily among women of elite rank or well-off non-elite households. Among these women, two who have their own rice fields sharecropped said that they were not farmers but housewives. Another woman said she was not a farmer because she runs a small shop by her house and is busy raising her daughter. However, she also manages rather large landholdings owned by her mother and attends harvests to oversee the work. Some well-off farmers who do not have to do field labour declared that it was more important to stay home and take care of their children (see also Hart 1991). One of these women owns a prosperous rice mill and another is a rice merchant. The rice merchant told me her husband does all the work, but when I pressed her about her business, she revealed that she has a number of clients from whom she buys rice at harvest. Her husband handles the processing and sale of rice at the mill. For these women, farming meant working in the fields, whereas managing those same rice fields meant they could redefine themselves as housewives. By claiming to be housewives, these women were highlighting their middle-class status and aligning themselves with the state ideology of domesticity for women.

Yet claiming the status of housewife was not simply a desire for higher status or a response to a state model. These women maintain their own sense of what a 'housewife' means. Lina, who works on her mother's fields and works for pay in other rice fields, said it was better to be a housewife. But she explained it to me this way, 'Of course you go to your rice fields. But you don't have to leave the house for so long. [You go] to the rice fields in the morning and return home in the afternoon.' Like Lina, several other women included work in their rice fields as part of being a housewife. 'Housewife' for them meant taking care of your children, your family and your rice fields. By incorporating their farm work into their notion of domestic work, these women farmers created a new definition of housewife. Although claiming to be housewives, a move that made their management of and work on their land invisible to the larger society, these women were not the housewives of New Order state ideology.

Conclusion

Indonesian state efforts to domesticate women have clear repercussions for working women, one of which is to reposition women's 'work' outside the household. If 1995 brought the 'Year of the Dual Role' for women (Saptari 2000b: 19), it cemented already established notions that 'work' was something separate from households (see Dawson ch. 2 of this volume). But despite the dominance of the state ideology of femininity and motherhood, it is not hegemonic in creating a particular type of Minangkabau woman. Minangkabau women have 'a multiplicity of feminine identities' (Sears 1996) to choose from and indeed all these representations operate to produce women's understandings of themselves as mothers, farmers and housewives. As Grewal and Kaplan (1994) note, local subjects are not just passive recipients of state and global discourses; each infiltrates the other. Women have not become the housewives and mothers of national fantasy, even when some of them claim to be. Rather than falling subject to state ideology, these women rework the concept of 'housewife' to incorporate their own productive activities into the definition of a modern 'housewife'.

For Minangkabau women farmers, representations of women as housewives or career women do not fit their understandings of themselves. Farm work is intricately woven with household, kin and labour practices, creating women's 'work' that belongs to households and extends beyond them through women's labour networks. Women farmers bridge binary distinctions of professional/ proletariat, owner/worker and housewife/worker through their complex production relations. Farming as work is not a simple category. Wolf notes for Java that 'singular categories (e.g. labourer, farmer, self-employed, informal sector) oversimplify a more complex situation' (1992: 51). Binary categories fall short of explaining the complexities of women's farm work. In Taram women farmers occupy multiple positions as landholders, owner-operators, sharecroppers and agricultural wage labourers, in many cases all at the same time. Average landholders, in particular, shift between owner and labourer, taking advantage of collective wage labour arrangements to increase income. These shifting relationships have helped not only to strengthen women's position on the labour market but also to lessen class differences.

Hegemonic state representations of women and work established by the New Order are clearly part of women's lives in West Sumatra and affect how they think about themselves and the claims they make about their farm work. But these representations are not simply reproduced by women farmers. Instead, women make sense of them in the context of their own labour as rice farmers, creating a new category of 'housewife' who is at once a farmer and a mother. Although the Indonesian state, through its policies and programmes, has fostered narrow definitions of 'work' as wage or salaried labour conducted outside the house and of women's farm work as 'family labour', work as a category of labour should incorporate the much broader range of productive activities and complex relations in which women engage. This discussion of women's farm work demonstrates that women are not always simply victims of poor economic conditions but are actively creating new work practices and labour networks. As they work to sustain their families, kin groups, and communities, Minangkabau women farmers maintain and manage multiple positions that bridge binary distinctions of work and labour.

Notes

1 See, for example, Hart (1986), Peletz (1988, 1996), Stivens (1996), Stivens *et al.* (1994), Wolf (1992).
2 See Hart's (1992) excellent analysis of the transformations in farming in Muda, Malaysia, where state and business interests were more successful in introducing combine harvesters.

3 See Blackwood (1999) for a more detailed discussion of the matrilineal relations of Minangkabau households.

4 I conducted fieldwork in the village of Taram in the easternmost district of the highlands of West Sumatra, Lima Puluh Kota, during the years 1989–1990 and 1996 under the auspices of LIPI, the Indonesian Institute of Sciences. Research and writing were enabled by grants from Stanford University, the East-West Center, the Woodrow Wilson National Fellowship Foundation, Purdue University and the Association for Asian Studies Southeast Asia Council. I use the actual name of the village where I worked, although the names of the hamlets within Taram and of people in the village have been changed to maintain their privacy.

5 Of the remaining households, nine have no income from land. Most of these are petty merchants or shop owners. Ten households in the hamlet were composed of civil service employees and their families. These included teachers at the local elementary school, several nurses and a doctor working at the state health clinic, and a police officer.

6 'Use rights' refer to the temporary right to grow rice on a piece of ancestral rice land. The produce from that crop is usually shared, with half going to the owner. Use rights are generally given only to close kin, in this study by the women landowners to a son or brother. A married son may ask for use rights to his mother's land, which he then passes to his wife for her to work. She keeps half the harvest and returns the rest to her mother-in-law. Use rights are sometimes given to men for the lifetime of their daughters and will be returned to the man's closest living kinswomen in his matrilineage when his daughters die.

7 The high rate of ancestral land ownership in Tanjung Batang is not representative of all hamlets in the village. Probably 50 per cent of all households in Taram lack ancestral rights to land and depend on sharecropping or other strategies to gain access to land. Tanjung Batang has a high percentage of elite and well-off families with land.

8 'Adult women' refers to married or unmarried women no longer in school or older than 18.

9 In 1990, 17 per cent of women and 21 per cent of men migrated in search of economic opportunities.

10 The figure is probably higher than 7 per cent because it relies on people's inclusion of such kin in their genealogies. There was no census available for that time period.

11 Only elites have the right to titles, lineage houses, land and other privileges that set them apart from the other kin ranks.

12 See, for example, Kahn (1980), Kato (1982), Tanner (1971).

13 Men also have exchange groups for ploughing.

14 Ancestral land cannot be sold. It can be pawned to provide cash but is never permanently alienated to someone outside the lineage. When the original landowners pay the pawn price, the person holding the land in pawn must return the land. Conflicts over land ownership, however, do occur when land has been pawned for several generations. If a sublineage dies out, the land is passed to the closest line within the lineage. A very few titled men, who have rights to a plot of land because of their responsibilities to the lineage, have been accused of using that land for their own profit, but these men do so to the detriment of their own sublineage. In addition, the Indonesian state has tried to institute individual land ownership through a programme of land registration. However, in West Sumatra, these efforts have generally failed, either because sublineages refuse to register land or because the names of all members of the sublineage are included in the registration. See further Benda-Beckmann (1979), Blackwood (2000).

15 During 1990 the average exchange rate was US$1 to Rp. 1,800. During 1996, it was US$1 to Rp. 2,800. Since the year 2000, the exchange rate has hovered around Rp. 9,000.

16 In 1996 women were paid Rp. 2,000 a day for planting or weeding. Given the rate of inflation, however, this amount was only a tiny increase over the wage paid in 1990.

17 There are some exceptions to this pattern for average women landholders. Older women and a small number of elite women did not sharecrop or participate in the collective labour groups as well.
18 About 30 per cent of women farmers in the well-off group work as owner-operators, as well as sharecroppers and, in some cases, labourers, which indicates that ownership of ancestral land is not the only avenue to wealth.
19 See Brenner (1998), Manderson (1980), Suryakusuma (1996) on the New Order state ideology of domesticity.

References

Bachtiar, H. W. (1967) 'Negeri Taram: a Minangkabau village community', in Koetjaraningrat (ed.) *Villages in Indonesia*, Ithaca, NY: Cornell University Press.

Benda-Beckmann, F. (1979) *Property in Social Continuity: continuity and change in the maintenance of property relations through time in Minangkabau, West Sumatra*, The Hague: Martinus Nijhoff.

Blackwood, E. (1995) 'Senior women, model mothers, and dutiful wives: managing gender contradictions in a Minangkabau village', in A. Ong and M. Peletz (eds) *Bewitching Women, Pious Men: gender and body politics in Southeast Asia*, Berkeley: University of California Press.

—— (1997) 'Women, land and labor: negotiating clientage and kinship in a Minangkabau peasant community', *Ethnology*, 36 (4): 277–93.

—— (1999) 'Big houses and small houses: doing matriliny in West Sumatra', *Ethnos*, 64 (1): 32–56.

—— (2000) *Webs of Power: women, kin and community in a Sumatran village*, Lanham, MD: Rowman and Littlefield.

Bray, F. (1983) 'Patterns of evolution in rice-growing societies', *Journal of Peasant Studies*, 11 (1): 3–33.

Brenner, S. A. (1998) *The Domestication of Desire: women, wealth and modernity in Java*, Princeton, NJ: Princeton University Press.

Deere, C. D. (1995) 'What difference does gender make? Rethinking peasant studies', *Feminist Economics*, 1 (1): 53–72.

Esmara, H. (1974) *The Economic Development of West Sumatra: collected papers*, Padang: Andalas University and Provincial Development Planning Agency, West Sumatra.

Grewal, I. and Kaplan, C. (1994) 'Introduction: transnational feminist practices and questions of postmodernity', in I. Grewal and C. Kaplan (eds) *Scattered Hegemonies: post-modernity and transnational feminist practices*, Minneapolis: University of Minnesota Press.

Hart, G. (1986) *Power, Labor and Livelihood: processes of change in rural Java*, Berkeley: University of California Press.

—— (1991) 'Engendering everyday resistance: gender, patronage and production politics in rural Malaysia', *Journal of Peasant Studies*, 19 (1): 93–121.

—— (1992) 'Household production reconsidered: gender, labour conflict, and technological change in Malaysia's Muda region', *World Development*, 20 (6): 809–23.

Hart, G., Turton, A. and White, B. (eds) (1989) *Agrarian Transformations: local processes and the state in Southeast Asia*, Berkeley: University of California Press.

Hefner, R. W. (1990) *The Political Economy of Mountain Java: an interpretive history*, Berkeley: University of California Press.

Hüsken, F. (1989) 'Cycles of commercialization and accumulation in a central Javanese village', in G. Hart, A.Turton and B. White (eds) *Agrarian Transformations: local processes and the state in Southeast Asia*, Berkeley: University of California Press.

Hüsken, F. and Kemp, J. (eds) (1991) *Cognation and Social Organization in Southeast Asia*, Leiden: KITLV Press.

Jay, R. R. (1969) *Javanese Villagers: social relations in rural Modjokuto*, Cambridge, MA: MIT Press.

Kahn, J. S. (1980) *Minangkabau Social Formations: Indonesian peasants and the world economy*, Cambridge: Cambridge University Press.

Kato, T. (1982) *Matriliny and Migration: evolving Minangkabau traditions in Indonesia*, Ithaca, NY: Cornell University Press.

Kearney, M. (1996) *Reconceptualizing the Peasantry: anthropology in global perspective*, Boulder, CO: Westview Press.

Koning, J., Nolten, M., Rodenburg, J. and Saptari, R. (eds) (2000) *Women and Households in Indonesia: cultural notions and social practices*, Nordic Institute of Asian Studies, no. 27, Richmond, Surrey: Curzon Press.

Manderson, L. (1980) 'Rights and responsibilities, power and privilege: women's role in contemporary Indonesia', in *Kartini Centenary: Indonesian women then and now*, Monash University.

Papanek, H. and Schwede, L. (1988) 'Women are good with money: earning and managing in an Indonesian city', in D. Dwyer and J. Bruce (eds) *A Home Divided: women and income in the Third World*, Stanford, CA: Stanford University Press.

Peletz, M. G. (1988) *A Share of the Harvest: kinship, property, and social history among the Malays of Rembau*, Berkeley: University of California Press.

—— (1996) *Reason and Passion: representations of gender in a Malay society*, Berkeley: University of California Press.

Reenen, J. van (2000) 'The salty mouth of a senior woman: gender and the house in Minangkabau', in J. Koning, M. Nolten, J. Rodenburg and R. Saptari (eds) *Women and Households in Indonesia: cultural notions and social practices*, Nordic Institute of Asian Studies, no. 27, Richmond, Surrey: Curzon Press.

Robinson, K. (1998) 'Love and sex in an Indonesian mining town', in K. Sen and M. Stivens (eds) *Gender and Power in Affluent Asia*, London: Routledge.

—— (2000) 'Indonesian women – from Orde Baru to Reformasi', in L. Edwards and M. Roces (eds) *Women in Asia: tradition, modernity and globalization*, Ann Arbor: University of Michigan Press.

Saptari, R. (2000a) 'Networks of reproduction among cigarette factory women in east Java', in J. Koning, M. Nolten, J. Rodenburg and R. Saptari (eds) *Women and Households in Indonesia: cultural notions and social practices*, Nordic Institute of Asian Studies, no. 27, Richmond, Surrey: Curzon Press.

—— (2000b) 'Women, family and household: tensions in culture and practice', in J. Koning, M. Nolten, J. Rodenburg and R. Saptari (eds) *Women and Households in Indonesia: cultural notions and social practices*, Nordic Institute of Asian Studies, no. 27, Richmond, Surrey: Curzon Press.

Scott, J. (1985) *Weapons of the Weak: everyday forms of peasant resistance*, New Haven, CT: Yale University Press.

Sears, L. J. (ed.) (1996) *Fantasizing the Feminine in Indonesia*, Durham, NC: Duke University Press.

Sen, K. (1998) 'Indonesian women at work: reframing the subject', in K. Sen and M. Stivens (eds) *Gender and Power in Affluent Asia*, London: Routledge.

Stivens, M. (1994) 'Gender at the margins: paradigms and peasantries in rural Malaysia', *Women's Studies International Forum*, 17 (4): 373–90.

—— (1996) *Matriliny and Modernity: sexual politics and social change in rural Malaysia*, St Leonard's, NSW: Allen and Unwin.

Stivens, M., Ng, C., Jomo, K.S, and Bee, J. (1994) *Malay Peasant Women and the Land*, London: Zed Books.

Sullivan, N. (1994) *Masters and Managers: a study of gender relations in urban Java*, St Leonard's, NSW: Allen and Unwin.

Suryakusuma, J. (1996) 'The state and sexuality in New Order Indonesia', in L. Sears (ed.) *Fantasizing the Feminine in Indonesia*, Durham, NC: Duke University Press.

Syahrizal (1989) 'Pola hubungan kerja dalam pertanian: studi kasus dalam masyarakat petani', unpublished thesis, Andalas University, Padang, Sumatra.

Tanner, N. (1971) 'Minangkabau disputes', unpublished PhD thesis, University of California Berkeley.

Tiwon, S. (1996) 'Models and maniacs: articulating the female in Indonesia', in L. Sears (ed.) *Fantasizing the Feminine in Indonesia, Durham*, NC: Duke University Press.

Weix, G. G. (2000) 'Hidden managers at home: elite Javanese women running New Order family firms', in J. Koning, M. Nolten, J. Rodenburg and R. Saptari (eds) *Women and Households in Indonesia: cultural notions and social practices*, Nordic Institute of Asian Studies, no. 27, Richmond, Surrey: Curzon Press.

White, B. (1989) 'Problems in the empirical analysis of agrarian differentiation', in G. Hart, A. Turton and B. White (eds) *Agrarian Transformations: local processes and the state in Southeast Asia*, Berkeley: University of California Press.

Wolf, D. L. (1992) *Factory Daughters: gender, household dynamics, and rural industrialization in Java*, Berkeley: University of California Press.

—— (2000) 'Beyond women and the household in Java: re-examining the boundaries', in J. Koning, M. Nolten, J. Rodenburg and R. Saptari (eds) *Women and Households in Indonesia: cultural notions and social practices*, Nordic Institute of Asian Studies, no. 27, Richmond, Surrey: Curzon Press.

2 Keeping rice in the pot

Women and work in a transmigration settlement

Gaynor Dawson

This chapter analyses the interface between the reproductive and productive work of women in a poor, remote transmigration settlement.[1] The transmigration programme saw the resettlement of millions of poor and landless people from densely populated to less populous regions of the Indonesian archipelago. The relocation of transmigrants to a distant rural settlement, in unfamiliar physical, social and economic surroundings, and away from extended family support, impacts on gender relations and increases the responsibility and burden for women as they perform the multiple tasks which are essential for their family's well-being and for keeping the cooking pot full. Their family's survival depends on how well they undertake their domestic and reproductive work, managing scarce household resources and caring for the family in locations where much of the infrastructure, communication and services are limited in comparison with the places from which they have come. However, it also hinges on their work outside the home. It depends on how they, together with their husbands, work their farms to produce food for consumption and for the market in conditions far different to those of the fertile soils and wet rice areas that they are used to in their villages of origin. It depends too on whether they are able to find income-earning work to contribute to the household budget in remote areas where industry and income-earning opportunities are scarce. It also depends on how successfully these women are able to form and maintain supportive social relationships with other transmigrant women who have originated from other regions and have different backgrounds.

In contrast to the situation in their original villages, in many cases women must perform their work without assistance from extended family. They often have no adult relative to care for children or to prepare meals for the family while they work in the fields or in paid labour. They have no help in caring for family members who are ill and nor do they have assistance in situations where medical treatment is expensive and hospitals are distant. While many women are used to working in wet rice cultivation in their home villages, they must learn new agricultural methods and skills to farm the dry plots of land in their new environs. Although many have experience in the informal sector as traders, service providers and in cottage industry on Java, their skills and experience are frequently not relevant in the new surroundings, where markets are limited and other settlers lack cash to buy their product. These transmigrant women also have to learn to interact with the local people, who are of different ethnicity, culture and language and to compete with them for work outside the settlement.

This reality of transmigrant women's work contradicts liberal economic perspectives of work performed by a self-interested rational male individual; it also contradicts Marxist perspectives of proletarianized male, or 'sexless', workers producing surplus value and engaged in class based struggles in the public sphere (Armstrong and Armstrong 1990: 14, 58; Kabeer 1994: 12, 45–6; Young 1993: 129). The work of women extends from paid and income-generating work to unpaid work which sustains and reproduces human life, attends to community obligations and establishes and maintains social networks. In contrast to men's work, women's work embraces a multiplicity of tasks which are often fragmented, may need to be performed simultaneously and which cover a longer period of the day. Unlike men, women cannot devote large blocks of uninterrupted time to the completion of a task. They have to be multi-tasked, flexible and efficient in order to satisfy the competing demands on their time and energy. Their work is unrelenting and often time consuming, and each aspect bears directly on others in the ways and spaces in which they are performed and managed.

This chapter describes the transmigration programme and the settlement to which the women and their families have been brought. It explores the ideals to which women are encouraged to aspire, the gendered power relationships enabled through these constructions and how these transmigrant women manage their work and time within this frame. Finally, the chapter explores the contrast between the situation of women whose husbands work away from the settlement and those whose husbands are present.

Transmigrating

In 1984, 430 families arrived in Harapan Jaya, a transmigration village in Riau Province, Sumatra.[2] These families were part of Indonesia's massive transmigration programme which operated to resettle nuclear households from the 'inner' islands to more sparsely populated, less developed areas in the 'outer' islands.[3] With significant World Bank and other international donor support, the programme accelerated rapidly in the late 1970s and 1980s during the period of the New Order and became an important element of the regime's national development efforts.[4] One of the many objectives used to justify the transmigration programme was increased food production, in particular wet rice, to achieve self-sufficiency in feeding the nation's growing population.[5] The settler smallholder farmers were to emulate the intensive food cultivation methods of Java, even though soil, climatic and marketing factors were quite different in most receiving areas. In what is often seen as a process of 'Javanization', the transmigrants were also supposed to introduce new and improved techniques of intensive cultivation to indigenous inhabitants, especially where shifting cultivation methods predominated. However, the land available for the settlements was usually in the least habitable, arable and accessible regions, making it almost impossible for many settlers to fulfil state expectations.

Towards the end of the Suharto regime, which coincided with the economic crisis of the late 1990s, opposition to the programme increased. Criticism grew more vocal about environmental degradation, the continuing poverty and deprivation in the settlements, the failure to alleviate population pressure in sending areas, the lack of suitable land, the impact on indigenous peoples and the increased social tensions in receiving areas. International donors' and lenders' support cooled and the massive general transmigration programme was closed in the year 2000.[6] However, transmigration is still being offered in a limited manner. For example, people living along the banks of rivers and drains in Jakarta were encouraged to transmigrate after massive floods inundated their homes in February 2007. The impacts which arose from the general programme are also on-going. To this day, there are tensions in many areas between transmigrant and local communities, which have resulted in violence and even death. Many transmigrants who remain in the settlements still struggle for an existence in the harsh surroundings and, in many locations, land clearing and inappropriate agricultural practices continue the process of environmental degradation.

The transmigrants who arrived in Harapan Jaya in 1984 were originally sent to Siak, a tidal swamp area on the coast. However, the land was frequently flooded and even when the settlers had good crops, traders found access to the settlement difficult so that produce was left to rot. They were unable even to maintain a subsistence livelihood, and exhausted any precious capital they had brought with them from Java. The government was forced to supply food rations for two years before a decision was made to move the transmigrants several hundred kilometres inland to Sungai Pagar. Harapan Jaya is the central village of seven which make up the settlement. Each household in the settlement was given 2 hectares of land: 0.25 hectare for a house and house garden; 1 hectare of cleared land ready for immediate planting; and 0.75 hectare of uncleared land in the surrounding forest for later development. They were provided with a rough house of wooden planks, corrugated iron roof and earth floor; agricultural tools and inputs such as hoes, seeds and fertilizer; a little furniture, a few kitchen implements and basic rations for one year.

Housing design and the availability of facilities such as water, sanitation, fuel and power are particularly important in the lives and work of women, issues to which the planners and implementers paid minimal attention. Water was a major problem. The government had failed to ensure that all domestic wells provided by the contractor held water. Water had to be collected from the dam or from public wells in the lower areas of the settlement for drinking, cooking, cleaning, bathing small children and watering livestock. Most people bathed in the dam or at wells which held water, or travelled several kilometres to a river in the next village. Sanitation was poor. Families were not provided with a toilet and some families used a convenient open spot in the house garden or fields, or went to the river to defecate. Other families dug pits in the house garden with some privacy afforded by a hessian or plank screen. The problems were compounded by corruption and lack of accountability in the preparation of the settlement.

The transmigrants had to adjust to their new physical, economic and social environment. While Siak had flooded, Harapan Jaya proved to be the opposite. It was hot and dry, with uncertain rainfall, and the soils and climate made it difficult to grow food crops. The settlers classified the red soils as 'hot' and infertile compared with the black 'cool' and fertile soils of Java. In addition, many of the plots of land which were supposed to be cleared and ready for planting when they arrived were overgrown with grass and had massive tree stumps in them which needed to be removed before the land could be ploughed. Most of the settlers had been farm labourers or tenant farmers on Java. They were familiar with wet rice cultivation, and those from the cool mountainous areas on Java had grown crops such as coffee, cacao and vegetables. However, due to poor design, the dam and irrigation canals in the settlement did not function properly. In addition, plagues of rats and elephants and wild pigs, which lived in the surrounding forest, destroyed any rice crops which did grow.[7] In the face of the failure to cultivate rice, secondary (*palawija*) crops became the dominant source of agricultural income for the settlers. These crops were mainly soybeans, chillies, cassava, maize, mung beans, peanuts and water melons. However, after initial good crops, yields declined rapidly as the nutrients leached out of the soil. Many families raised small livestock such as chickens, although these were regularly decimated by disease. Some household heads were given cattle through a cattle distribution scheme funded by the International Fund for Agricultural Development (IFAD). Fruit trees, such as rambutan and jack fruit, also became a secondary source of food and income for some families.

The marketing of farm produce, which is critical to an agricultural settlement's economy, requires good access and a confluence of buyers and sellers. Unlike Java, transportation and communication were difficult. The settlement was located 12 kilometres from the main road. Access was along a gravel track which entered the forest about 60 kilometres south of Pekanbaru on the main road to Teluk Kuantan. The track was difficult to traverse in the wet season when rains turned the surface to mud and floods covered the low-lying sections.[8] Although there was a market in the settlement, it was not one that had developed naturally over time at a crossroads or other place where traders met. The traders who entered the settlement were from other ethnic groups, principally Minang, Batak and Malay. The transmigrants had to establish relationships with them and were in a poor bargaining position. There was sometimes the feeling that they were being cheated and that prices were too low. Transmigrant traders, both women and men, who went outside the settlement to sell and buy in the local rotating markets also had to familiarize themselves with different produce and prices, and establish relationships with buyers from other ethnic groups.

Situating transmigrant women

In the production and reproduction of gender relationships and inequalities, the institutions of family and household are core locations. However, families and households are not discrete entities. They are part of a wider society. As elements of that wider society they are both conduits for, and products of, its social, economic and political forces and values. Within family and household, intimate and personal relationships mesh with these external forces to organize the ways in which women and men go about their daily lives and to shape the power relationships between them. Social meanings are constructed and conveyed which mould the ways women and men think about themselves in their particular historical time, location and environment. Differences are created in how women and men are able to mobilize and use the resources available, and social controls are exercised over women's labour, bodies, sexuality, reproduction and choices (Kabeer 1994: 58, 66).

The way the state constructs and operationalizes 'the household' and the roles of its members in the transmigration programme reinforces prevailing ideologies on the distinct roles of women and men. This separation in the roles, where men are the income earners and public representatives of the family while women are concerned with domestic matters, appears to be a natural outcome of biological difference. In these complementary roles, women are 'embodied' as mothers and reproducers of human life, the managers of the domestic realm with responsibility for the minutiae of everyday life. On the other hand, men are released by women's labour and concern with the 'dirt' and detail of life so that they are above everyday concerns and can undertake work which accrues status and behave as if they are 'disembodied' rational, self-interested agents of development in liberal economic theory (Armstrong and Armstrong 1990: 14, 58; Errington 1990: 6–7).

Within the transmigration programme the family/household is a primary target and instrument for government. Transmigration policy and documents reflect a conventional bureaucratic conceptualization of the nuclear family household as uniform, constant and discrete. This ideal is a hierarchical and asymmetrical arrangement in which the man is located at the apex as head (*kepala keluarga* or KK) with priority in entitlements to its material resources. As household head, he has the designated role of income earner and representative of the household in the public domain.[9] On the other hand, the woman rarely emerges except to be assigned the subordinate position of household manager with responsibility for domestic work and child care. The identification of the male household head enables a simple direct line of authority and communication to be established between the state and the household through which directives and resources from the state can be channelled. The household head is identified as the landowner on the land title given to the transmigrants and he is asked to participate in projects introduced to improve the settlement's economy. The household head also has authority to speak for other household members in the public domain on matters including labour commitments to development activities, and to make unilateral decisions concerning farming activities. In this way women's labour can be spoken for and commitments made in her name. In addition, she can be excluded from income-earning opportunities in which her husband, who is viewed as the household's income earner, represents her.

While this concept of a male-headed nuclear family household has been the standard for transmigration policy and programme implementation, in reality, household composition and structure in the settlement varies over time, shifting in relation to the life cycle of household members and according to socio-economic pressures and opportunities. This has implications for gender power relations. For example, men often leave to seek income-earning opportunities outside the settlement. Women whose husbands are away are situated in different power relations within their household and in the public domain compared with women whose husbands are always present. Married daughters and daughters-in-law, especially those whose husbands are absent, who live with parents and parents-in-law also have different obligations and pressures to those women living with their husbands in their own household.

By the 1990s, the structure and composition of households in the settlement had shifted in contrast to the nuclear family household model used by transmigration planners to calculate labour availability.[10] While the majority of households in Harapan Jaya were still nuclear households with husbands living and working in the settlement, there were a significant number of households where the woman was the head. Poverty and poor agricultural conditions meant that many married men took opportunities to earn money outside the village. During a period of a year, over a quarter of male heads of households worked away for various periods of time, some only briefly and others almost continuously. Women in these households became *de facto* female heads in their husbands' absences and the main source of agricultural labour for the family. In addition, about 5 per cent of households were headed by widowed or divorced women as *de jure* heads of household.

The standard male-headed nuclear household model had implications for the allocation of state resources. Decisions as to who was to be included in projects, such as the cattle distribution project, were at the discretion of village authorities and relevant government officials. Participation usually correlated with the power and influence wielded by the household head and the strength of his links to local authorities. Women who were *de jure* household heads were entitled to participate in village development activities but they were usually not invited or were not confident enough to attend or list their interest. Furthermore, these women were not considered farmers in their own right, nor to have the farming expertise required to participate, even though they might be quite capable and want to be involved. One woman explained her objection to women's exclusion from the cattle distribution project and her determination to confront this narrow thinking: 'The government thinks that we [women] are less responsible – for instance, they think that if the cow escapes at night a woman would be frightened to go looking for it. However I have bought a cow myself privately – not from the project. If I lose it, it's my loss.'

In addition to male-headed nuclear, extended and female-headed households, another form of household within the village was the polygynous household, where men spent part of their time with each wife (8 per cent of married women had been a co-wife at some time). The prospect of a husband taking another wife was greatly feared by women in the settlement. It meant loss of status, indignity and the likelihood of economic and emotional disadvantage. It also had significant impact on women's labour, usually increasing it to make up for the loss of some of the husband's labour time. In polygynous relationships, it was unusual for wives to live in the same residence. However, in one case in a neighbouring village, two co-wives lived together, apparently harmoniously, with their husband. The first wife in this unusual case had not been able to have children. She had agreed to her husband taking a second wife who then bore children in a situation with some parallels with the Western concept of surrogate motherhood. The first wife was happy to stay at home and look after the children and work with her husband in the fields while the second wife worked for wages in a rubber plantation to provide cash to help support the household.

In the idealized, dichotomized and stratified gender relationships, all parties appear to be in equilibrium in their allotted places. Conflict and disharmony between the sides is discouraged. Although in reality there may be conflicting interests, they are suppressed in order that a state of social harmony prevails within the household and in the wider community (Guinness 1986: 131–2; Sciortino and Smyth 1995: 2). In Harapan Jaya, women could not conceive of themselves as individuals, separate from family and household and with the possibility of competing or conflicting needs or status. Their reference point was themselves as wives and mothers of a family, a role which they saw as their destiny. When asked what characteristics made a 'good wife', women in the village would respond with answers such as 'loyalty', 'obedience', 'politeness', 'a woman who waits for her husband's orders', 'a woman who helps her husband', 'a woman who cares for and guides her children', 'a woman who is good at managing the household'. Yet when they were asked what were the characteristics of a 'good woman' they were at a loss. To be seen as an individual woman, not in the role of a wife and mother, was in a sense pre-discursive, something which hadn't been thought of before (White 1992: 8). Implicit in women's responses to the definition of a 'good wife' are the ideal feminine characteristics of submission and dependency on men, of selflessness, and the view that women can only be identified, and only identify themselves, through their reproductive work as wives and mothers. These responses were internalized and readily available. They are encountered by women every day of their lives in the ways in which 'womanhood' is constructed in the formal and informal discourses of religion, the media and daily life and through the state and its specific operationalization of this construction in the transmigration programme.[11]

This is a 'master narrative' (Hart 1991: 94) which prescribes the ideals, the standard, to which women should aspire and live. These ideal qualities are also available to be used by others to control and discipline women to live up to them and at the same time to excuse men. For example, Ibu Mus, whose husband frequently went to live with other women, leaving her to ensure the survival of herself and her two children, was told by her father to spoil her husband, to cook what he wanted to eat and to take better care of his needs so that he would not live with other women. It was not her husband's behaviour which was the problem in her father's eyes, but that Ibu Mus was not being a sufficiently 'good wife'. However, there were varying degrees of adherence and resistance to the ideal. For example, Ibu Niam recognized her difference and stated outright that she was the driver in her household while her husband was the pillion passenger (*dia naik ojek*). She felt that although she was seen by others as dominant, as the 'driver' in the family and sometimes as harsh, her difference was accepted because she made efforts to help her neighbours and was very active in the community, so that others did not think she was 'bad' (*jelek*). The implications of this were, however, that if she hadn't maintained such good social relationships, the fact that she didn't fit the ideal could have been used against her.

In contrast to the clearly articulated and restricting ideals set for women, the roles for men did not constrain but gave them freedom and privileges. Unlike women, men were not identified as belonging to, or dependent on, someone else. They were seen as the family breadwinners, whether this was actually the case or not, and this gave them status. As head of the household, they were the ones valued as being their families' income earners and decision makers, while other family members were in their shadow. Men's status and understandings of how they should behave meant that they could determine the rules and allocate resources as they wished, and in this way they could preserve their position. Men attended and spoke in village meetings and formal occasions where important decisions were made and men had the freedom to move at will both within the settlement and outside. Men set the ideals and standards for themselves and, unlike the situation for women, there was no-one else but themselves to enforce these standards. They had greater independence, choice and opportunity to avoid responsibilities and obligations.

Juggling work and time

The notion of work is conventionally seen and constituted through a male lens (Armstrong and Armstrong 1990; Kabeer 1994; Scott 1995). Its forms have reality in a male world-view – as productive labour most often producing exchange values; as linear activities which continue to a completion point; and as single tasks which are worked at continuously for a large part of the day. Such understandings of the nature of work are inadequate when considering the reality of much of women's work, which is cyclical and unending, and where activities in a day are multiple and often performed simultaneously. Where women are concerned, the concept of work must also be extended beyond productive and income-producing work. Unless the worth of their unpaid work is acknowledged, the labour, time and energy of those who carry it out are devalued. One important aspect of women's unpaid work in Harapan Jaya was to foster and maintain social networks within the village. This was essential to ensure that resources were available in place of the neighbourhood and family networks which they had left behind in Java. Collective activities in which women participated, such as *selamatan*, mutual labour exchanges between households (*royongan* or *sambatan*), prayer groups (*yasinan*), and savings and loan (*simpan pinjam*) or rotating credit groups (*arisan*), strengthened inter-household reciprocal relationships. Women gained opportunities to tap into a range of material and emotional resources outside the household in time of crisis and this gave a better sense of security to women in those households living on the edge.

The range of women's work can be conceptualized as reproductive and productive, where reproductive labour includes childbearing and child care, domestic maintenance activities, and community and social obligations, and productive labour includes production for the market as well as for household consumption. However, we cannot talk of these aspects of women's labour as divorced from one another. They are closely interconnected and bear directly on one another in the ways and the spaces in which they are performed and managed under conditions imposed by overarching socio-economic, cultural, generational and gender relationships. When a woman marries, according to Indonesian marriage law, she formally becomes a housewife (*ibu rumah tangga*). This concept of *ibu rumah tangga*, which is reinforced through state policies, programmes and laws, as well as the mass media and religious teachings, reflects elitist ideals of what a married woman should do. As *ibu rumah tangga*, she is the person responsible for the smooth running of the household and ensuring that the needs of its members, in particular her husband, are satisfied. The role of income earner and family breadwinner is allocated to the husband. However for women, especially poor women, an ever-present tension exists in juggling the role of housewife/mother with the role of producer and income earner in order that the family can survive. In Harapan Jaya, women cooked the meals, washed the dishes, cleaned and tidied the house and lit the lamps in the morning and evening. They carried clothes to the well, dam or river to wash. They collected wood for cooking fuel and water for drinking and cooking. They shopped for food at small kiosks and the market. They cared for and raised children. They tended the sick. They managed the household finances and directed the labour of other household members who were available to assist them.[12] In addition, most women worked the land, raised livestock or were involved in trading and other income earning activities.

In the settlement, as elsewhere in Indonesia, children were important to couples since the family was not seen as complete without children to continue the family line. They were a sign of the couple's suitability to one another, of the woman's fertility and the husband's virility. When children were young, mothering responsibilities were in tension with the need for women to contribute to family production and finances. Unlike Java, where children are frequently left with grandmothers in their mother's absence, there were often no grandparents or other adult extended family members living in the settlement.[13] Older siblings, especially girls, were the main carers of young children and babies, which meant they bore great responsibility. In the absence of other care-givers, fathers were also more likely than on Java to look after children out of necessity. However, leaving young children behind when working was seen as not being consistent with motherhood and there was an element of anxiety for mothers about any accidents or illnesses that might befall the child in their absence. Children were seen as important to the work that needed to be done within the family. As they grew older, children were expected to help in the fields, and daughters, in particular, were expected to care for parents in their old age. Both sons and daughters were also expected to contribute money to the household if they obtained paid work. Daughters were encouraged to help in the house from a young age and looked after younger siblings from the age of six or seven. Although boys were also sometimes asked to help, it was more difficult for mothers to access their labour for domestic tasks because, unlike girls, they were often playing away from the house. 'Boys only return to eat', was mothers' frequent lament.

Domestic and child raising work were central to women's sense of identity. This was the role which was clearly prescribed for them. Women spent an average of over three hours every day on domestic and child care work, although this varied from woman to woman, depending on factors such as the number of small children they had to look after, or the number of other women in the household who could assist them. Women protected their domestic role, particularly the work in the kitchen. Many believed that housework was their own business and should not to be done by men except under exceptional circumstances, although men and boys might help sometimes with the arduous work of collecting wood and water.

> It is harmonious [*rukun*] for a husband to help ... but the kitchen, that is the business of the woman herself. For men, their work is to gather wood and so on, that is the business of men. But men cannot do the business of cooking. What is his wife for?
>
> (Ibu Katini)

> I don't think men should do the housework because housework is women's work. Sometimes I ask him to help though, for instance to get firewood or water from the well. If I am sick he cooks and does the washing if I am not able. I don't think he likes to help in the house though – men are slow workers if it is housework!
>
> (Ibu Sudarwati)

Even though women might work in the fields, in the market, on nearby plantations, trade in neighbouring villages and so on, they were physically associated with the environs of the house and its responsibilities. This view enabled men to escape and excuse themselves from housework. Ignoring the reality of his wife's work in the fields, one husband articulated this perception: 'It's difficult for a man to help in the house because he isn't there a lot of the time. Isn't the house the woman's place?'

The case of Ibu Sairah, a trader, illustrates how, even when women are absent from the home for much of the day, they continue to feel responsible for its smooth running. Ibu Sairah traded with settlers in a newly established transmigration settlement about 10 kilometres away in the forest. She woke at 4.30 am to cook breakfast and lunch for her husband and two sons. After eating breakfast herself, she packed the containers on her bicycle with the goods she would sell, such as *tahu* (tofu), *gula merah* (coconut palm sugar), coconuts or water melon and left at about 5.30 in the morning while it was still cool. She returned to the house at about 3.00 or 4.00 in the afternoon, cooked the evening meal, cleaned the house and washed the clothes. When I asked why her husband and sons did not help her she said, 'Javanese men don't know how to cook and, anyhow, my husband works in the fields all day. The one helping out should be my married daughter, Paijem, who lives next door.'

However, it was not really that men did not know how to do domestic work if necessary. In situations where there were no women present, men were forced to take the work on themselves. Widowers or men living in logging camps or working as construction workers in town cooked, cleaned, washed and so on. On a visit to a village midwife, I found her husband, Pak Syamsuddin, mending the seam of his trousers because he wanted to wear them to go out. His wife was massaging a woman who had just given birth and was not at home to sew his pants. Pak Syamsuddin's comment was that sometimes he felt like a widower, not a husband, when his wife had to attend someone who had given birth and he was left to look after such domestic matters.

Generally, an ideal model of a cooperative and fair working relationship between husband and wife was held amongst the transmigrants, both women and men. However, women's critique of this model sometimes emerged, in particular in regard to their husband's assistance with domestic work. Mbah Mul and some of her neighbours initially portrayed the workings of their households in its archetypal form with their husbands cooperating and sharing the burden with them. But when I asked what their husbands actually did in the house Mbah Mul elaborated:

> If I was in the fields, and hadn't come back, and my husband went to the forest and returned first, and ... [at this point another woman joined the conversation, speaking and laughing simultaneously with Mbah Mul, indicating the 'insider' joke status of their common view] ... he was thirsty but there wasn't any water – he would boil the water!

To these women, a husband 'cooperated', but only minimally, and only when they were not in place to do that work. They observed that the primary drive for a man to act only came from the satisfaction of his own needs, rather than attending to the wants and comforts of other members of the household as was commonplace for women.

In addition to their domestic work, many women in Harapan Jaya spent long periods in the fields, labouring alone or alongside their husbands. They made farming choices such as what crops were to be planted, supervised labourers in their fields, negotiated with traders about the price for the harvest and discussed planting schedules and agricultural questions with their neighbours and cultivated the house gardens.[14] Some women were also responsible for taking care of livestock. In many cases, women also identified and managed additional crops to the major crops. Long beans, chillies, vegetables and coffee, and small livestock, provided a regular income for women. The daily work required was regular and of shorter duration compared with the intermittent periods of intensive and lengthy work involved in major crop production. Cultivating these crops enabled women to plan and accommodate their other work and responsibilities more easily. Yet despite women's involvement in farming and other income-earning activities, such as trading and cottage industry, men were usually seen by both women and men as the household's income earner and farmer. Women's significant contribution to agricultural production and to the income of the household was unacknowledged.

This view was reflected in state interventions. Women were ignored in activities such as farming extension, the cattle distribution programme mentioned earlier and projects to introduce tree crops.[15] All these programmes, which were designed to increase productivity and household income, were directed to the male household head who was perceived as 'the farmer'. This gave men access to and control over the benefits which might eventuate. As Ibu Sudarwati stated matter-of-factly, 'My husband owns the cow ... and he is the one who will sell it in the future. It was he who signed for it, not me.' Nevertheless, although women did not usually participate in government agricultural and livestock schemes or related training, women such as Ibu Sudarwati were often expected by their husbands to take care of livestock or look after the crop. They undertook this work as obedient wives and with the expectation that some or all of the profits would come back to the family, whether or not it actually did.

Control of their work time and the protection of their right to stop work when they wanted were of critical importance to most women, enabling them to better manage their diverse responsibilities and to integrate their work inside and outside the home. Trading and cottage industry were activities which enabled women to have flexibility, to have direct access to income and to diversify their sources of livelihood so that they were not as dependent on agriculture. However, even though many women had engaged in these activities on Java, only a few women in the settlement were able to successfully enter these economic niches because of their lack of start-up capital and the limited market and cash in the settlement. Working daily for an employer was viewed negatively by most women because of its lack of flexibility, and they resisted the idea of having a boss who could control the type and length of their work. Women frequently commented on the difficulty, when working under someone else, of taking time off for reasons such as illness, or for household or community obligations, or merely to 'rest'. Some women were also aware of, and concerned about, the exploitative labour relationships to which they could be exposed and said that they preferred not to work for someone else who would keep the profits of their labour. However, even in their own farm households, women's labour was often directly or indirectly subject to another's decision.

Within the unequal gender power relationships of the household and the complementary ideal models of 'the good wife' and the 'equitable and cooperative household working unit', many women felt that they must comply with their husbands' demands on their labour. Women were compelled to complete domestic work in order to live up to the image of being 'a good wife' and their productive labour was frequently accessed by husbands to work in the fields. The presence of a man was likely to add to the time that a woman spent on both domestic and farm work.[16] Ibu Siti, whose husband had left her to take another wife, contrasted how her life had changed after he had left and she had taken control of her labour time:

> My work is a lot less now and I can rest when I want to. Before, I was always working in the fields – mornings and afternoons. Now I can decide when I want to rest and I don't have to do things like wash his clothes. Before I was thin, now I am getting fatter!

The need to perform both productive and reproductive work was at times questioned by some women. Productive work in the settlement was usually hot, dirty and unpleasant and, in combination with women's reproductive labour, was often onerous. Preference for being a housewife and just working in the home was sometimes expressed, especially by younger women with small children. However, on hearing one woman express this view, her elderly neighbour quickly challenged her, refuting the elitist concept of 'housewife', and drawing on the village ethos of the cooperative relationship between wives and husbands:

> If you stay in the house and don't go to the fields, you give up your reason for being.... Farmers have to work cooperatively, not like an official. An official goes to the office while his wife works in the house, cooks and buys things.

In this view the productive work of farming gave meaning to a woman's life in the village. It was the essence of her being, without which she was not complete. It was only in non-farming, elite households that it was appropriate for women to relinquish their productive work and become dependent housewives and consumers.

When husbands work away

Poverty and the failure of agricultural production were perpetual concerns for the settlers. How to increase the cash income of the household was a never-ending question. A frequent solution to the issue was for husbands to search for work outside the settlement: husbands from 28 per cent of households in the village sought work outside the settlement over a period of a year. In this situation where men worked away and women were left to maintain the home and agricultural production, there were implications for household gender relationships. In such an acute model of a public/private division, men's working life was markedly separated from their domestic and family life, which was sustained by women. The farm became the base to which they could retreat, a haven maintained and secured by the efforts of their wife and family in their absence.

Decisions as to whether husbands or wives would work away were shaped by meanings, expectations and differentials related to gender identity. Despite the fact that, on Java, women's absence from the household in their circular migration for work was generally accepted, few married women worked outside the village in jobs which required their overnight absence.[17] Conventional belief and official rhetoric underscored women's primary responsibility for care of the house and children. The lack of grandmothers and other extended female family in the settlement constrained women's choice to work away in comparison with the situation on Java, where children were often left in grandparents' and other family members' care for extensive periods while mothers found work elsewhere (Hetler 1986). Views about women's sexuality and vulnerability when not under the protection and supervision of their husbands and fathers also curtailed their movements. This was exacerbated by the fact that, compared with their areas of origin on Java, there were less likely to be kin and neighbourhood linkages outside the village that could provide an acceptable base and would protect their reputation.[18]

Another consideration for a woman was what her husband could do with the household's economic resources if she were away. This fear was underpinned by the commonly accepted and formal presumption that the married man, as the head of household and landholder, represented the collective interests of the household and had privileged right to its property. In practice, these are two aspects of gender ideology and rhetoric which are potentially contradictory. One woman expressed concern that if she were away, her husband would sell some of the land in her absence. Another recounted how her husband had sold furniture and started to break up the house to sell iron roofing, wooden beams and even nails when she worked as a trader outside the settlement. Her husband also sold her chickens and a tape recorder which she had bought through her trading efforts. As her neighbour commiserated, 'If a wife leaves her house, her household suffers (*susah rumah tangganya*)!'

Nevertheless, a number of women, especially those without young children, stated that they would like to work away to gain access to the greater financial benefits available outside the village. It was their husbands who opposed them, telling the women that their obligations as housewives precluded them from working outside the transmigration settlement and warning them that they would not be successful. As Ibu Bariah stated:

> I have always wanted to work away but I can't do it. My husband says that I can't. He says that I would be shy and it would be difficult to get a job. He says not to go away to work, that I have to work here at whatever I can find. I have to stay here to look after the children and the farm. However, he likes to work away. He doesn't want to farm.

The combined burden of domestic and agricultural work where there was limited on-farm labour available was hard for many women whose husbands worked away. The difficulties experienced by women whose husbands were absent, but who kept up their work as farmers, were intensified by the lack of support from agricultural extension workers. While many would have liked to have access to the extension workers to help them manage farm production, they were not invited. Most women relied on male relatives, neighbours and husbands on their return to communicate important agricultural information, such as planting schedules and new varieties of crops.

In addition to domestic and productive work, women had to fill in for absent husbands' community work obligations (*kerja bakti*). Women cleared the verges of their yards themselves but if they were not able to participate in other required community work and there was no male relative who could substitute, they were obliged to pay someone to work in their husband's place or to provide cigarettes or drinks for the work party. In this situation, women – especially those with small children – were unable to continue much of their productive work and often became dependent on their husbands' earnings as the burden of caring for home, children and farm production without the labour support from husbands, extended family or the state, became too great to manage. Almost half of these households did not cultivate the larger plots provided for crops, although their house gardens were cultivated to some extent and they were able to obtain some of their consumption needs or sell produce for cash. Significantly, one-third of women were completely dependent on their husbands' remittances to feed and maintain their families. A young woman whose husband often worked outside the village said,

'I prefer to just mess around in the house. I can't do everything myself.' Another stated, 'My work is cooking, looking after the children, cleaning – just working in the house.'

There was a delicate balance between the benefits and costs of men working away, especially for those women who were largely dependent on husbands' incomes. Many women had no contact with their husbands outside the village and did not know where their husbands were or for how long they would be away. Some husbands returned with no money, some were injured or fell ill. Remittances to the family were sent at the husband's discretion or not at all. Dependent on husbands sending money for everyday needs, women often suffered as they waited, not knowing when money would come, or when their husband would return. Ibu Mistia's experience exemplifies the anxieties and stress which some women endured while their husbands were away. Her husband had left to work outside the village shortly after she gave birth to their fourth son. She heard nothing from him and received no money for three months. With a newborn baby to care for, as well as three other children under 11 years, Ibu Mistia could do little agricultural work except plant some vegetables in the house garden. The two fields the family owned were uncultivated. Her 10-year-old son helped around the house and earned about Rp. 2,000 per week preparing cabbages and onions for a stall owner at the weekly market. This, the only cash they had, was used to buy a little food. The family had no other relatives in the settlement who could give support. Most of their needs were obtained by borrowing from neighbours and obtaining credit from shop owners and traders. The willingness of these others, who were also often not well off, could only be stretched so far and then Ibu Mistia was forced to look for someone else who would be willing to help her.

With husbands working away, a crucial aspect of women's control and power within the family was removed. Managing the household's finances to meet daily needs and ensure the survival of its members was an important element of women's role as housewife.[19] For women in the settlement, the security to be gained by their management of household finances, even though the amount was meagre, was highly valued and tightly guarded.[20] Most were against any idea of men handling the household monies and they generally considered men incapable.[21] As Ibu Sairah caustically remarked, 'When a man has the money, he has plenty of cigarettes, not like when a woman manages the money. If a man has the money, it frequently doesn't reach the kitchen!' However, for women whose husbands worked outside the settlement, the balance in control over, and access to, household finances shifted considerably.

Men who earned money away from the village had direct access to the bulk of household income and command over its allocation. In control of much of the family's earnings, they were the purchasers of luxury items such as stereos and televisions which they found in the towns through which they travelled. This contrasted with the situation where household income was gained in the village and its amount and use was relatively open to the scrutiny of both husband and wife. Where husbands were in the village, women knew if their husbands were working and how much they would earn. They knew when crops or livestock were sold, and even if they were not involved directly in the bargaining, they could estimate the expected value and had greater access to the funds that were realized, although they might still need to cajole their husbands to get the money from them. Living and working in places distant from the settlement, men's freedom not to disclose income and to use wages as they liked was much greater. Many women said that they did not know how much their husbands earned, how much they spent or what they spent it on when they were away. There was also the chance that men would enter into relationships with women outside the village or would never return, leaving women who were dependent on them destitute.

Conclusion

In the unfavourable agricultural conditions of the settlement, most transmigrant families lived on the margins, lacking resources and assets which they could mobilize in times of need, vulnerable to shock and emergencies such as illness or crop failure, and with little power to change their situations. In this context, women's labour was essential to farm production and part of their identity as farmers. Women saw their farm work and other income-earning activities, such as trading, as an important way they could help to ensure that there was enough food to feed their families. However, continued engagement with work was important to women for other reasons as well. Many women also saw their productive work as a means of retaining their independence. Uncertainties and vulnerabilities, not only of agricultural production, but also within marital relationships, meant that women's capacity to keep working and productive, even if the marital relationship broke down, was an important means of protecting themselves and their families from suffering and destitution. The lack of a family support network within the settlement made this even more crucial.

The vulnerability of women and their families was most evident in situations where women did little productive work and became dependent on remittances from husbands who worked away from the settlement. If money was sent regularly, women managed to live comfortably, although they and their families were still exposed to indebtedness and hunger if husbands became ill or were injured. However, where men were unreliable in remitting money, women who had no other source of livelihood suffered the deprivations of severe poverty with their families. The exposure of women and their families to uncertainties and destitution was more acute in the settlement, where households did not have the extended family support networks of their original homes in Java. In emergencies, people had to rely on the support of others to whom they had limited social connection. Women, such as Ibu Niam, saw their work in forming and cementing relationships as an important responsibility, and as a means of gaining respect and status in the evolving community. Such relationships had the potential to give women access to emotional and material support where necessary.

Women's work in the settlement was closely circumscribed and organized through material conditions and necessity, and also by social norms and conventions. It was characterized by lack of choice and opportunities in comparison with the authority, freedoms and wider opportunities available to men. Women were constantly cognizant of their responsibility to be a 'good wife': of attending to the needs of others and ensuring that the domestic arena functioned seamlessly and effortlessly for their husbands. Whatever productive and income-earning work was undertaken by transmigrant women, the domestic responsibilities of managing the home were constantly present in their minds – other work was juggled to accommodate housework. Household management tasks and child care were the core aspects of their identity as married women. Regardless of whether women undertook the work themselves or had someone help, they were always responsible for ensuring that it happened. In addition to the limited numbers of other family members available to assist, the lack of infrastructure in the settlement and the poor housing conditions added to the difficulties of this work.

The reality of life in the transmigration settlement challenged the state's model of distinct roles and responsibilities for men and women within the household. While 'good wives' were typically represented as their husbands' submissive, quiet and obedient followers, taking care of domestic work, these transmigrant women living at the vulnerable margins of a subsistence economy often behaved in very different ways. They continually manoeuvred their time, resources and their labour. They were assertive and forceful, ingenious and resourceful, and ultimately they, not the male 'income earner', ensured their household's survival by keeping the cooking pot full. Their capacity to achieve these outcomes in the arduous conditions of the transmigration village in many cases masked the failure of husbands and other family members to contribute sufficiently to the sustainability of their households.

Notes

1 The primary research for this chapter was conducted in a transmigration village in Riau Province, Sumatra, between 1991 and 1993. Data were collected by a village census, and three socio-economic surveys, a marital survey and five time-allocation surveys of a stratified random sample of households drawn from the census. An assets index was used to rank households. Data were also collected by qualitative methods: interviews, informal discussions and observation.

2 Approximately 46 per cent of the transmigrants in the village were Central Javanese, another 46 per cent were East Javanese, and 3 per cent were Sundanese. Five per cent of the original households were local Malay-Minang families, included as part of the policy of including local people in the transmigration scheme. However, with the exception of one local family who established a successful shop in the market, all the local transmigrants quickly sold their plots and left the settlement.

3 The 'inner' islands included Java, Bali and Lombok, while 'outer' islands included Sumatra, Sumbawa, Sumba, Sulawesi, Kalimantan, West Papua, Maluku, Flores and Timor.

4 'Colonization', later to become the transmigration programme, was commenced by the Dutch in 1905 as part of their Ethical Policy. It aimed to bring poor families from Java to work in the plantations in Sumatra with the ideal of giving them a better standard of living. However, it also provided cheap and compliant labour power for the expansion of colonial plantation development. The transmigration programme was continued by Sukarno but in a limited way. A decade after the New Order came to power, the

programme was substantially accelerated with plans for the movement of millions of people. Even though implementation fell far short of planning, in the 15 years between 1974 and 1989, 873,000 families (3.5 million people) were transmigrated. These figures can be compared with 136,483 families (about 674,000 people) who were transmigrated in the previous 25 years (Adhiati and Bobsien 2001).

5 Numerous aims were used to justify the transmigration programme: to alleviate population pressures in densely populated islands of Java and Bali; to provide landless families with farm land so that they could improve their socio-economic situation; to move people who were living in critical areas such as on the slopes of volcanoes or who had been displaced by natural disasters; to relocate people from lands planned for development such as dam building; to populate and develop the Outer Islands; to increase productivity, especially of rice, in regions outside Java and Bali; and to populate borders and areas which were considered security risks.

6 Transmigration continues in a limited form with the resettlement of refugees and displaced persons from areas where there is internal disruption and insecurity, and the establishment of settlements along international borders, and to provide labour for commercial development.

7 Dwindling forest habitat caused by clearing for plantations, logging and settlements, increased the likelihood that elephants and pigs would search for food in the settlers' fields.

8 The local population of the area are mostly Malay and Minangkabau who are clustered in villages along the main road from Pekanbaru. They earn a living cultivating small holdings of rubber, secondary crops such as corn and working in oil palm and rubber plantations. Construction in towns, land clearance and logging are other opportunities for waged work. Plywood and pulp factories also absorb wage labour from the area, but these are located over 200 kilometres away.

9 In fact, transmigration and newspaper reports usually refer to the number of KK or household heads (*kepala keluarga*) as a substitute for the word 'family'. The household head represents the household and all other family members become invisible.

10 The availability of household labour to work the farm was calculated using a 'man day' as the measure. Each household was assumed to have three children able to work. Women were calculated as giving 0.6–0.8 of a man day of labour and children 0.3–0.5 of a man day (Dawson 1994: 73).

11 Some examples of how a constructed 'woman' is mediated follow. In women's prayer meetings (*yasinan*) in the village, male religious leaders instructed women that they must take care of their husbands and raise their children well, while no reference was made to women's other roles. A popular Javanese saying is, 'Wherever a husband goes in life, whether to heaven or hell, a wife will follow' (*swargo nunut, naroko katut*). This saying reinforces the dependency, powerlessness and submissiveness of women to their husbands. Religious texts such as the Qur'an and the state's Marriage Law No. 1 of 1974 and regulations (PP No.9 1975; PP No.10 1983) also focus on women's responsibilities as dutiful wives and mothers.

12 While most domestic work and child care took place in and around the house, the fields were also extensions of living space for many families who temporarily lived in huts to protect their crops from pigs, elephants, birds and rats during the growing season. The daily rhythm of family life continued there and women interspersed their work in the fields with their usual domestic work and care for children. However, food was usually still cooked in the house by women and brought to the fields for family members' consumption.

13 A marital history survey in May 1993 found that on Java grandmothers were the main alternative child carer in 78 per cent of cases compared with 33 per cent in the settlement.

14 Women with babies, the elderly, or those with other income-earning work, such as trading or cottage industries, were usually not as actively involved in agriculture in the fields

as others; however, most of them made extensive use of the diverse resources of the house garden.

15 Cattle and tree crops were introduced to the settlement under the Second Stage Development Programme designed to assist poverty-stricken settlers to improve their economies.

16 Evidence from five time-allocation surveys conducted throughout the agricultural calendar between December 1992 and October 1993.

17 In only one case in the sample used for the research did a married woman work away from the village and was absent from her household overnight.

18 Hetler (1986: 251) found in her research in Central Java that security was felt to be a problem for female circular migrants from the village and that 72 per cent stayed with kin or friends when they were away from home.

19 Eighty-four per cent of married women surveyed said that they 'held' or managed the household purse.

20 Having this responsibility was a double-edged sword. Women were obliged to ensure that there was money coming in to the household. Dariman, a young man aged 19, recounted how his mother was frequently angry with his father, himself and his brothers and sisters when there was little cash available for the household's needs. She berated them regularly about finding daily labouring jobs so that they could each contribute some cash. Women were expected to obtain and conserve money for the family's everyday subsistence needs yet have enough available to satisfy their husband's requests. While women handled barely enough money for the household's essential requirements, husbands usually kept their own pocket money or were given money for cigarettes and other needs when they asked. This could place stress on women and lead to conflict when women refused to give their husbands money. Even if women refused to give money, they were still in a weak position. Men could obtain credit from traders and shops or borrow at high interest rates, sometimes for gambling. The responsibility for repayment of these debts usually fell on women.

21 Indeed, some men felt uncomfortable about holding money. Pak Syamsuddin remarked, 'I get a little [money] from organizing birth certificates. People might give me Rp. 500 or Rp. 1,000 and I use that to buy cigarettes. But if I get Rp. 5,000 I give that to Mbah because if I hold any money I get stressed (*panas pikiran*).' However, as Keeler (1983: 5) remarks, this is also 'a sign that he is above materialist calculation' and the everyday petty details to do with running the house. His dignity might be compromised by having to undertake such 'inconsequential' tasks.

References

Adhiati, M.A.S and Bobsien, A. (eds) (2001) *Indonesia's Transmigration Programme – An Update*, prepared for Down to Earth, July. Online: http://www.dte.gn.apc.org/ctrans.htm (accessed 6 August 2005).

Armstrong, P. and Armstrong, H. (1990) *Theorizing Women's Work*, Toronto: Garamond Press.

Dawson, G. (1994) 'Development planning for women: the case of the Indonesian transmigration program', *Women's Studies International Forum*, 17 (1): 69– 81.

Errington, S. (1990) 'Recasting sex, gender and power: a theoretical and regional overview', in J. M. Atkinson and S. Errington (eds) *Power and Difference: gender in Southeast Asia*, Stanford, CA: Stanford University Press.

Guinness, P. (1986) *Harmony and Hierarchy in a Javanese Kampung*, Singapore: Oxford University Press.

Hart, G. (1991) 'Engendering everyday resistance: gender, patronage and production politics in rural Malaysia', *Journal of Peasant Studies*, 19 (1): 93–121.

Hetler, C. B. (1986) 'Female-headed households in a circular migration village in Central Java', unpublished PhD thesis, Australian National University.

Kabeer, N. (1994) *Reversed Realities: gender hierarchies in development thought*, London: Verso.

Keeler, W. (1983) *Symbolic Dimensions of the Javanese House*, Working Paper 29, Chicago: Centre of Southeast Asian Studies, Anthropology Department, University of Chicago.

Sciortino, R. and Smyth, I. (1995) 'The triumph of harmony: the formal denial of domestic violence on Java', paper presented at the workshop on Indonesian Women in the Household and Beyond: reconstructing the boundaries, Leiden: Leiden University, 25–9 September.

Scott, C. V. (1995) *Gender and Development: rethinking modernization and dependency theory*, Boulder, CO: Lynne Rienner Publishers.

White, S. (1992) *Arguing with the Crocodile*, London: Zed Books.

Young, K. (1993) *Planning Development with Women: making a world of difference*, London: Macmillan.

3 *Dukun* and *Bidan*

The work of traditional and government midwives in Southeast Sulawesi

Simone Alesich

> My mother was a *dukun*, but I didn't want to become one. It is very demanding work. You can be called upon at any time, day or night.
>
> (An elderly woman in Buton)

Women assume most of the responsibilities for healing work in rural Southeast Sulawesi. Two types of women healers, the biomedical, government-trained midwife, or *bidan*, and the traditional healer and birth attendant, the *dukun*, between them provide the majority of healing services in rural villages. Healing can be considered an extension of women's work and women's roles in the Indonesian state, and in the local communities where the healers live and work. In examining healing work in rural areas we are encouraged to reconsider the notion of work, and how it can be defined and experienced in different ways. The type of work performed by these women healers differs significantly from women's labour force participation in predominantly urban areas (see Hay 1999). In particular, the *dukun*'s position as a healer is not so much a job as a personal identity in the village where she lives, and a way of interacting with others. The same can be said at least in part of the *bidan*, since she must also live and establish social relationships in rural villages.

The Indonesian Department of Health plays an important role in the training of both *bidan* and *dukun*, and in determining their relative importance vis-à-vis the state. This was particularly apparent in the New Order period of government (1966–98). The history of maternal health service provision in rural villages in Indonesia is long and convoluted. The literature (e.g. Cholil *et al.* 1998; Hunter 1996) indicates that the late Dutch colonial period was the earliest time when an effort was made to coordinate birth attendant services in a centralized manner in the archipelago. The state has embraced, and rejected, the skills and knowledge of indigenous/traditional or village healers at various times since then. The colonial era saw the first effort to train midwives to replace healers in village areas, with the establishment of a 'School for Indigenous Midwives' in 1852 (Cholil *et al.* 1998). Subsequently, the colonial regime conducted training of indigenous healers in biomedical practice. After independence in 1945, and particularly during the New Order period, policies established by the Dutch were continued in various forms by the Indonesian state. In the 1970s the national midwife scheme was disbanded and emphasis was placed on hospital deliveries for all births (Geefhuysen 2000). Later, the Department of Health began to train traditional healers (*dukun*) in biomedical practice (Grace 1996). The government midwife programme was revived by the Department of Health in 1989, with an estimated 56,000 'young midwives' (*bidan*) placed on government contracts between 1991 and 1997 (Geefhuysen 2000: 63). Biomedical training of *dukun* was phased out during the 1990s. While many of the changes to the maternal health service programme in Indonesia have been made in response to current global trends, as well as the perceived failure of previous schemes, this programme of maternal health training has had a significant impact at the local level in rural villages across Indonesia.

Southeast Sulawesi is a sparsely populated, relatively poor province of Indonesia, which has received scant attention in both academic literature and government programmes. Like many provinces of Indonesia, it is on the outskirts of

Figure 4 Bidan Nila.

development, with mostly rural inhabitants working in subsistence and cash-crop farming. The two villages where I conducted fieldwork are in fairly remote, rural areas at two ends of the province.[1] One is a Butonese village, in the mountainous area between the port city of Bau Bau and the new district capital of Pasarwajo. The village does not share the sea-faring reputation of much of Buton, and villagers mostly farm dry rice and corn, and make *arak* (a type of liquor distilled from the lontar palm). The other is a Tolaki village up near the border with central Sulawesi province, and about 100 kilometres from the coast. It is a flat area, ringed with high mountains. The young men collect rattan and villagers farm dry rice and mung beans along the wide river nearby. Both villages are in 'uplands' areas, far from the coast; both are far from subdistrict health centres (*pusat kesehatan masyarakat – puskesmas*) and both have government midwives living in their villages. Southeast Sulawesi has historically been neglected by health services from the national government (Kristanto *et al.* 1989) although it has been involved in the various waves of midwifery training.

Figure 5 Dukun Hana.

At the time that I conducted fieldwork in 2004, approaches to training traditional and biomedical midwives were changing yet again. Government midwives were being recalled for additional training by the district Departments of Health across Southeast Sulawesi province, partly in response to a general concern that the midwife placement scheme had not produced the reduction in maternal mortality for which the Department had hoped. After the end of the New Order period, the process of decentralization began to change the way that the state interacts with rural villages, with the new structure of the Department of Health placing much greater responsibility on district (*kabupaten*) health offices, for example, for training and budget allocation. This chapter is written within the context of the current training situation, with reference to the historical context outlined above.

My analysis will consider the *bidan* and *dukun* as representing two different types of healing in Southeast Sulawesi, one type of healing sponsored by the state, and the other produced locally. The state has projected particular ideas and practices of women's work in the area of health, resulting in the female-dominated *bidan* phenomenon. The state has also redefined the role of the *dukun* according to state-sanctioned definitions of local healers. These state-sanctioned ideas draw on idealized concepts of the community and 'the village' in Indonesia (e.g. Bowen 1986; Li 2001; Warren 1993). Such state models of the village are often contested at a local level, and increasingly so in the decentralized era. This has implications for the roles that the *bidan* and *dukun* play in the local community. I will begin by considering in turn the *dukun* and *bidan* in my two field sites, the type of work that is performed by each, and how they interact with their clients, the state and the villages where they live and work. I consider how their work has changed over time, and discuss the implications of this for women's own understandings of their work and the roles they play in rural Southeast Sulawesi society. One important aspect of healing to consider is the connection between the healer, healing practices and the patient. Healing work cannot be separated from membership of a particular community, a healer's relationship with her clients, and connections to other parts of her life.

Healing as work

Healing can be classified as 'work', in a fashion similar to factory labour or rice production. Analyses of labour in industrial economies place a great emphasis on productive work for a wage. This has been challenged by feminist scholars, who argue for unpaid work, such as housework, to be included within the definition of 'work' (Bullock 1994; Pringle and Game 1983). Adkins (1995) elucidates the difference between 'manufacturing' and 'service' work, demonstrating that the latter is a growing area within the labour market, and one dominated by women. Part of the service provided to a client includes an aspect of the identity of the worker – such as her reputation or her rapport with clients (see Urry in Adkins 1995: 8). Healing can be seen as a type of service work, where the person of the healer and her relationship to the client is much more significant than in other types of (productive) work. Moreover, the work of the healer itself has particular attributes which the healer carries into the rest of her life, and her working and non-working lives inform one another. A large proportion of healers in Indonesia are women, and their healing role is seen by the community, and the state, as compatible with their identities and designated functions as women.

The healing practice of the *dukun*, the female traditional healer, is an integral part of her identity and relationship with others in rural villages. *Dukun* are expected to be available at any time, day and night, and remuneration for their services is often nominal or symbolic. The *dukun* has an important position in rural society as a powerful figure who can summon spiritual authority and heal people. She is related to many of her clients, who explicitly use this familial connection to seek her services. She is descended from a family of *dukun*; thus her practice can be classified as an inheritance, and a woman descended from *dukun* often faces much pressure from the community to become one herself. She is trained by elders of that *dukun* family in a form of apprenticeship (see also Laderman 1983). In the area of childbirth, both the *dukun* and *bidan* are variously entrusted with the responsibility of ensuring the well-being of the mother and child. The *bidan* embodies the government health system and the authority of the government in the village. According to the government, the *bidan* is responsible for attending all births in villages, with the *dukun* only present as an assistant. However the ideals and practice of village health are embodied in the *dukun*, and her behaviour reflects the strength and authority of local health practice within the village. A majority of villagers express a preference for having a *dukun* attend births, whether or not the *bidan* is present. Yet the practices of both healers are ambiguous, since they are affected by both the authority of the state and the local community where they live.

For women in rural areas of Indonesia, working for some form of remuneration complements their other responsibilities as mother, wife and housekeeper. Although some women in Southeast Sulawesi work as waged labour in the forestry industry or road construction, for example, a large proportion of women work in occupations where they can concurrently look after children, their husbands and their households. This includes operating small shops from their houses or nearby markets. In both villages where I lived, small shops (*kios*) in the front of houses were a frequent sight. These are primarily – and sometimes solely – the responsibility of women (see also Indraswari 2005). Healing is one such occupation which dovetails in with other areas of women's lives, since the typical work venue is her own, or another villager's, house. However *dukun* work can be very demanding, such as when a *dukun* is called to attend the birth of a woman in a distant field (*kebun*), and she must be available to assist women in labour at any time.

The *Dukun*

Dukun Hana welcomed me into her house in some embarrassment, commenting on its shabby appearance, before offering me a chair in the front room. Her grandchildren played in the front yard and around our feet a number of small kittens mewed and explored. Hana is a Tolaki woman of probably about 50 years of age, who has lived in the northern part of Southeast Sulawesi province her whole life. She is a senior *dukun* in her village, called to assist births not only here but in a number of villages across the province where her skills are known. Hana laughed as she told me stories of births that she had attended and of her own labour, in the way of older women who are confident in their own society, able to laugh at their own actions and to proclaim that they sailed through their labour with ease. Extending her own lack of concern with pain, Hana told me about a recent accident where she had been badly hurt, and 'nearly died', when she left the village to assist a woman in child-birth some hours away. She smiled at me again, and walked into the back room to prepare a placenta for burial.

The *dukun*, or traditional healer, is a common figure in rural life in Southeast Sulawesi. Indeed, women with specialized skills in attending births in villages are found across Asia. They have been generalized by development literature into the category of 'traditional birth attendant', which ignores the specificity of their roles in the communities where they work (see Pigg 1995). *Dukun* is an Indonesian term for this type of healer, a woman who attends birth, among other healing services. Confusingly, *dukun* is also a term used widely in Indonesia, and historically in anthropological literature, to refer to sorcerers and magical practitioners (see for example Geertz 1964). Some authors have used local terms, such as *belian* in Lombok (Hay 2005) to remove the confusion used by the term *dukun*. Since my ·fieldwork was conducted in two different areas of Southeast Sulawesi, the local terms for *dukun* differed: *osando* in Tolaki and *bisa* in the Wakaokili dialect used in the Buton village.[2]

The demanding nature of *dukun* work in Southeast Sulawesi villages means that it tends to be performed by older women, who have lesser responsibilities for chil-dren and the household. *Dukun* are typically past the age of having children, 'usu-ally between about 50 and 70 years of age' (Grace 1996: 151). Older *dukun* are greatly revered for their experience and knowledge, referred to as *dukun senior*. Being married, with children, and generally older, *dukun* escape the condemnation that women in some societies have in terms of working outside the normal occupa-tions of women (in child rearing and household tasks). Their status as older women, and mothers, means that they are able to leave the village to attend births (in other villages or in distant fields), and to work at night as well as during the day. This can be considered less acceptable for younger women (for a discussion of the problems of night-time work see Nilan and Utari ch. 7 of this volume).

I visited Hana's latest client in her front bedroom: a young unmarried woman, the *dukun*'s niece, who had fled to her aunt's house to give birth because she had concealed her pregnancy from her parents, fearful of her father's reaction to her pregnancy. I later watched as Hana washed the new baby's placenta carefully, using water, salt and dried mango (a type of *asam* or sour dried fruit) before wrap-ping it in a white cloth (white cloths are also used for burial) to bury it. The placenta was buried by a man, since the baby was a boy. The placenta is referred to as *kakak* – older sibling – and it will guard the baby against illness as it grows (for discus-sions of the meaning of the placenta in other parts of Indonesia, see Grace 1996; Niehof 1985; Parker 2002). The *dukun* prepares the placenta for burial as part of her role in assisting women, usually relatives, with the birth process. The authority and healing skills of the *dukun* can challenge the lack of authority women generally hold in village society. In this case the *dukun* harboured her niece in her house, protecting her from the violent intentions of the girl's father. Such a role may be destabilizing to the male-dominated social order in villages in Southeast Sulawesi.

The education and training of *dukun* lie outside the formal government system: *dukun* are trained in a type of apprenticeship with an older *dukun*, often a member of their own family (see Grace 1996; Laderman 1983). Laderman outlines in some detail the rigorous apprenticeship of a *dukun* in Malaysia (where she is called a *bidan kampung*), which has many regional similarities to *dukun* training in Indonesia. *Dukun* in the village learn a number of specialized skills which are common to *dukun* in Indonesia more generally; these skills include herbal or traditional medicine, spiritual healing, massage and birth attendance. Laderman argues against assumptions that *dukun* are untrained, suggesting that it is 'an expression of cultural bias in favour of formal schooling over apprenticeship' (1983: 119). While there are a few male *dukun* in Southeast Sulawesi, the majority are women and it is generally seen as inappropriate for a man to deliver a baby, 'unless he is a doctor', as one informant commented. The birth process is considered the preserve of women. It is almost exclusively female *dukun* who brace the legs of the woman giving birth, assist in delivery and sit in the birth room. As older women too, *dukun* attend births having experienced childbirth themselves, and are therefore seen as the appropriate people to guide younger women and impart their knowledge of post-partum care. A number of *dukun* have commented that attending births caused their own childbirth labours to be particularly severe, one Tolaki *dukun* saying, 'attending births is a *pamali* (something forbidden). When I attend births the sickness of other women transfers to me, making my own labour more difficult.'

Although knowledge of spiritual and traditional medicinal practices is held by a number of people in the village, *dukun* are set apart by the extent of their knowledge and experience (Hay 2005). A *dukun* must be skilful in wielding ambivalent spiritual power to help their clients (Slamet-Velsink 1996). When attending births, *dukun* use their spiritual knowledge and experience to protect the woman and her child's spiritual and physical health. Grace argues that *dukun* 'speak the same language, literally and metaphorically' as their clients (1996: 164), offering reassurance to the woman giving birth on a number of levels, in a way that cannot be duplicated by the *bidan*. This link between spirituality and health is important in traditional health practice, since 'health represents cosmological harmony' (Aragon 1992: 333). The prayers that the *dukun* chant in Southeast Sulawesi are Islamic, and *dukun* like Hana have strong connections to Islam. Hana competed in Qur'an recitation competitions as a girl, although she does not hold a formal position in the Islamic faith, since these are reserved for men. Islam is linked to local beliefs in Southeast Sulawesi, as it is in other parts of the country.

The differences in spiritual healing between Butonese and Tolaki villages reflect local differences in cultural practices and spiritual beliefs. These different types of spiritual powers are employed by the *dukun* to protect her client, the birthing woman, from harm. *Dukun* not only protect pregnant and labouring women from spirits: their spiritual healing extends to other types of spiritual disturbance in

Figure 6 Birth ceremony attended by *dukun*.

village society. For example, a Tolaki man who kept seeing the ghost of a dead person, and fainting, was ritually washed by a *dukun* to cure him of this disturbance. Dukun Hana explains, 'The *bidan* and the *dukun* must work together. The *dukun* does not know how to inject people with syringes, and the *bidan* does not know how to perform spiritual healing (*tiup-tiup*).' While some *bidan* may make an attempt to cater for spiritual needs when attending births (Parker 2003), this is not generally seen as typical by villagers. Village women who give birth in hospital, for example, do not observe the same post-partum practices as women who give birth in the home, and their recovery is assisted by pharmaceuticals from the *bidan* rather than traditional remedies, such as washing with hot water, by the *dukun*.

Dukun work is not something that can be set aside at the end of a day: it is an important aspect of the way that *dukun* define their relationships with others and establish their identity in the village. As a vocation which is inherited, *dukun* are aware from an early age of the expectations placed on them to follow in the footsteps of their elders. As the quotation at the start indicates, one woman from a family of *dukun* resisted the pressure from the community to become a *dukun*, arguing that the work was too demanding. This is a story common to other parts of Indonesia, such as Bali (Connor 1983: 62–3). Within a Southeast Sulawesi village, there are particular families of healers – although all villagers seem to be related to a *dukun* in some way, even if only through marriage or via a distant relation. In some cases, a *dukun* from a neighbouring village will be preferred to attend a birth over a local *dukun* due to a closer familial connection with the family concerned.

Hana was frequently called to attend births in her natal village, some hours distant. Virilocal residence is common in Southeast Sulawesi, and women retain links to their own village. In the case of polygynous marriage (also common in Southeast Sulawesi), some wives may remain in their natal villages after marriage.

There have been a number of efforts to train *dukun* in government-sponsored biomedical practice since colonial times in Indonesia. Currently, the Indonesian government advocates *dukun* training in non-clinical skills, particularly training in her relationship with the *bidan*. *Dukun* have responded to recent government pressure for non-clinical training in a number of ways. Some have attended the training and continued to practise as before. Others have relished the new knowledge and potential opportunities that this training has provided, particularly younger *dukun* who lack authority in terms of their own *dukun* practice in the village. A senior *dukun*, Hana has strenuously resisted any government training, declaring proudly that she has not attended any training sessions at any time, now or in the past. Hana is one of the most-respected *dukun* in her community, which is reflected in the patronage that she has in the village as well as praise from the health establishment. However, she feels dismissed by the government health system, and she is acutely aware of their interest in limiting her role in attending births. She said that the *puskesmas* (subdistrict health centre) 'told me I am the best *dukun*. But they do not listen to me, they don't give me the equipment I need, that I ask them for.'

The healing practices of *dukun* and *bidan* are remarkably different, including their understandings of healing and their relationship with the community. One key concept in *dukun* practice is the idea of matching a treatment to the patient. This is often referred to in Indonesian as being *cocok* or 'compatible'. While the *bidan* will usually dispense some sort of medication to each patient – often just vitamins – the *dukun* tailors the treatment of each illness to the perceived cause, whether physical or spiritual, in conjunction with the patient's 'unique individual circumstances' and their relationship to their environment, community and belief system (Slamet-Velsink 1996: 75). When villagers assisted me in one village when I was ill, they deemed Western pharmaceuticals to be more *cocok* for me, arguing that traditional remedies were less likely to be effective than medicine from my own world of Western biomedicine. For those villagers, I was connected to a different environment, community and belief system to them, as evinced by my white skin, Christianity and status as a foreigner. This was further reinforced to them by the atypical nature of my illnesses, such as violent reactions to certain foods and frequent dizziness, which they did not experience.

The *Bidan*

As noted earlier, government training schemes for midwives have been in place in various forms in Indonesia since the Dutch colonial period. The most recent effort, from 1989 onwards, has involved a concerted placement of midwives directly in villages, rather than in health centres (*puskesmas*) or hospitals as in previous schemes. *Bidan* in both of the communities where I conducted research trained under the post-1989 midwife placement drive, which involved school-leavers being given one year of midwifery training before being placed in remote villages. These young women had grown up in cities distant from the communities where they were now based. They faced a number of challenges in assimilating to the new village environment: they were not local, and as young, often unmarried, women, they were not seen as having any particular authority in the area of childbirth practice. After all, what do unmarried women know about childbirth practice? *Bidan* are rarely located in one village for longer than five years, requiring them to continually re-establish their basis of authority in new locations.

Ten to fifteen years after the most recent policy was introduced, however, *bidan* like Nila have extensive experience in delivering babies in rural environments, and have built up relationships with the communities where they work. Nila is a young Butonese woman from the large city of Bau Bau. She spent a year in midwifery training and was then placed in two villages, one on the nearby island of Kabaena and one in Buton, each for a period of five years. She was recently placed in a new village in Buton and now begins the difficult task of getting to know her new village and her new clients, and of establishing herself as a unique service provider in the wake of a popular previous midwife. A Tolaki *bidan*, in a different district of Southeast Sulawesi, resisted the pressure from the Department of Health to move to a new village, preferring to remain in an area where she was familiar with the local population. Both she and Nila are from cities, now placed in rural villages some distance from their homes, where they have no family. For Nila, not knowing the local language makes her task even more of a challenge. Villagers are most critical of village *bidan* who are unsuccessful in assimilating into the community, rather than those who are inattentive to village health concerns (see also Laderman 1983). 'She is only here two or three days a month ... she doesn't come and talk to us' were the most common complaints about midwives. Popular *bidan* were praised thus: 'She would come into my house and help herself to food from my kitchen. She was just like family.' While she separates her work and social life while in the city, or training, in the village she is the *bidan*, addressed as such, and called on at all hours in the midwife's house, where she lives and practises.

Like the nurses in rural Java described by Sciortino (1995), *bidan* are subject to a strict hierarchy in the government health system, and they come somewhere near the bottom. They spend much of their time carrying out orders from above, whether from the district office of the Department of Health (Dinas Kesehatan Kabupaten) or the subdistrict health centre (*puskesmas*; see also Habsjah and Aviatri 1996). *Bidan* conduct government health activities such as the monthly outreach clinic for maternal and child health (*pos pelayanan terpadu – posyandu*) in the village, assisted by a team from the *puskesmas*. They attend monthly meetings at the *puskesmas* where they report on their progress, including the death and birth statistics of the villages for which they are responsible. When the Department of Health recently decided to conduct retraining of *bidan*, the *bidan* themselves had no opportunity to contribute to the timetable established for the retraining. One *bidan*'s schedule was determined as three days training, three days working, per week. Since her training was some six hours away from the village where she worked,

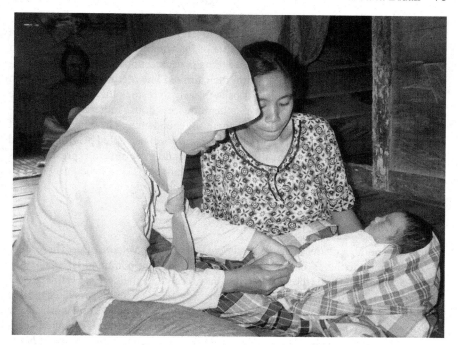

Figure 7 Bidan giving an injection.

this involved two days of travel a week, three days of training and two days of working in the village. Her commitment to both job and training would need to be high – given that she had no time off, and two long days of travel a week. She consequently visited the village once a month, spending a maximum of two or three days there before returning to the city.

Although there is a Midwives' Association of Indonesia (Ikatan Bidan Indonesia), which ostensibly represents the interests of *bidan*, this does not appear to be active in Southeast Sulawesi and *bidan* have limited bargaining power vis-à-vis the Department of Health (see Habsjah and Aviatri 1996). This particularly relates to contract *bidan* who are placed in villages. All *bidan* are initially employed on five-year contracts, after which they theoretically sit an exam and become fully fledged public servants in the Department of Health. In reality, *bidan* contracts are renewed, and *bidan* find it difficult to break into the public service. *Bidan* who have achieved public servant status have much greater authority than contract *bidan*, partly due to their guaranteed employment status.

For the *bidan* themselves, living in villages and 'going down' (*turun*) (Grace 1996: 150) to the people is not always a preferred career option, with many *bidan* trying to obtain public servant status, so that they can remain in the city. Nila said that she felt 'bored' being in the village all the time, frequently journeying to Bau Bau on weekends. However, living in villages gives Nila a kind of independence for which many *bidan* expressed a desire; moreover, this is a kind of independence that is not easily achieved by unmarried women in much of Indonesia. Although there is pressure on *bidan*, like all women, to get married and have children, even unmarried *bidan* are given the exalted title of *ibu* (mother/Mrs) when working in the village. Running a small business of selling pharmaceuticals indicates the entrepreneurial nature of many *bidan*, using their limited knowledge of general health practice and utilizing their frequent trips to the city to restock their supplies. Some *bidan* that I spoke to preferred to live in the midwife's house rather than with a village family, saying that they valued their independence. The phenomenon of unmarried *bidan* is sufficiently common to be fairly well accepted by villagers, and the respect given to *bidan* as health practitioners and government representatives generally protects them from criticism and speculative gossip (particularly regarding unmarried *bidan*) when they are required to work at night.

The *dukun* and *bidan* compared

There are a number of areas where the work of the *dukun* and *bidan* differ. These areas primarily relate to their relationship with their clients in the communities where they work. Such areas include the remuneration they receive for their services (financial or in-kind); the ratio of *dukun* and *bidan* to villagers; the access villagers have to their services; and the role they play in the communities where they live and work. There are often several *dukun*, but usually only one *bidan*, in any village. Their client-seeking methods differ partly on this basis, since villagers often have no choice of *bidan* but many choices of *dukun* in one village. However, the *bidan* can improve the quantity and frequency of her clients through establishing links with the community, and making villagers and their families feel comfortable visiting her to seek assistance. As a *bidan* is 'only' a midwife, she is often seen as extraneous to daily village needs. Although at the time of birth, the *bidan* can provide invaluable support, for the majority of the time she must earn respect through assisting villagers in everyday health matters. Thus she gives injections of vitamins to elderly people who are 'feeling weak', antibiotics to those suffering boils, and dressings for men involved in motorbike accidents. In this way she builds an additional role for herself in the village.

Since a *dukun* has, theoretically, much competition in the village from other *dukun*, she must establish her status in a number of ways. One of these is to appeal to her family connections, since she usually attends births of relatives, as discussed above. Another way to establish her status is through age and experience. Older, more experienced *dukun* are referred to as *senior*, and they are called to attend births in other areas as well, usually where they have family connections. As well as experience, developing a reputation as a successful and competent *dukun* helps her establish a client base (see Laderman 1983). Maternal deaths may harm the perceived competency of a *dukun* in the eyes of villagers, as Hay (1999) suggests in Lombok. There were no maternal (or infant) deaths during my fieldwork, and descriptions of other deaths ascribed blame to a variety of sources, such as 'she was too short' or 'she gave birth far from the village'.

Bidan have a full-time job as a midwife and general health provider, while *dukun* work in the fields or other occupations in addition to their healing work, to support their families. This is partly a result of their different remunerations for healing work. *Bidan* receive a wage for part of their work from the Department of Health, including services to the health centre (*puskesmas*). They are also paid by families for attending births at a rate set by the district government. The rate set in districts in Southeast Sulawesi in 2004 was around Rp. 200,000 (approximately US$22), but this varies in practice according to the ability of families to pay, and may be as low as Rp. 50,000 to Rp. 100,000. In late 2004, certain districts introduced financial support for poor families, waiving the fee for attending childbirth (for a foreshadowing of this policy see Cholil *et al.* 1998). Instead, the *bidan* was paid for these deliveries by the Department of Health, once the births were reported at the health centre (*puskesmas*).

Payments for *dukun* are much less standardized, partly because they lie outside the official government system. When attending births alongside *bidan*, *dukun* may be allocated part of the attendance fee: an estimated sum of Rp. 25,000 to Rp. 50,000. One *bidan* qualified this, adding, 'except where the *dukun* is a member of the family'. Herein lies one of the greatest obstacles to financial remuneration for *dukun* in childbirth services: they generally attend the births of members of their family, and are thus not formally paid. However, as a service to their family, attending a birth is unparalleled and *dukun* may receive much informal support and payment in other ways, such as financial assistance for herself or her children, from extended family members. When a *dukun* attends a non-family member who 'has money', that person will pay for her services. While the *bidan* is able to separate her professional and personal lives in the village, the *dukun* cannot often do so in the same way, given that her clients are frequently relations. *Dukun* work is an important aspect of her relations with others, which she maintains through childbirth attendance and other healing work.

Interaction

Given the long history of both *bidan* and *dukun* in the provision of healing services in Indonesia, it is inevitable that they have to work with one another. In working with one another, they have the opportunity to develop attitudes about the work and role of the other in comparison to themselves. In the post-1989 period, when the village placement of midwives scheme has been in full force, with a majority of target villages covered by a *bidan* by 1996 (Cholil *et al.* 1998: 26), *dukun* and *bidan* have had more opportunities to work beside one another than before and observe each others' practices. Laderman (1983: 108–9) argues that villagers felt that 'most of the [*bidan*]'s services were superfluous, duplicating those of the [*dukun*]' in rural Malaysia. This was not the case in Southeast Sulawesi. In fact *dukun* tended to consider that *bidan* provide an entirely different service to that of the *dukun*. In the area of childbirth, *dukun* considered *bidan* to have an important role in providing an injection to assist with the avoidance of post-partum haemorrhaging (usually due to retained placenta). Hana told me, 'I never feel comfortable delivering babies if there is no *bidan* present, in case there is post-partum haemorrhage' (*pendarahan*). She elaborated further, telling me that there were two types of post-partum haemorrhage, one that was caused by spirits – which she could cure – and one that was a 'doctors' type' that could be cured by injection. This is presumably a concept that was developed in response to the advent of injections for post-partum haemorrhage. However, neither the *dukun* nor the community believed that the *bidan* could replicate the role of the *dukun*: after all, she is neither knowledgeable about traditional medicine nor able to conduct spiritual healing. At the time of giving birth, in particular, a *dukun* provides essential spiritual protection for the woman giving birth that the *bidan* is unable to give.

Although literature on the *bidan* and *dukun* suggest that *dukun* may resent the imposition of *bidan* in the villages where they practise, this is not overtly shown on a daily basis. *Bidan* tend to be dismissive of village health practices, including those of the *dukun*, but not consistently so. Nila was likely to condemn village health practice one day as 'backward' or 'ignorant', and tell me the next day that 'a *dukun* could attend a birth by herself if she were away from the village'. In fact current government policy emphasizes the fact that a *bidan* must always be present at a birth. Government policy cautions against *dukun* practice as 'dangerous', 'unsafe' or 'ignorant' (Cholil *et al.* 1998; see also Pigg 1995), and this feeds into *bidan* training and practice. National policy makers and health practitioners in Indonesia show little enthusiasm for the idea of involving traditional practitioners (Grace 1996: 145; Parker 2003; Sciortino 1995). Health personnel in Southeast Sulawesi were consistently critical of *dukun* practice and general health practice in the village. Such attitudes have been common since colonial times, but were reinforced in the New Order period when village practices were directly subsumed under the authority of the state. Current government attempts to incorporate *dukun* into the official health system are little more than veiled attempts to remove their practice altogether. Recent training of *dukun* is limited to instructions about working with *bidan*, as their assistants, rather than clinical training.

Traditional healers who stand outside the government health system are able to have more independence in their work, but their skills are unlikely to be recognized as a valid form of healing by the state. In comparison to other types of traditional health practitioners, such as male spiritual healers or bone-setters, *dukun* are more easily incorporated into the modern health system, since their role is seen by the state as comparable to biomedical midwives/*bidan*. The skills of other traditional healers, particularly those working primarily with spirits, are not so easily identified, and cannot be incorporated into the biomedical system. This has advantages and disadvantages for *dukun*: for example, their skills can be recognized by the government health system, but those skills can also be downgraded and criticized by that system in comparison to the skills of the government-trained *bidan* (see Sarwono 1996).

This is not to say that *bidan* and *dukun* do not work together well in everyday life. Although *dukun* are aware of the criticism of their practice from the health establishment, they refer patients to *bidan* and are respectful of their knowledge and practice. The *bidan*, in accordance with government policy, work with *dukun* in a way that shows respect for their age and status in the community.

However, the fundamental differences in their training, and in their healing practices, mean that in most cases, except childbirth attendance, *bidan* and *dukun* are considered to be separate and independent health providers in their own right. Since a *dukun*'s identity and skill derives from the village-based knowledge system, her type of healing work is generally considered more effective by clients. Speaking the language of villagers, patients of *dukun* are able themselves to see the benefits of her healing. The efficacy of *bidan* practice is often much more unclear in the eyes of villagers, deriving as it does from biomedical knowledge to which villagers have no access. Vitamins and other oral medication, in particular, are not seen as particularly effective, and are quickly discarded if no physical change is discerned by the patient.

The increase in numbers of *bidan* present at village level has changed the nature of *dukun* work, primarily because villagers no longer have to rely on *dukun* as the sole providers of childbirth and general health assistance. While *dukun* have certainly not retired from practice, as the Indonesian government would prefer, on a number of occasions women in my fieldwork areas preferred to give birth with only a *bidan* present. Certainly *bidan* have demonstrated to villagers that their commitment to assisting villagers is comparable with *dukun*: on one occasion a *bidan* travelled by boat to assist a woman in labour in a field. Most commonly, *bidan* and *dukun* attend births together, or the *dukun* attends births without a *bidan*. The main factor preventing the increase in *bidan* attendance at births is that they are so often not in the village when births occur. With pressure to retrain, family located far away and the discomfort many *bidan* feel in living in rural villages, *bidan* tend to be in the village on a limited basis, at best. As a result, *dukun* are still used because they are always present in large numbers to ensure that all women can be assisted in childbirth.

Healing as women's work

Connor argues, in the case of women healers in Bali, that healing work can be seen as an extension of women's work in rural villages, since 'ideological constructions of gender' shape the types of work that women do, which includes the practice of healing (1983: 54). As Bullock argues 'women's jobs echo their responsibilities' to family and the wider community (1994: 2). *Dukun* and *bidan* in Southeast Sulawesi perform healing work which extends from community perceptions of women's roles in their communities and from the naturalized, and government-promoted, ideal of women as carers – particularly as carers of their families. Communities prefer to ascribe the reasons for a gendered division of labour to biological difference, although 'there is nothing inherent in a job that makes it male or female' (Pringle and Game 1983: 23).

In villages of Southeast Sulawesi, women are expected to care for their families, particularly once they are married. This idea is by no means confined to Indonesia, or Asia. As Mason (1996: 16) notes, the idea of 'women's caring psyche', which has been naturalized into women's role as carers of their families, has been a focus of feminist writing in many parts of the Western world. Women's role as carer is linked to their responsibility for the health of their family. Responsibility for health and illness is often viewed in terms of ideas of personal responsibility and morality (Blaxter 1997). While living in a Tolaki village, I commented that I had not seen the woman who lived next door recently, and the village head told me that she had taken her teenage daughter to start high school in the district capital, about four or five hours away. Her husband always walked unsteadily and appeared to have had a stroke; consequently he rarely went out. A few days later the village head's wife's brother-in-law went to the house next door. He was the cousin of the woman in question. He came to our house afterwards, and told us that the man and his son were very sick and couldn't leave the house. There were only the two of them, and there was no one to look after them. The village head was critical of the woman who had left her husband and son to fend for themselves. 'It's a pity she's not here to look after them,' I agreed, 'But it's not her fault they got sick.' 'You don't under-stand,' the village head replied. 'You can't just go and leave your family if you're married. That's your responsibility.' Knowing a number of men who regularly left their families by themselves, including a number who had multiple wives, this seemed to be an accusation of gender-specific neglect, reflecting the idea that it is the particular duty of women to be responsible for marriage and the household. In this case, the woman's role as wife and mother, and her role as carer, are conflated as one.

In the two villages that formed my field sites, the process of childbirth reflects strongly on women's role in society. As one *dukun* commented to me, 'childbirth is the role of women'. This is not always the case, however, as Nourse (1989: 108) notes in her study of two communities in central Sulawesi. There, childbirth 'is associated with continuity and fatherhood', while the mother's role is diminished and problematized. In one of the communities that Nourse discusses, male *dukun* deliver the baby, reinforcing the connection between childbirth and men, and the important role that men play in the childbirth process. In these communities, men are associated with a caring role, while women are seen as neglectful. This contrasts with the idea of women as carers of their families, tenable in Southeast Sulawesi, in Indonesia more generally. Girls often begin to perform household duties at an early age (see Laderman 1983), and from an early age they are taught the skills to care for their families. Yet, despite the fact that she may have been keeping house for a num-ber of years, it is not until marriage, and particularly childbirth, that a girl officially enters into womanhood in Indonesia. In Southeast Sulawesi, unmarried women – and men – are treated as children, while parents are given the exalted title of 'mother-of' (or 'father-of'). This practice of teknonymy indicates the prestige of parent status. Therefore the act of childbirth is very significant for young women: it signifies the achievement of a higher, adult status in the community. Childbirth is not only an affair of women; it is considered one of their main roles. Older women, moreover, have much greater authority than younger women and are often present in numbers at a birth, particularly when a new mother needs to be instructed in ways to care for her child. This includes *dukun* along with other older women.

Rural women enact their roles as wives, mothers, household managers and citi-zens through a state-sponsored discourse of the ideal family, communicated through the institution of the PKK (Pembinaan/Pemberdayaan Kesejahteraan Keluarga – Family Welfare Movement). Although many PKK activities and roles are supported by the community generally – such as the roles of women as mothers, wives and household managers – the state inscribes a particular role for women in these areas, which they enforce through PKK. While recent changes have been made to PKK – including a name change to incorporate the idea of 'empowerment' (although the acronym remains the same), and a more democratic structure (PKK 2001) – the PKK in Southeast Sulawesi operates much as before. As wives and mothers themselves, *dukun* are incorporated into this projection of state ideology onto Indonesian women. The self-sacrificing nature of their work reflects the idea that women should serve their families and the state.

Women take on particular roles in healing practice, reflecting gendered connections made of women with earthly pursuits, such as cooking and childbirth, and men with the spirits – such as their role in religious leadership (see Hay 2005; Niehof 1985). The Indonesian state reinforces the idea that the appropriate role of women is healing, in particular attending births. The *bidan* is the primary government health provider in rural villages, and it is an almost exclusively female profession. Although men work as doctors in health centres, male health workers infrequently go to villages, usually only for the monthly health outreach clinic, to dispense medication and medical advice. On a daily basis, the female *bidan* provide most health services in the village, defining their role as one exclusively performed by women. The exclusive training of *dukun* rather than male traditional healers by the Department of Health reinforces this emphasis on women as healers in the official government view. In contrast, most male healers fall into the category of spiritual healers, and many are directly associated with formal, institutionalized religion. In the case of Southeast Sulawesi, most male healers are also *imam*, Islamic religious leaders. *Dukun* incorporate both practical aspects of healing – such as the use of herbs, and massage – and spiritual healing. Spiritual healing is used to combat illnesses caused by spirits (*roh halus* and *setan*), encounters with spirits of villagers who have recently died and illness caused by sorcery – such as curses and love spells. Both *dukun* and *imam* are called upon to address illnesses with a spiritual cause. However, there is a strong attempt to demarcate, or to 'outline a balance of power', between male and female healers, as there is in Lombok (Hay 2005: 27). In the case of one illness in Buton, an *imam* was called in preference to a *dukun* because his powers of spiritual healing were seen as more potent.

Old or young, women are expected to work hard throughout their lives: when children, they must work for the household of their parents; when married, they work for their own families and households. As Laderman suggests, 'Women must be sick indeed before they abdicate their daily tasks' (1983: 12). The traditional self-sacrificing 'nature' of women is noted by Cholil *et al.* (1998); this is characterized as a typical feature of Indonesian women. Women who are not self-sacrificing are condemned, as the story about the absent wife above shows. The hard work of women, including *dukun*, demonstrates the extent of their caring commitment to their families. *Bidan* are similarly expected to work hard and be committed to the communities where they live, although *bidan* prefer to come and go when attending births rather than staying for the full length of labour like *dukun*. Like doctors in a hospital, they come in at the last moment to supervise the final stages of labour. Standing outside the village community, *bidan* have less pressure to work in a self-sacrificing way to help others than do *dukun*. This is not to say that *bidan* do not work hard, but because they are not members of the community they have different expectations placed upon them to fit into its established division of labour.

The *dukun* and *bidan*, themselves, express satisfaction – and frustration – in their work as healers in rural Southeast Sulawesi villages. *Dukun* Hana makes many personal sacrifices in her work: she travels far, and was recently injured badly in an accident while travelling to assist a woman giving birth. Yet she is proud of her work, and proud of her independence from the government health system. 'I have never attended any training,' she told me. Discussions with Hana elicit a wealth of knowledge about childbirth practice and its relationship to spirituality. 'I started working as a *dukun* when I was still a girl,' Hana said. 'I was trained by my mother, who was also a *dukun*.' *Dukun* birth practice has changed over time, such as cutting the umbilical cord. 'They used to bite it,' Hana tells me, making a face. *Bidan*, too, are proud of the work they do, and the independent lifestyles they are able to achieve in the village. Some are frustrated. *Bidan* Nila expressed her boredom in living in the village, and her desire to study further rather than practise in a village setting. 'Like you,' she said to me, referring to my own education. Healing work provides an opportunity for young women from city areas to become *bidan*, and healing gives *dukun* greater status within their own communities. For women, though, in any type of profession, work must be negotiated around the expectations placed upon them (by villagers, and the state) to take on their primary gender role as wives and mothers. Nila married in 2004, and was expecting a baby the last time I saw her. It remains to be seen if she will be able to maintain her position as a *bidan* in the village, particularly with her husband resident in the city of Bau Bau. Only married women whose husbands are willing to live in their work area seem to successfully maintain their work as a village *bidan*.

Conclusion

Healing, like other forms of service work, relies on the connection between the person, the work and the client for whom the work is performed. These connections are particularly salient in rural areas of Indonesia. In the case of both the *dukun* and *bidan*, relations with the communities where they work are important for establishing a successful healing practice and being sought after as health providers. However, the connection to clients remains much more important for the *dukun* than the *bidan*, since the *bidan* is an outsider in terms of her residency in the village and her biomedically based health practice. The *dukun* is strongly linked to the community and her clients through her membership of the community in which she resides, the language and practice of healing which is based in that community and the familial ties she has with many of her clients.

The post-1989 government programme, which promotes residency of *bidan* in rural villages, has changed the way that health work is performed, with communities less engaged with the healing process when it is performed by the *bidan*. There has also been continual pressure from the Indonesian government – and its health workers – for *dukun* to cease or reduce the scope of their healing practice. However villagers are arguably less likely to prefer health practices such as biomedical practice that do not engage with villagers and local knowledge. Villagers are more likely to seek health services from, or to patronize, a health worker who has closer ties to the community, and to quickly reject healing practices with which they do not have a connection, or of which they have no understanding. In addition, *bidan* are still simply not in the village often or long enough to take over the function of *dukun* completely. It seems that *dukun* will continue to play an important role in healing in rural Indonesia in the future.

Southeast Sulawesi villagers and the state both see the healing work of *dukun* and *bidan* as arising naturally from the caring role of women in the community. Village communities also emphasize the role of female healers in bodily processes and male healers in spiritual and cerebral processes (Niehof 1985). This is particularly the case with childbirth attendance, and is reinforced by the fact that childbirth is seen to be exclusively a female affair. Unlike male doctors in hospitals, female *bidan* reinforce this connection between women, healing practice and childbirth attendance that has been established by *dukun* practice. Women working in healing practice also reflect the state production of the Indonesian woman as one who cares for her family and is dutifully subservient to the overarching state. The healing work of *dukun* and *bidan* sustains some gender stereotypes while challenging others. In this way their work replicates community values while also extending the role of women in village society, and within the Indonesian state.

Notes

1 Fieldwork was conducted in two rural villages of Buton district and Konawe (formerly Kendari) district for a period of twelve months from January to December 2004. Fieldwork was conducted as part of a PhD in Anthropology at the Research School of Pacific and Asian Studies, Australian National University. Fieldwork funding was provided by the Australian National University. Names used in this chapter have been changed to respect the privacy of fieldwork informants.
2 My fieldwork was conducted in the Indonesian language, making *dukun* the logical term used by villagers for traditional healers when speaking with me. In addition to this, I use the term *dukun* here because it is a term with all the connotations of spiritual and magical power, a term used to connote backwardness by the state and development agencies conducting maternal and child health projects. Rather than use a neutral term I choose to use a loaded term with significant meaning for villagers, anthropologists and modern health practitioners.

References

Adkins, L. (1995) *Gendered Work: sexuality, family and the labour market,* Buckingham: Open University Press.

Aragon, L. V. (1992) *Divine Justice: cosmology, ritual and protestant missionization in Central Sulawesi*, Indonesia, Urbana–Champaign: University of Illinois.

Blaxter, M. (1997) 'Whose fault is it? People's own conceptions of the reasons for health inequalities', *Social Science & Medicine*, 44 (6): 747–56.

Bowen, J.R. (1986) 'On the political construction of tradition: gotong royong in Indonesia', *Journal of Asian Studies*, 45 (3): 545–61.

Bullock, S. (1994) *Women and Work*, London: Zed Books.

Cholil, A., Iskandar, M. B. and Sciortino, R. (1998) *The Life Saver: the mother friendly movement in Indonesia*, Yogyakarta: Galang Communication.

Connor, L. H. (1983) 'Healing as women's work in Bali', in L. Manderson (ed.) *Women's Work and Women's Roles: Economics and Everyday Life in Indonesia, Malaysia and Singapore*, Canberra: Australian National University.

Geefhuysen, C. J. (2000) 'Safe motherhood in Indonesia: a task for the next century', in M. Berer and T. S. Ravindran (eds) *Safe Motherhood Initiatives: critical issues*, Oxford: Blackwell Science.

Geertz, C. (1964) *The Religion of Java*, London: Free Press of Glencoe.

Grace, J. (1996) 'Healers and modern health services: antenatal, birthing and postpartum care in Rural East Lombok, Indonesia', in P. Liamputtong Rice and L. Manderson (eds) *Maternity and Reproductive Health in Asian Societies*, The Netherlands: Harwood Academic Publishers.

Habsjah, A. and Aviatri, M. F. (1996) 'Suara bidan tak terdengar', in M. Oey-Gardiner, M. L. E. Wagemann, E. Suleeman and Sulastri (eds) *Perempuan Indonesia: Dulu dan Kini*, Jakarta: PT Gramedia Pustaka Utama.

Hay, M. C. (1999) 'Dying mothers: maternal mortality in rural Indonesia', *Medical Anthropology*, 18 (3): 243–79.

—— (2005) 'Women standing between life and death: fate, agency, and the healers of Lombok', in L. Parker (ed.) *The Agency of Women in Asia*, Singapore: Marshall Cavendish Academic.

Hunter, C. (1996) 'Sasak identity and the reconstitution of health', unpublished PhD thesis, University of Newcastle.

Indraswari (2005) 'Women and warung in an urban kampung', unpublished PhD thesis, Australian National University.

Kristanto, K., Makaliwe, W. H. and Saleh, A. K. (1989) 'South-east Sulawesi: isolation and dispersed settlement', in H. Hill (ed.) *Unity and Diversity: regional economic development in Indonesia since 1970*, Singapore: Oxford University Press.

Laderman, C. (1983) *Wives and Midwives: childbirth and nutrition in rural Malaysia*, Berkeley: University of California Press.

Li, T. M. (2001) 'Relational histories and the production of difference on Sulawesi's upland frontier', *Journal of Asian Studies*, 60 (1): 41–66.

Mason, J. (1996) 'Gender, care and sensibility in family and kin relationships', in J. Holland and L. Adkins (eds) *Sex, Sensibility and the Gendered Body*, London: Macmillan.

Niehof, A. (1985) 'Women and fertility in Madura', unpublished PhD thesis, University of Leiden.

Nourse, J. W. (1989) 'We are the womb of the world: birth spirits and the Lauje of Central Sulawesi', unpublished PhD thesis, University of Virginia.

Parker, L. (2002) 'The power of letters and the female body: female literacy in Bali', *Women's Studies International Forum*, 25 (1): 79–96.

—— (2003) 'Developing an indigenous modernity: birth in Bali', *Journal Antropologi Indonesia*, 70: 20–40.

Pigg, S. L. (1995) 'Acronyms and effacement: traditional medical practitioners (TMP) in international health development', *Social Science & Medicine*, 41 (1): 47–68.

PKK (2001) *Pemberdayaan dan Kesejahteraan Keluarga PKK: Pedoman Umum*, Jakarta: Tim Penggerak Pusat, PKK.

Pringle, R. and Game, A. (1983) *Gender at Work, Sydney: George Allen and Unwin*.

Sarwono, S. (1996) 'Personalistic belief in health: a case in West Java', in P. Boomgaard, R. Sciortino and I. Smyth (eds) *Health Care in Java: past and present*, Leiden: KILTV Press.

Sciortino, R. (1995) *Care-takers of Cure: an anthropological study of health centre nurses in rural Central Java*, Yogyakarta: Gadjah Mada University Press.

Slamet-Velsink, I. A. (1996) 'Some reflections on the sense and nonsense of traditional health care', in P. Boomgaard, R. Sciortino and I. Smyth (eds) *Health Care in Java: past and present*, Leiden: KILTV Press.

Warren, C. (1993) *Adat and Dinas: Balinese communities in the Indonesian state*, Kuala Lumpur: Oxford University Press.

4 Poverty, opportunity and purity in paradise

Women working in Lombok's tourist hotels

Linda Rae Bennett

Young women in Lombok often romanticize working in the international tourist industry, imagining the more exciting lifestyles that may ensue from their close association with the relative freedom, affluence and modernity of tourists. And yet competition for paid work in tourism is fierce, job insecurity is a structural reality of the industry and women's wages do not guarantee affluence. This chapter explores the gap between popular imaginings of the tourist industry and women's actual participation within in it, resisting both the romanticization and the victimization of women working in tourism. It explores the realities of their lives through an ethnographic lens that privileges women's own interpretations of their desires, experiences and opportunities as they are linked with (but not wholly determined by) their employment. It examines the consequences of Indonesia's recent economic crisis and dramatic downturn in international tourism, and the pragmatic compromises that women have made in recent years in light of the increased insecurity of their employment. Working in the tourist industry impacts significantly on many key life decisions for women – decisions about their residence patterns, roles in the family, their choice of partner, family planning and how they manage child care. Of particular interest is the ways in which participation in the tourist industry shapes public perceptions of women's sexuality and respectability, and how this impacts upon their relationships with men. This chapter thus explores how women's work is enmeshed with almost every aspect of their lives, and examines how the interrelated themes of opportunity, autonomy and agency are manifested in relation to women's work.

This chapter derives from ethnographic data collected from participant observation and repeat in-depth interviews with 15 women in full-time employment in tourist hotels on the eastern Indonesian island of Lombok. The interviews were conducted between June 2004 and August 2005 and observations of women working in this area have been ongoing since 1995. At the time of data collection, my informants were between the ages of 20 and 32 and working in hotels in a range of positions including as waitresses, receptionists, kitchen hands, cooks, cleaners and book-keepers/accountants, as managers and in public relations. In reality, the work required in any one of these positions necessitates undertaking a variety of tasks incorporating duties from several job descriptions. Women's and men's roles in tourism on Lombok are also typically gendered and closely mirror the gendered division of labour observed in Balinese tourism by Long and Kindon (1997). Women generally engage in the kinds of labour described above that are understood to be more feminine and aligned with the domestic sphere, while men tend to monopolize work that is thought to be more dangerous, to require greater physical strength or to involve greater spatial and temporal mobility. Typically masculine occupations in Lombok's tourist industry include those of *jaga malam* (lit. night watchman, or security guard), drivers, gardeners, maintenance staff and guides. However, despite these gendered tendencies in the tourism workforce, there is a range of occupations in which women and men overlap and compete for jobs, including management, accounting, table waiting, cooking (although qualified chefs are usually men), cleaning and reception duties. Below, I describe women's perceptions of their career opportunities compared with their male peers employed in similar positions.

The women whose experiences and perspectives are represented in this chapter are all Muslim and are primarily of Sasak ethnicity, although three women have mixed Sasak and Javanese ethnic backgrounds. The Sasak are the indigenous inhabitants of Lombok. Although they constitute roughly 90 per cent of the island's population, they remain economically and politically marginalized.[1] I chose informants employed in budget, mid-range and top-end hotels in order to compare their experiences across different economic brackets of tourism. A number of women interviewed had shared workplaces and staff from a total of 12 hotels participated in this research. The marital status of the 15 women whose lives are featured in the chapter is varied, including single, engaged, married and one woman in a *de facto* relationship.[2] All informants speak English, as well as Indonesian and various regional languages such as Sasak, Balinese and Javanese. Interviews were conducted in a mix of Indonesian and English, reflecting the eagerness of these women to practise their English skills.

Senggigi beach, the setting of this chapter, is one of three key tourist locations on Lombok. It is the most developed in terms of its infrastructure and the presence of large international hotel chains and the high levels of service they offer. Senggigi is approximately 30 minutes by car from the island's airport, and an hour's drive from Lembar harbour where the ferry from Bali docks. It is generally the first stop-over for tourists arriving in Lombok. The two other most popular tourist destinations in Lombok are the three small *gili* (islands), Gili Meno, Gili Air and Gili Trawangan, that lie off the west coast of Lombok, and the village of Kute, a surfing destination on the southern coast. International tourism in Lombok has been organized in a more restricted and localized manner than has been the case for its near neighbour, Bali (immediately to the west), and is far less integrated with the local economy than is the case for Bali. Although individual villages in Lombok's interior do specialize in handicrafts such as pottery, wood work, rattan weaving and cloth weaving, these villages have not shifted their production and local economies to the extent that they are heavily reliant on tourism for survival. The majority of Sasak live in rural areas, at subsistence level, and are impacted upon by globalization to a much lesser extent than those women living and working in tourist locales.

Reliance on the tourist dollar is greatest in areas that focus on supplying accommodation, food and recreation for the tourist market, and for this reason these areas have been most affected by the serious downturn in tourism from 1998 onwards.

Political economy and international tourism in Lombok

Prior to 1998, earnings from and investments in international tourism on Lombok were steadily improving (BPS–NTB 1995). In this climate of optimism, Lombok was expected to significantly expand its tourist industry, an expectation that was supported by regional government initiatives, local business and both local and international investment (Director General Tourism Lombok 1997). The economic downturn and escalating inflation that ensued in Lombok and across Indonesia had disastrous consequences for investment in tourism. This was accompanied by constantly depressed demand from international tourists stemming from a series of unfortunate events that undermined public perceptions of the safety and desirability of holidaying in Indonesia. These events include Indonesia's economic crisis and the associated political upheaval that facilitated the downfall of the New Order regime in 1998, as well as the military interventions required to bring about East Timorese independence (granted in 1999). The single most devastating event in terms of deflating international tourist demand was the Bali bombing in Kuta on 12 October 2002, which was explicitly aimed at taking tourist lives. This attack drastically undermined foreign perceptions of Indonesia's ability to ensure domestic security against terrorist attacks. While Bali has a predominantly Hindu population, Lombok's population is 90 per cent Muslim. Due to Westerners' heightened perceptions of their vulnerability in relation to Muslims, Lombok's safety as a tourist destination became a subject of international concern. Many of my informants who had been working in Senggigi prior to the Bali bombing noted that they encountered explicit anti-Islamic attitudes from international guests for the first time following the bombing.

The downturn in tourist demand in 2003 was so marked that numerous tourist businesses went bankrupt. Many were forced to reduce operating costs by limiting services and retrenching staff, and significant numbers of tourist-oriented developments were abandoned. In recent years, empty hotels, bungalows, retail outlets and abandoned building sites have come to pepper the Senggigi landscape, invoking an atmosphere of stagnation and decay. Following widespread bankruptcy, the value of local land and businesses depreciated rapidly, resulting in significant changes to the composition of tourism investment. In 2005, Indonesian investment remains depressed; Australian investment also remains below pre-2002 levels; while European investment in hotels and eating venues has risen markedly. Investment by the local Chinese community appears to have been sustained and is now mirroring that of expatriate investors from Northern European countries, particularly Belgium, Germany and the Netherlands. Since the first Bali bombing, locals have also noted fluctuations in tourist demand connected with the threat of SARS in 2003, the avian bird flu since 2003, and the recent spate of drug arrests of Australians in Bali. Locals working in Lombok's tourist industry are particularly annoyed at the impact of one recent drug conviction lamenting that 'Corby is not good for business'.[3] They express frustration that a few *nakal* (naughty) tourists endanger the image of the whole industry and in turn endanger their livelihoods.

Notable shifts in the composition of the local workforce have occurred in response to these upheavals. Previously, a large number of Balinese and Javanese were employed in Lombok's tourist industry and they outnumbered the Sasak who were less able to secure formal positions. In response to severe economic downturn, many Balinese and Javanese have returned to their islands of origin in search of better opportunities, and some who had financed their own tourist ventures were compelled to relocate due to bankruptcy. Simultaneously, the skills base of locals has been steadily improving. Sasak youth have invested in English language skills and hospitality training, making them more competitive with peers from other islands. The fact that the vast majority of Sasak begin their working lives from positions of relative disadvantage, compared to those of other ethnic groups on Lombok, tends to engender patience when seeking employment and often a stoic sense of determination to succeed or endure in the face of difficult financial circumstances. In response to the broader socio-economic conditions, which has created heightened and continued job insecurity, some women within Lombok's tourist industry have made strategic compromises to guard their longer-term interests.

Working conditions

The working conditions reported by women working in Senggigi are remarkably similar across different hotels and occupations, and indicate high levels of awareness among women of their rights as workers, as well as fairly consistent industry standards. All of the women interviewed earn a basic wage (before travel and food allowances) of between Rp. 300,000 and 1,000,000 per month, with only two of the women earning over Rp. 500,000.[4] More than half of my informants were being paid at (or above) the *upah minimum regional* (UMR – minimum regional wage), and those who were being paid under the minimum were aware that they were making a salary sacrifice. The reasons women were willing to accept less than the minimum wage include securing employment in an environment of fierce competition, lack of previous experience, the expectation that their wages would increase over time, and an agreement with hotel management that their wage will return to the minimum when business improves. Those women earning under the minimum wage have a greater reliance on tips to supplement their income. While all of the women interviewed would be happy with higher wages, none of them described their wages as exploitative and those who are being paid below the minimum all clarified that it is their choice to accept a lower wage. It was common for women to remind me that the wages they would receive for parallel work outside of tourism would be significantly lower (usually 50 per cent of rates in the tourist industry), and that they felt very fortunate to be in full-time employment. Thus, women's interpretations of their economic situation are generally shaped by their awareness of the wider socio-economic environment.

Women who were called upon to work overtime during high season reported that they are paid for the additional hours worked, and generally receive higher rates for overtime on public holidays. Waitresses in particular are often required to be on standby for large functions and during high season, and tend to view this as an opportunity for earning more rather than as an imposition on their recreational time. All of the women who chose to share details of their work lives were in full-time positions, indicating the preference of hotels in the area for employing staff on a full-time rather than a part-time basis. Apparently, there is a perception amongst management that full-time employees are more reliable and loyal than part-time staff. Regardless of whether women are employed on a contract or permanent basis, as full-time employees they are entitled to 10 days paid annual leave, plus additional leave for *hari merah* (lit. red days, public holidays and religious celebrations, known elsewhere in Indonesia as *tanggal merah*). However, women working in hotels often have to negotiate which *hari merah* they can take off as hotels still need to maintain a skeleton staff on public holidays.

A full working week for hotel employees is typically six days, with eight-hour shifts per day. Women's shifts are varied and begin in the morning, at midday and in the early evening to accommodate the almost 24-hour demand for tourist services. All of the women reported being entitled to take breaks for food, rest and prayer during their eight-hour shifts. Although none of the women reported taking breaks over 30 minutes long, many take breaks opportunistically to accommodate for fluctuations in guest demand. While women's breaks tend to be short, they also tend to be self-monitored, and are not formally recorded via time sheets or other means. Many of the women have permission to eat meals supplied by their hotels. For some employees, simple meals are prepared for staff, while others are allowed to eat kitchen surpluses or food rejected by guests. Women whose hotels provide simple but fresh food for their staff greatly appreciate this benefit. These women noted that the availability of food means they do not waste time looking for meals outside the work place. This ensures that they do not skip meals and thus have higher energy levels on the job.

All but one of my informants is supplied with a uniform by their hotel and most of the women are satisfied with what they are required to wear. However, two of the younger waitresses interviewed, who work at a nightclub/restaurant attached to an up-market hotel, are required to wear short black fitted skirts (above the knee) and both stated they would prefer to wear jeans or longer skirts. These women change out of their uniforms before returning home as they feel embarrassed to be seen on the street in short skirts. When I inquired as to whether they had mentioned their concerns over the uniform to the hotel management, they informed me that the management 'does not care' (*tidak peduli*), as they are trying to promote a new more 'Western' image for the restaurant/nightclub. Their hotel management explicitly utilizes the attractive bodies of its female staff as part of its marketing strategy, despite women's reluctance to present themselves in such a way.[5]

All of my informants agreed that women's legislated right to three months' paid maternity leave is generally honoured for hotel employees who are in permanent full-time positions (Heti's experience narrated below is an exception to this rule). A number of the younger women, who are still employed on a contract basis, explained that entitlement to maternity leave was one of their primary motivations for seeking permanent positions. This reflects the unanimous desire of the women I interviewed to continue working once they are mothers. With regard to sick leave, most hotels accept absences of one day without requiring documentation. For absences of two or more days a doctor's certificate is required to ensure that there is no wage deduction. The acceptance of routine sick days by hotel administrations in Senggigi is necessary and indicative of the generally poor health status of women on Lombok, who suffer from regular gastrointestinal disturbances, respiratory tract infections, anaemia and a plethora of other common but plaguing health complaints related primarily to poverty, poor water sanitation and dietary deficiencies.[6] None of the women interviewed acknowledged their specific entitlement to menstrual leave when discussing their rights to recreation and sick leave (cf. Lahiri-Dutt and Robinson ch. 6 of this volume). They do, however, believe that common physical symptoms associated with menstruation, such as fatigue, stomach and back pain constitute reasonable grounds for taking sick days. Thus, while menstruation is understood as legitimate grounds for leave from work duties, this understanding is not formalized by women or their employers and absences of more than one day still require a medical certificate.

When I asked women how they perceived their employers or hotel management, their responses were overwhelmingly positive, describing their superiors as 'good', 'fair' and 'ideal'. The only issue that invoked intensely negative reactions among most of the informants was their experiences of on-the-job training prior to being hired by hotels. Several of the younger women described the common practice of not paying hospitality trainees a wage, from anywhere between three and six months, as 'exploitation' (*eksploitasi*). Although trainees typically receive a food and travel allowance, my informants pointed out that this did not cover their living expenses and that the hours worked as a trainee are equal to those worked once they are hired. This practice is considered to be particularly unfair when on-the-job training does not result in employment, which means that women often work unpaid for months on end with no long-term gain for their labour. Ironically, it appears that the top-end hotels with the largest profit margins have the longest training and probationary periods and the lowest rates of hiring staff after their training is completed. In both policy and practice, top-end hotels were reported to offer the least favourable working conditions, despite their desirability in terms of perceived job security related to higher levels of foreign investment and wealthier guests.

Indonesia's minimum wage legislation requires equal pay for equal work between the sexes in the tourist industry. All of the women interviewed confirmed that they are receiving equal pay to that of their male peers and do not perceive any gender asymmetry in opportunities for career advancement. They explained that prior work experience, performance, English-language skills and duration of employment are the determinants of promotion, pay increases, bonuses and gaining permanent as opposed to contract positions. My informants did note that women tend to attract more frequent and larger tips than men, but as tips are typically shared equally between all staff on a monthly basis, the advantage of women attracting more tips is shared by male staff as well. When I inquired as to why women attract more tips, my informants provided two common responses, the first being that women are more attentive to tourists'/guests' needs than men. The second response was that, because men typically pay most of the bills, they are more likely to tip women than men because of their assumed heterosexual attraction to women.

Women's narratives about their working conditions in Senggigi tourist hotels refute any simplified assumptions of gender inequality in employment opportunities. Women possess a strong sense of their entitlement to equal pay for equal work, and although some are prepared to accept below minimum wages, they are adamant that such compromises are equally likely to be made by male peers. The women articulate an explicit choice to accept reduced wages in the short term in order to maximize their long-term prospects (as is the case for Ria and Heti below). This choice is based on economic pragmatism and is not perceived by women as a form of gender disadvantage.[7] My informants also understood that opportunities for career advancement are parallel for women and men, although a number of informants suggested that women are likely to advance more rapidly than men due to their 'more diligent' (*lebih rajin*) attitude to work. Notions akin to a 'glass ceiling' for women working in tourist hotels were not deemed relevant to these women's experiences and aspirations. My informants were quick to provide examples of women in management and other positions of relative power within their hotels. Of the twelve hotels in which my informants are employed, seven have women in management positions, and in five of the hotels women are solely responsible for the day-to-day management of the establishments.[8] Moreover, my informants did not construct motherhood as conflicting with their career aspirations, despite the fact that they all wish to have small families.

Work and life trajectories

Ria is a single 20-year-old Sasak woman who has been working as a waitress at the mid-range, boutique Hotel Rainbow for two years since her graduation from high school.[9] When Ria and I first met she had just graduated from high school in the central Lombok town of Praya where she had come top of her class in English. On the basis of this achievement (and because her rural family were too impoverished to consider tertiary education), Ria was recommended as a trainee to Hotel Rainbow, where she completed three months of on-the-job training. Ria worked six days per week and received only a travel and food allowance for the duration of this work experience, when she was fortunate to be offered a one-year contract as a waitress. She now earns a wage of Rp. 300,000 a month and receives an additional Rp. 120,000 for her travel and food allowances. Her total monthly income with tips is thus between Rp. 420,000 and Rp. 500,000 (US$47–56) per month and her basic wage falls Rp. 55,000 below the national minimum standard. Ria is aware of the minimum wage and is hopeful that her wage will be increased to the standard if she continues to impress the hotel management.

Ria is the youngest of 10 children; her mother is widowed; and her siblings who are all married are rural labourers living at subsistence level. In many senses, Ria is the pride of her family: she is the first child to have completed high school with outstanding results and the first to have earned a wage in the formal sector. Yet this achievement is not without its sacrifices: Ria must live independently from her extended family to gain employment in the tourist industry and must travel for a full day to return home if she wishes to see her family. Going home is difficult when she works six days per week. After two years of this independent living, Ria has finally adjusted to life in the coastal locale of Senggigi and has made good friends whom she trusts. Initially, as an outsider, Ria was the target of constant gossip, most notably from other young women who had tried but failed to secure work in tourist hotels and who spread rumours that Ria's success was related to sexual liaisons with men within the hotel where she works. Ria found this gossip extremely difficult to endure and was cautious about making friends due to her confusion over who could be trusted and her fears that she may attract further gossip. It is only in recent months that her extraordinary homesickness for the intimacy and support of her family and village life has dissipated. The emotional and social opportunity costs of working in tourism for Ria have been significant up to this point.

However, the financial hardship Ria experiences in supporting herself without any additional income or family assistance is the key concern that emerged from our dialogue. One of Ria's disappointments is her inability to save money. Her initial hope was that her wage would be sufficient to enable her to send money home to her mother on a monthly basis. To date this has been impossible. Ria was unprepared for the cost of living in the semi-urban environment of Senggigi, where basic food stuffs require cash (credit and barter are not an option as is the case in villages) and the cost of renting a room is inflated due to high demand for accommodation. Two-thirds of Ria's basic monthly wage is dedicated to renting her living space, a single room that she shares with a close female friend who is also a waitress. All of Ria's disposable income is required for food, transport and other basic living costs; additional expenses such as health care costs or clothing are extremely difficult to manage. As a result, Ria tends to suffer ill-health without being able to seek appropriate medical consultations or to afford treatments such as iron supplements for anaemia or antibiotics to treat severe infections.

Ria is also keenly aware of the ways in which the sexual economy of tourism creates both opportunity and disadvantage for young women such as herself. When lamenting her economic hardship, she pointed out that local sex workers could earn up to a million rupiah per night with international clients. Ria has regularly observed relationships between sex workers and their clients who are guests at her hotel, and has been propositioned by guests dining in the restaurant on numerous occasions. Ria expressed her views on the risks associated with sex work in the following way:

> I understand why they [local female sex workers] do it. I earn less than half a million a month, but they can earn a million in one night. I receive many offers from male guests to sleep in their room or to be their girlfriend. But I know this

is dangerous. Once you do that you can never go back. Your reputation is ruined and I would lose this job. It's not just my problem if I do that [sex work] – the hotel and my family would also experience shame. I would lose my friends here in Senggigi too. If you bring this kind of shame you get thrown out, you cannot find respectable work again. Also no one will marry you. Some girls do find Western husbands, but that is very rare. Usually their Western boyfriends just leave them when it's time to go home. It's very dangerous. No local man will consider them after that.

(Interview with Ria, July 2005, Senggigi)

The slippage between sex work and relationships with Western men is notable in Ria's discussion. Both premarital relationships with Westerners and sex work hold significant stigma for women. Relationships with Westerners are assumed to involve sex, due to local perceptions of the immorality associated with the West and with international tourism, an association that is reinforced by Western tourists' highly visible consumption of drugs, alcohol and sexual services. In the local sexual culture, and in terms of the social regulation of sexuality in Islam, paid sex and premarital sex are both technically considered *zina* (fornication).[10] Sadly, the reputations of all local women who work in the tourist industry are affected by proximity to tourists. No evidence of actual sexual relationships with tourists is required for the wider community to make unfavourable assumptions about the character of women who work in tourist establishments. Ria's interpretation of the risks of sex work focuses on the social opportunity cost for women whose reputations are degraded by sexual stigma. Interestingly, she did not mention the health risks associated with sex work (such as exposure to STIs including HIV) or the physical vulnerability of female sex workers to abuse by male clients.[11] Ria revealed how opportunity for women working within hotels is explicitly linked with maintaining a favourable sexual reputation, and how a compromised reputation represents a real threat to their employment and marriage prospects. The same cannot be said for men working within tourist hotels, as the social regulation of male sexuality is far less of a concern for employers and the local community in general.[12]

Ria explained that her choice to seek a career in tourism has influenced both her own spouse ideals and the kind of man who is likely to be interested in marrying her. She is convinced that no man from her village of origin would consider her as a prospective bride while she remains employed in tourism and that her reputation has been compromised simply by living independently before marriage in the morally questionable environment of Senggigi. However, Ria does not express any sense of regret over altered perceptions of her marriageability within her village. She explained that her own desires have shifted and that she wishes to marry a man who is a wage earner, and who has had exposure either to tourism or the more cosmopolitan urban environment of the island's capital city, Mataram. Ria is also explicit about the fact that she will exercise much greater autonomy in choosing her marriage partner than would have been the case if she had remained in her village. In the village, choice of partners is often restricted by limited mobility, a narrower social circle, stronger social censure of courtship and greater family involvement in marital choices.

Ria believes that a marriage between two people with similar educational and work experience is more compatible both in economic terms and in relation to life aspirations. She feels that men who are familiar with tourism or have worked in tourism are less likely to judge her sexual reputation harshly and more likely not to question that she is still a virgin. Maintaining her virginity until marriage is important to Ria. For this reason, she has had only two short-term casual dating relationships with local men in the Senggigi area. Ria explained that she is careful to protect her sexual reputation by ensuring that she is always chaperoned by a friend if she dates, by avoiding alcohol and cigarettes, and by dressing modestly in jeans or long pants.[13] Ria is comfortable wearing her uniform, which is a long fitted skirt to the ankles and a matching blouse with sleeves reaching to the elbows.

In terms of her motherhood aspirations, Ria wishes to have only two children and hopes to continue working once she is a mother, although she would ideally like to find more secure and highly paid work. Becoming a *pegawai negeri* (public servant) is her long-term career goal, due to the security and respectability such jobs offer in contrast to working in the tourist industry. Overall, Ria perceives her decision to enter tourism as a good one and believes her prospects have been enhanced by her job and exposure to new people and life experiences. Ria describes the most enjoyable aspect of her job as making friends with guests and learning about the world beyond Lombok. However, she sometimes feels envious of the affluence and freedom of these Western friends. For locals, the cost of participating in tourist-oriented entertainment is high and they are largely excluded from enjoying the nightspots, cafes and restaurants where they make their living.[14] Despite the economic hardship and insecurity of her current position – she has a twelve-month contract – Ria feels fortunate to have a job in the current economic downturn. She enjoys earning her own money and is relieved not to be an economic burden to her extended family, a position in which many unemployed, unmarried women find themselves. While often frustrated by her lack of disposable income, Ria remains optimistic about her future, her ability to support herself until marriage and to contribute to family income once married.

Heti is 28 years of age and married to Firda, with whom she has a 7-year-old son, Alit. Both Heti and Firda are Sasak, were born and raised in Mataram, and have full-time jobs in tourism. Firda is employed as a chef at a local five-star hotel and Heti now works as a receptionist-cum-manager at the local budget Hotel Sunshine. This is Heti's sixth year of employment at Hotel Sunshine. She was originally employed as a waitress in the hotel where Firda still works. The couple met when Heti was just 20 years old and began their courtship through flirtations at work, sending innocent messages such as 'hello' and '*apa kabar?*' ('What's the news?' or 'How's things?') to one another via their workmates. After several months, Firda offered to chaperone Heti home after work and she accepted. This quickly led to her family's acceptance of Firda as a prospective husband and the couple's marriage within six months of meeting.[15] Heti describes their attraction as immediate or '*langsung*', akin to Western notions of love at first sight. She enjoys joking with Firda that she had initially hoped to marry a Westerner but found him to be irresistible. Heti also explained that her parents were very relieved when she married Firda, as they had feared her choice to work in tourism may compromise her marriage prospects. Before she was married, Heti's father apparently encouraged her to find alternative, more respectable work. Their concern dissipated with the marriage and conception of her first child.

While marriage was advantageous to Heti in terms of finding love and securing her social status, it was also initially disadvantageous to her career. The policy of many top-end international hotel chains is not to hire married couples or immediate kin within the one establishment or within the same department of very large hotels. Consequently, Heti and Firda had to choose which one of them would leave the security of their employment. They decided together that it was more strategic for Heti to resign as she expected to become pregnant after the wedding and would thus be leaving work temporarily to have their child. As Firda was still completing his chef's apprenticeship when they married, it was a safer investment in the future for him to obtain his qualifications at the hotel where he had begun his training. Heti expressed considerable annoyance at having been forced to make this decision, as she wanted to continue working until the third trimester of her pregnancy to save money to support her child. Due to the marriage and her compulsory resignation, Heti also lost her entitlement to maternity leave, which she felt was very unfair after having worked at the hotel for two years. Heti expressed her frustrations with the five-star hotel policy in the following way:

> It's just stupid. What do they think we will do? Obviously if we are married we have more than one future to think about. If we make a mistake it will affect our partner. So who is going to do that? It's a very insulting policy.

> My place of work now is just the opposite. We are like a family. It's my sixth year now and I feel very loyal to my boss. We all feel loyal. Everyone works hard. Not because they are forced to, but because we all want the business to succeed.

> Those big hotels have everything back to front. They treat you like you are bad, like you are a thief. Does that make people loyal? I don't think so. Also they have very high staff turnover. How can you create a happy work place when the staff are always changing? How can you expect loyalty when there is no security? If Firda gets the opportunity to work at another hotel with the same wage I will encourage him to leave.

> (Interview with Heti, August 2005, Senggigi)

In her current position at Hotel Sunshine, Heti has considerable autonomy and authority in her job. She makes reservations, welcomes guests, completes their registration, tends to their inquiries, makes bookings for any additional services they require, and is responsible for processing guest accounts, documenting daily expenses and supervising other staff when the manager is not present. She works six days per week and is employed permanently, though her initial three months of employment were on a contract basis as a probationary measure. Heti remembers initially having been overwhelmed by the variety of tasks she now undertakes with ease. She describes her current position as far more interesting than waitressing because of its variety and her ability to complete tasks as she deems necessary, without being subjected to the constant supervision she experienced in her previous job. However, she also describes her supervision of the ten other employees at Hotel Sunshine as one of the least enjoyable aspects of her job. Although she considers her relationships with the other staff to be very good and 'family-like', she still feels uncomfortable when she must correct or discipline her workmates. This discomfort is indicative of strong cultural preferences for avoiding direct conflict or shaming individuals through public criticism.

Her relationships with hotel guests are sometimes contested. Heti feels that good experiences with friendly, polite guests and the friendships she often develops with them are the most rewarding aspect of her job. Conversely, she experiences having to deal with rude and difficult guests as the least pleasant aspect of her job. Heti's strategy for understanding guest relations is to study and respond to people in terms of their cultural and class characteristics. She has developed many cultural generalizations about her guests from different countries and has her own theories on how best to deal with people from different backgrounds. Heti explained to me that this strategy is 'like a game'. It keeps her interested and allows her to see the bigger picture so that she does not have to respond to negative behaviour in a personal way. When I asked Heti what her ideal employment would be, she responded with humour – 'to do research on tourists'. I am sure she would excel at this. Heti also confirmed that she was very satisfied with her current job despite the fact that she would be happier with a higher wage.

Heti is currently paid at the standard monthly rate of Rp. 475,000, and generally receives anywhere between Rp. 10,000 and Rp. 100,000 in tips per month. Prior to 2002, Heti and the rest of the permanent staff at Hotel Sunshine were all receiving above the minimum wage. Following the serious slump in tourism after 2002, the owner and staff of Hotel Sunshine consulted over how best to keep the business afloat and avoid forced dismissals. The staff came to an accord, which involved the decision not to dismiss any employees, but for all to accept a 20 per cent decrease in wages until the hotel's turnover improved. Heti described this process of decision-making as being very family-like, where the focus is placed on the welfare of the group rather than on individuals and decisions are made with the long-term benefits in view. In 2005, Hotel Sunshine was able to halve the reduction in wages to 10 per cent, and staff are now hopeful that the improving climate for tourism will soon result in a return to full wages. There is strong consensus at Hotel Sunshine that the business would not have survived the slump had the management failed to include the staff in its decision-making and survival strategies.

While Heti's wage has been reduced over the past four years, Firda's wage has steadily increased due to his incremental advancement to a fully qualified apprentice, assistant chef and now head chef. The position of head chef became available when Firda's hotel reduced its employment of more expensive expatriate staff to cut costs. Thus, while Heti suffered in the short term due to the tourism slump, Firda has gained significantly from the recent downturn. The couple's combined income has been sufficient for them to buy land and build a home in a relatively cheap urban complex between Mataram, where their families live, and Senggigi, where they both work. They were able to save enough for a deposit and borrowed the additional amount through a fixed-term five-year bank loan. It seems likely that Heti and Firda will own their home within the next two years, although they are finding it extremely difficult to meet both their mortgage repayments and basic living costs. Heti described the anxiety she feels over meeting the monthly repayments as being like 'unable to breathe' (*tidak bisa bernafas*). Often they must turn to relatives for assistance with meeting household bills. They are extremely fortunate to have affluent, middle-class families who are in a position to assist them.

Heti cites their financial concerns as her primary reason for deciding not to have another child. Both she and Firda feel satisfied with their son, Alit, and have high ambitions for his education: they want him to attend a private school once he reaches secondary level and eventually to be tertiary educated. They are both able to work because Heti's mother cares for Alit after school and during the evenings if necessary. This free child care also involves Alit spending regular time with his cousins, which his parents feel is extremely important for his emotional well-being as an only child. When Alit was six months old, Heti had a *spiral* or inter-uterine device (IUD) inserted for free at the local *puskesmas* (primary health care centre). To date she has not presented for a follow-up appointment although she knows she is due to have the IUD removed this year. Heti confided that she was not comfortable with her consultation with the midwife when the IUD was inserted and that she would prefer to attend a private clinic for her next family planning appointment. She estimated that the cost of the appointment and replacement of the IUD would be a minimum of Rp. 70,000 and expected that she would need at least two more months to save this amount of cash. Thus, regardless of this family's dual income and middle-class aspirations, the cost of basic health care still represents a significant outlay that is not necessarily within the means of their immediate disposable income.

Regardless of the differences in monthly income and living situations between Ria and Heti, both value their participation in the tourist industry highly. Both say that their greatest concern is financial strain, despite being in full-time employment. Ria and Heti's life experiences highlight that economic opportunity is a key motivation for women working in tourism. However, this economic opportunity is frequently coupled with poverty or financial hardship even though women are able to generate their own income.

Work and sexual politics

My informants unanimously agreed that sexual harassment is common in their work environments, although women used the local terms *diganggu* (to be annoyed, bothered or harassed) and *kelakuan yang tidak cocok* (inappropriate behaviour) to describe their experiences, rather than the English term 'sexual harassment'. Women experience unwelcome attention in multiple forms, including compliments on their appearance, repeated invitations to join guests socially, guests purchasing them unwanted drinks and food, guests remaining until closing time and attempting to convince women to accompany them, derogatory sexual comments, offering women money for sex, and physical transgressions such as touching, grabbing and pinching women. The women I interviewed were particularly offended by touching on the buttocks. When women described their experiences of sexual harassment, they also elaborated on their responses and strategies for dealing with unwanted attention. These typically involve informing male guests that they are married (regardless of whether or not they are), asking a work friend to take over serving the customer and making sure they always have an escort on the way home. The final resort is to report the matter to a superior. However, there appear to be very few incidents when women officially report harassment by guests. This is largely due to the fact that women generally feel that their work peers look out for them: they feel a shared sense of awareness of the willingness of their friends (both male and female) to intervene to protect them. This typically involves a friend taking over the job or accompanying the target of harassment so that she feels safe. Such a strategy presupposes that the person responsible for the harassment is external to the workplace and is positioned as a guest.

When I asked women what they would do if harassment was by a workmate, most said they would probably leave their jobs if the problem was ongoing. A deeper exploration of women's thinking behind such a response revealed that women have no confidence in the effectiveness of formalized processes for addressing workplace harassment. This lack of confidence is indicative of the reality that formalized processes for the resolution of such misconduct are not functional or are functioning poorly in Lombok. This is due to low awareness of sexual harassment legislation, a lack of appropriate institutional structures, and the lack of conflict resolution skills required to formally resolve such issues. It also reflects cultural preferences for more informal modes of conflict resolution, indirect or circumscribed modes of communication, and the desire to avoid public shaming.

In the local context, women's preference for resigning if faced with serious harassment from a colleague should not be simply interpreted as a passive or subordinate course of action. In most cases, women suggested that they would resign without giving notice or explanation to employers if they were subjected to harassment by colleagues. The silence associated with such a resignation and the independence of a decision made without consultation with superiors is described by women as a deliberate strategy of disengagement. This indicates that women are '*tidak tertarik perhatikan hal seperti itu*' – not interested in dealing with this kind of problem. The implicit message conveyed is that such problems belong to those responsible for the harassment and that women are simply not willing to waste their time addressing the problem. To understand such action as a form of deliberate disengagement, as opposed to a forced retreat, acknowledges women's agency in workplace relations. It also signifies what various commentators have observed in other non-Western settings (Parker 2005): that women's agency operates in culturally specific modes that typically reflect distinct modes of communication, the ways in which social relationships are structured locally, and also women's understandings of gender identity.

Through discussions with women about different types of hypothetical sexual harassment, they revealed that the most common and generally most offensive instances of harassment are committed by guests who are local Indonesian men. My informants noted the hypocrisy of such men, who typically label women working in tourism as morally questionable due to their association with Western men, whilst demonstrating significantly higher levels of sexual aggression towards these women themselves. Local women are particularly offended and distressed by sexual harassment from local men because they expect men who understand the sexual etiquette of their culture to adhere to appropriate behaviour. When local men harass women working in tourist hotels, these women feel that the protection they typically associate with belonging to the local community is compromised. A number of informants commented that sexual harassment by local men is most pronounced in situations where alcohol is consumed, and suggested that local guests appear to have a lower tolerance of alcohol than international guests. Several of my younger informants who work in hotel bars, where alcohol (and not food) is the primary attraction, also expressed their preference for finding work in hotel restaurants rather than in hotel bars in order to minimize their exposure to sexual harassment.

The routine experiences of sexual harassment described by women in Senggigi reveal the complexity of power relations exercised through gender and postcolonial hierarchies in the context of tourism. While Western male tourists clearly exercise the greatest economic power in relation to both local women and men, their economic dominance does not necessarily translate into an apical position in an absolute gender hierarchy in terms of their relations with local women. Despite the vast financial resources of most Western guests compared to those of locals, local women working in tourism tend to experience less gender discrimination in the form of sexual harassment from Western men than they do from local men. Local women feel most compromised and disempowered by local men who harass them, regardless of the relative economic equality between local women and men. When local men 'sling mud' at local women in the form of sexual harassment and innuendo, this stigma is more likely to stick to women's reputations than is the case if Western men, who are temporary guests less bound by local sexual culture, engage in the same kinds of behaviour. The dual burdens of protecting their sexual reputations and avoiding or limiting the impact of sexual harassment are an ongoing fact of life for women working in an industry that is innately associated with sexual stigma. Women's constant negotiation of the sexual politics embedded in tourism is an aspect of their working lives that all women described as undesirable and taxing, although economic difficulties remained the greatest overall life concern expressed by these women. The sexual double standards of the local culture function in a manner that intimately links women's sexuality with their career opportunities, in a manner that does not apply to their male peers.

A related issue is the issue of reproduction and motherhood. All of the women interviewed discussed family planning in positive terms and described access to contraception as essential to their participation in paid work and the sustainability of career opportunities. The four women among my informants who are using contraception made the decision to do so independently or in consultation with partners, and none experienced any resistance from partners in relation to their family planning choices. Regardless of whether women are already mothers or have yet to become mothers, they all stated their desire to continue working once they have children. For those three women who are mothers, child care is provided by female relatives or domestic helpers. These mothers feel secure that their children are being well cared for and did not express any negative sentiments about their preference to continue working. Additionally, none of the working mothers felt pressure from their spouses not to return to work after the birth to their first child and all returned to full-time work within twelve months of giving birth.

Despite my informants' constant engagement with modernity through the globalized tourist economy and pleasure culture of international tourism, their identities are significantly removed from the state-conceived notion of women within the 'small and prosperous' modern Indonesian family, which is based on a strict gender division of labour between the private and public spheres (Sullivan 1994: 127). While many of the women employed in tourist hotels have middle-class aspirations, they are unimpressed by the official model of a middle-class family, in which men are expected to provide the family income and women's roles are ideally confined to the home. Not only do these women enjoy working in the public sphere, but also the nature of their work makes them highly visible to the public eye. This high degree of visibility does not generally cause women discomfort, provided that they are free to determine their self-presentation. The two young women discussed above, who are required to wear short skirts while working, clearly do feel discomfort. Because of hotel policy, their right to manage their self-presentation has been compromised.

When I questioned women about how many children they would like, all but two felt that 'two children is enough' (*dua anak cukup*). They explained that this family size is more economically viable than larger families. Half the women also mentioned that it would be more difficult to find child care and return to work if they had more than two children. Hence, it appears these women are indeed choosing to create 'small' and hopefully 'prosperous' families, yet in ways that do not reflect a passive consumption of state ideology. Rather, their version of the small family norm involves a complication and contestation of ideal female roles in the family. Two of the women, who were already mothers, felt that one child was enough and cited the cost of rearing children as the primary motivation for having only one child. However, the two women who were satisfied with one child also expressed broader life aspirations that would involve considerable savings. These aspirations included their own desires to travel abroad and to undertake tertiary study, as well as wanting their children to receive costly private education.

The two women who are satisfied with one child have boys, aged 6 and 7, and gave birth in their early 20s immediately after marriage.[16] Their success in family planning through long-term contraceptive use highlights a significant commitment to limiting family size to one child and a high degree of reproductive autonomy for these women. These two women's articulation of personal desires and their willingness to dedicate personal (and family) income to the realization of such desires represent another stark contradiction with state ideals of femininity based on the philosophy of women's self-sacrifice to the family (Djajadiningrat-Nieuwenhuis 1987: 44). For these women, the articulation of personal aspirations is not viewed as a threat to family well-being, precisely because women's heightened awareness of family welfare guides them in the pursuit of such aspirations. Moreover, the fact that women earn their own income appears to support their (and their partners') sense of entitlement to invest in the realization of women's desires.

Conclusion: opportunity, autonomy and agency

The life trajectories of all the women I interviewed in Senggigi indicate that the economic opportunity associated with working in tourism guarantees neither financial security nor affluence. Working within tourist hotels does, however, provide many women with the foundation for developing greater economic autonomy both before and within marriage. However, it is important to contextualize the notion of economic autonomy for these women in terms of the almost-universal economic interdependence of women with their families regardless of their marital status. For instance, Heti requires frequent economic assistance from her family and receives free child care from her mother, and is also expected to respond to any financial emergency that might arise in the extended family – such as her father's short-term hospitalization for severe gastroenteritis. While Ria has not managed to send regular savings to her mother, she dedicates most of her meagre excess income to purchasing basic food supplies such as sugar, coffee and oil for her family, which she delivers to the village on her rare visits home. Ria and Heti are on 'economic standby' for family emergencies and special events. For instance, Ria purchased and delivered the sterile water, razor blades and antibiotics required for the circumcision of three male cousins.

The economic autonomy of Sasak women needs to be understood in relation to the spectrum of family and communal relationships in which women are constantly engaged. This is because social and economic relationships are primarily structured around collective needs and not individual desires. In this context, it is not feasible to speak of women's economic autonomy in absolute terms; it is more accurate to compare the degree of economic autonomy experienced by different women. It is clear that women employed on a full-time basis within Senggigi's tourist hotels are able to make a more significant contribution to their household income than would be the case if they were unemployed or employed in parallel jobs outside of the tourist sector. Participation in formal labour in the tourist sector also appears to improve women's long-term prospects for increasing their income. These women describe relatively high levels of economic autonomy in deciding how their income will be distributed to meet both personal and family needs. Their articulation of individual desires, such as the dream of travelling abroad or the aspiration to undertake tertiary study indicates that women are comfortable expressing their desires and possess a sense of entitlement to invest their income in the pursuit of such desires. Comparing the economic circumstances of single and partnered informants reveals that the opportunities for saving and capital accumulation are much greater for women who have partners who are also in full-time employment. For single women who live independently from their families, opportunities for saving are limited by the high cost of independent living in Senggigi. Single women who are able to reside with their local families are sometimes in a better position to save, and yet this is not always the case as living with their families often brings a higher level of economic obligation to directly support the family. Despite the difficulty of saving for women working in tourist hotels, the goals of saving for the future and for investing in a home are universal among my informants.

Women's engagement with tourism also shapes their life trajectories in relation to their reproductive and sexual autonomy. Exposure to a wider spectrum of people through their work also equates with exposure to an expanded pool of potential marriage partners. Participation in paid work appears to encourage women's preference for finding partners who are also wage earners. Among my informants there is a definite preference for choosing their own marriage partners, although family approval of spouses remains a key consideration. Women's ability to mix with more men, to choose men who share similar economic expectations and opportunities, and to exercise greater independence in their final choice of partner amounts to a relatively greater degree of sexual autonomy than is often the case for women who are unemployed and who work only in the home prior to marriage. Single women who reside independently of their families in order to work in the tourist industry are also in a position to exercise greater sexual autonomy in their premarital relationships than would be the case if they were living under direct parental supervision.

Reproductive autonomy and women's continuing participation in the tourist industry are inextricably linked. All of the women who participated in this research expressed positive attitudes towards family planning and their intent to practise family planning once married. Women explicitly articulated that they would not be in a position to continue their careers in the manner they wish, without the ability to successfully control their fertility. The reproductive autonomy of my married informants was respected by their partners, who supported their wives' decisions both in relation to family size and contraceptive use. These women's strong sense of entitlement to both motherhood and work is manifest in their desire to have small families. None of the women interviewed was reluctant about motherhood, or viewed motherhood as a signal to end their working lives. These women are keenly aware of the fact that exercising reproductive autonomy is pivotal to maximizing their career opportunities. Likewise, the availability of affordable child care is understood as crucial to women's opportunities. Hence, women's preference for small families is motivated by a combination of factors including their desire to continue working once mothers, the cost of child rearing, the cost of child care and their desire for economic security and prosperity.

Women working in this milieu are subjected to continual sexual harassment and sexual double standards that their male peers do not have to endure. The sexual double standards embedded in local culture render women particularly vulnerable to sexual innuendo, gossip and stigma simply through their association with the tourist industry. It is only women who are required to constantly protect and defend their sexual reputations to ensure that their job prospects are not damaged by sexual stigma, and, conversely, to protect their marriage prospects from the stigma attached to their work. Thus, the prime location of inequality identified by women working in tourist hotels is in the realm of sexuality, where women are required to maintain the public performance of sexual purity in order to successfully negotiate both their career and life prospects. The sexual inequality experienced by women working within Lombok's tourist industry does not, however, indicate that women are necessarily passive or powerless in response to sexual harassment at work. Women's reactions to unwanted attention from international guests typically involves collaboration with workmates and reflects conscious strategies for ending or avoiding harassment. Such responses indicate women's propensity to exercise agency, or their 'socio-culturally mediated capacity to act' (Ahearn 2001: 112). The notion of agency as a mediated form of action is highly relevant also to women's distinct response to the problem of sexual harassment perpetrated by male colleagues. As discussed above, the strategy of resignation without consultation or warning is not constructed as a passive response by women working in Senggigi. In such a scenario, the choice of deliberate disengagement is most accurately understood as an explicit action, rather than as an enforced retreat. It is only when the socio-cultural context of workplace relations, gender dynamics and culturally determined modes of communication are adequately understood, that we can precisely identify and describe women's agency in a manner that is relevant to their own perceptions and experiences.

Notes

1 For comprehensive discussions of the socio-economic and political status of the Sasak, see Judd (1980) and Grace (1997).
2 Cohabitation prior to marriage in Lombok is rare and attracts significant social sanctions for women. For details of the consequences of cohabitation for young women see Bennett (2005b). The one informant interviewed for this research who was in a *de facto* relationship resides with her Western boyfriend, whom she hopes to marry. She has been severely stigmatized for her choice to cohabit out of wedlock. However, she has not yet been forced to marry as Western men are far less vulnerable to the kinds of social pressures placed on local men to marry women with whom they cohabit prior to marriage.
3 Australian citizen Schapelle Corby was convicted in May 2004 of having imported 4 kilograms of marijuana into Indonesia in her boogie board case. On 17 April 2004 another nine Australians, referred to as the 'Bali 9', were arrested for heroin smuggling at Denpasar airport.
4 At the time the data for this chapter were compiled, US$1 was equal to approximately Rp. 9,000.
5 The explicit use of female bodies and beauty as a marketing strategy by this establishment is evident both on the printed vouchers that are given out on the street to potential

customers and in the conversational hooks used by the young men who give out these vouchers to tourists. The vouchers picture cartoon images of young, scantily clad female bar staff, while the men who tout for customers regularly describe this bar as having the most 'beautiful', 'hottest' and 'sexiest' waitresses and bar staff on the island.

6 The poor health status of Lombok's inhabitants is reasonably well documented largely due to the high number of internationally sponsored health/development projects that have attempted to ameliorate the primary causes of mortality over the past 15 years. In the province of Nusa Tanggara Barat (NTB), the life expectancy for women is 47.3 years and 44.6 for men, both of which are significantly lower than the national figures of 61.5 years for women and 58.1 years for men (BPS–NTB 2000). Key indicators of the population's persistently high morbidity and mortality, particularly among rural Sasak, include the very high provincial maternal (750 deaths per 100,000 live births) and infant mortality rates (110 deaths per 1,000 live births), which are significantly higher the national averages and among the worst in Indonesia (World Bank 2000). Hepatitis B is also endemic in Lombok, due to the reuse of infected needles for immunization and injections in primary health centres (Adlide 1996). Anaemia among women (and pregnant women) is also very high, as is the number of children born with low birth weights (Hull *et al.* 1999). Acute gastroenteritis and respiratory tract infections are chronic for much of the population due to environmental factors, and continue to be major causes of fatality among infants, young children and the elderly, who are the most physically vulnerable members of Sasak society (Nelson *et al.* 2000; Sutanto *et al.* 2002). Outbreaks of dengue fever and malaria still occur with regularity on Lombok and often go untreated due to the limited capacity of health services and the poverty of rural Sasak (Hijaz 2005).

7 See Lock and Kaufert's (1998) edited volume *Pragmatic Women and Body Politics* for a range of explorations of women's pragmatism in varied cultural contexts.

8 The gender equality experienced by women in Senggigi in relation to hotel management diverges from the findings of Long and Kindon (1997: 104) in Bali, where men were found to be approximately twice as likely to be the primary or sole managers of *losmen* and bungalows as women are.

9 Pseudonyms have been used to replace the names of all informants and hotels in order to protect the confidentiality of individuals and businesses.

10 For a more thorough definition and discussion of *zina* in the Indonesian context see Bennett (2005a).

11 In 2001 the World Health Organization estimated that around 120,000 Indonesians were living with HIV/AIDS. More recent research has described Indonesia's HIV epidemic as explosive; infection rates are highest among female sex workers and intravenous drug users in urban areas (Dowsett *et al.* 2003). The most up-to-date data available on HIV infection and risk in Indonesia is published in the National Behavioural Surveillance System surveys on an annual or biannual basis. However, to date these surveys are based only in very large cities and focus on groups considered to be at high risk of contracting HIV/AIDS.

12 In the locale of Northern Bali, Jennaway (2002) has also observed the gender differentiated risks associated with engagement in tourism. She describes how young women's sexual reputations are acutely vulnerable to association with tourism – while the reputation of young men is not prone to the same kind of censure.

13 See Parker (1995) and Bennett (2005a) for extensive discussions of idealized femininity and women's sexual reputation in Indonesia.

14 See Bennett (2005a: 68–72) for details of the dual economy of Lombok's international tourist industry and the economic marginalization of locals in this economy.

15 For a description of contemporary courtship practices on Lombok see Bennett (2002) and for details of more traditional courtship practices in the 1970s see Ecklund (1977).

16 While both of these women have sons, there is no evidence to suggest that their satisfaction with having one child is based in, or supported by, any cultural preference for boy children. If Sasak do express any preferences regarding the gender of children it is typically to have children of both sexes in the family.

References

Adlide, G. (1996) *Giving Children a Health Start, AusAID Report*, Canberra: AusAID.

Ahearn, L. (2001) 'Language and agency', *Annual Review of Anthropology*, 30: 109–29.

Bennett, L. R. (2002) 'Modernity, desire and courtship: the evolution of premarital relationships in Mataram, Eastern Indonesia', in L. Manderson and P. Liamputtong (eds) *Coming of Age in South and Southeast Asia: youth, sexuality and courtship*, London: Curzon.

—— (2005a) *Maidenhood, Islam and Modernity: single women, sexuality and reproductive health in contemporary Indonesia*, London: Routledge/Curzon.

—— (2005b) 'Patterns of resistance and transgression in Eastern Indonesia: single women's practices of clandestine courtship and cohabitation', *Culture, Health and Sexuality*, 6 (4): 6–12.

BPS–NTB (Biro Pusat Statistik Nusa Tanggara Barat) (1995) *Nusa Tenggara Barat Dalam Angka – 1995*, Mataram: BPS–NTB.

—— (2000) 'Regional profile: Nusa Tengarra Barat, BPS'. Online: http://www.bps.go.id/profile/ntb.shtml (accessed 19 October 2001).

Director General of Tourism Lombok (1997) 'Bahasa, Budaya dan Parawisata', paper presented at Seminar Internasional: bahasa dan budaya di dunia Melayu, Univeristy of Mataram, 16–18 June.

Djajadiningrat-Niewenhuis, M. (1987) 'Ibuism and priyayization: path to power?', in E. Locher-Scholten and A. Niehof (eds) *Indonesian Women in Focus*, Dordrecht: Floris Publications.

Dowsett, G., Grierson, J. and McNally, S. (2003) *A Review of Knowledge about the Sexual Networks of Men Who Have Sex with Men in Asia*, Melbourne: Australian Research Centre for Sex Health and Society.

Ecklund, J. (1977) 'Marriage, Seaworms and Song: Ritualized Responses to Cultural Changes in Sasak Life', unpublished PhD thesis, Cornell University, Ithaca, NY.

Grace, J. (1997) 'Health, development and Sasak women', unpublished PhD thesis, Murdoch University.

Hijaz, T. (2005) 'Indonesia: Chikungunya spreads in West Lombok.' *EINet News Briefs*, 8 (9). Online: http://depts.washington.edu/einet/newsbrief39.html (accessed 21 March 2006).

Hull, T., Roosmalawati, R. and Djohan, E. (1999) 'They simply die: searching for the causes of infant mortality in Lombok', *Development Bulletin*, 48: 25–9.

Jennaway, M. (2002) 'Inflatable bodies and the breath of life: courtship and desire among young women in rural North Bali', in L. Manderson and P. Liamputtong (eds) *Maidenhood, Islam and Modernity: single women, sexuality and reproductive health in contemporary Indonesia*, Richmond: Curzon.

Judd, M. (1980) 'The sociology of rural poverty in Lombok, Indonesia', unpublished PhD thesis, University of California Berkeley.

Lock, M. and Kaufert, P. (eds) (1998) *Pragmatic Women and Body Politics*, Cambridge: Cambridge University Press.

Long, V. and Kindon, S. (1997) 'Gender and tourism development in a Balinese village', in M. Thea Sinclair (ed.) *Gender, Work and Tourism*, London: Routledge.

Nelson, C., Sutanto, A., Gessner, B., Suradana, I., Steinhoff, M. and Arjoso, S. (2000) 'Age-and cause-specific childhood mortality in Lombok, Indonesia, as a factor for determining the appropriateness of introducing haemphilus influenzae type b and pneumococcal vaccines', *Journal of Health Population and Nutrition*, 18 (3): 131–8.

Parker, L. (1995) 'Conceptions of femininity in Bali', paper presented at the Third International Bali Studies Workshop, University of Sydney, 3–7 July.

—— (2005) 'Introduction: introducing women's agency', in L .Parker (ed) *The Agency of Women in Asia*, Singapore: Marshall Cavendish.

Sullivan, N. (1994) *Masters and Managers: a study of gender relations in urban Java*, Sydney: Allen and Unwin.

Sutanto, A., Gessner, B., Djlantik, I., Steinhoff, M., Murphy, H., Nelson, C. *et al.* (2002) 'Acute respiratory illness incidence and death among children under two years of age on Lombok island, Indonesia', *American Journal of Tropical Medicine and Hygiene*, 66: 175–9.

World Bank (2000) 'Reproductive Health Table 2.16'. Online:http://www.worldbank.org/data/wdi2000/pdfs/tab2_16.pdf (accessed 15 August 2000).

5   Industrial workers in transition

Women's experiences of factory work in Tangerang

Nicolaas Warouw

Tangerang, approximately 35 kilometres to the west of Jakarta, is one of Indonesia's foremost manufacturing centres. However, local residents rarely work as factory workers in the industrial establishments surrounding their neighbourhoods. Instead, migrants – many of them women – comprise the majority of the labour force in the factories across the region. Unlike rural 'factory daughters', who are able to commute daily to work (Wolf 1992), these urban migrant workers establish a relatively permanent urban existence far away from Indonesia's rural hinterland. Factory work exposes these urban migrant workers to very different conditions and experiences from those of the rural settings in which they grew up.

A factory shares characteristics of a 'total institution' in Erving Goffman's (1971) sense. Individuals are detached from the larger society, and from their previous existence, and are placed in circumstances designed to sustain industrial production. Women workers' incorporation into the industrial institution is marked by symbolic rituals imposed by corporate agencies, which strip away their identity and individuality. For Foucault, this enables authorities to create subordinate individuals as the object of power, as 'docile bodies' whose initiative has been taken away and replaced by 'new forms of knowledge' – just as rural children are introduced to the 'new mechanisms of power' that regulate their minds and bodies so they conform to the corporate project of commodity production (1991: 155). The internalization of these mechanisms is accomplished through the habituation of the self to capitalist production (Braverman 1974). The significance of habituation is not merely related to the technological transformation, but also to the conditioning of workers so that they become an extension of the machinery they operate.

Habituation is achieved by training the workers to appreciate the precision of task execution measured by the clock in order to ensure a product's progression through the assembly line (Thompson 1967). The conception of time in industrial production trains and transforms the agrarian body into a capitalist instrument, whose movements are synchronized with the rhythm of the shop-floor. In pre-capitalist Southeast Asian societies, a 'sense of time and rhythm' is expressed in different ways, ranging from a time division based on Islamic prayer times to time measurement based on the smoking of a cigarette (Ong 1987; Wolf 1992). The transition to capitalist production forces rural subjects to reorganize their everyday lives in accordance with clock-based time partitions. A factory also imposes industrial disciplines that meticulously define individuals' every single movement in order to maximize their utility to production. The implementation of these disciplines requires surveillance machinery, which, along with time-based organization and habituation to routine operations, make up what Foucault terms 'the calculated technology of subjection', which replaces 'traditional ... violent forms of power' (1991: 221). In labour-intensive industries, the deployment of these surveillance mechanisms is imperative to ensure that control remains intact at every level of the hierarchy.

This chapter explores young women's experiences of the processes that integrate them into the logic of commodity production. It begins by describing the set of rules that compels female workers to adjust to industrial discipline and the work rhythm of the factory. Their incorporation takes the form of industrializing rituals, marking the transition from a rural, agricultural existence into working subjects. During this process, workers are expected to embrace the new capitalist arrangement, leaving their past behind. Particular rituals mark the stage of transition, which Turner (1967) describes as 'liminality'. The chapter then turns to the experiences of women on the shop-floor as they adjust to the industrial realm in which the surveillance apparatus continually disciplines them. The chapter argues that although factory work provides urban migrants with the sense of 'uplift' from their rural (agricultural) existence, they do not feel attached to their jobs, and have no intention of becoming fully integrated into their factory employment. The women whose stories form the basis of this chapter consider factory work as transitional, and not an endpoint in itself. This perception signifies women's covert resistance to industrial capitalism, expressed when they refuse to fully incorporate their selves into the industrial regime of 'knowledge' and 'power' (cf. Foucault 1991).

Young women's reluctance to fully engage in the industrial system also relates to their exposure to global culture, which they have experienced since childhood as a consequence of 'the urbanisation of the rural' (Young 1994). As a result of this exposure, many urban factory women perceive migration to the urban centres as a lifestyle choice rather than as a journey simply to pursue economic gain. On the one hand, this reproduces the experience of Wolf's rural Javanese factory daughters, who saw their work as a way to increase their 'buying power' so they could conform to 'modern style' (Wolf 1992: 193). At the same time, however, this agenda of modernity provides workers with a defence mechanism in the face of the pressures of industrial work. For these women, the 'urban' represents both an aspiration and a future (Hadiz 1997: 124; Hull 1994: 5), and factory work is a way to mediate their connection with modernity. This view reflects women's liberty to make own interpretations about their mobility, and their capacity to bring about change into their lives.

This chapter, set in the context of the post-1997 Asian financial crisis, is based on nearly eleven months of ethnographic fieldwork conducted between 2000 and 2001. During that time I engaged in the activities that define the everyday lives of workers: queuing at the wells; walking to the workplace; eating at the food stalls; shopping at the malls or the market; watching TV, video compact discs and karaoke; gossiping; and waking up at dawn to dine during the fasting month. It was not merely these activities that have informed my understanding of woman subjects; it was the verbal exchanges that occurred amidst this bustle that created an entrance for me to 'the conceptual world' (Geertz 1973: 24) in which migrant factory workers are situated. The majority of women whose stories and experiences follow worked in the textile, garment and leather industries. Most had arrived in Tangerang as fresh migrants from rural areas and had only worked in factories for one or two years – or even less – when I first met them. These women came from rural areas in Java and the outer islands. They varied in age between their late teens to their mid-20s, and most had completed their secondary education. The majority were unmarried, although married couples with infants were not uncommon. These complexities represent the heterogeneous community of migrant workers in the area, and are indicative to the different reasons women have chosen to move to Tangerang, and their expectations of work.[1]

Learning to work

It was nearly seven o'clock in the morning when thousands of factory workers streamed into a badly maintained street on their way to an industrial cluster in the south of Gambir neighbourhood in Tangerang. A Korean-owned shoe factory; a subcontracting factory producing Nike shoes; a Chinese under-licence motorbike factory; a factory producing oil-drilling components for a transnational oil company; and a Korean-owned leather golf glove factory – among others – are located in this cluster. The complex also includes the giant industrial compound of the locally-owned PT GHTG Group, whose products range from tyres to sanitary pads. The noise of machines, the sight of factory smokestacks issuing forth thick, dark smoke, and the heavy container trucks and recent-model cars (owned by the companies' top executives) all symbolize the grandeur of industrialization.

The factory gate where the workers sign up for one domain, and leave the other, is located here. Lining up in front of the gate – often in long queues that spill into the street causing traffic jams – is a morning ritual that all workers must undertake before they are allowed to enter the factory premises. When they enter, workers wear an identity badge, normally attached to their uniform pocket, which is checked by the company's security officials. The identity badge, although small in size, can determine the fate of an individual since failure to wear it affects a worker's personnel record, which is considered when the 'season of dismissals' comes, particularly if the employer is facing economic difficulties. For a newly recruited worker, who has worked for less than two years and only has temporary status (*buruh harian*), such a mistake will delay promotion to a permanent position (*buruh tetap*). Even those with no intention of pursuing a career in the factory have to comply with the policy since salaries are paid on presentation of the badge to the company's cashier. Lengthy preparations for work in substandard accommodation and the limited availability of public transport make it difficult for workers to arrive at work on time. Under this pressure, failure to carry their badge seems excusable, but such an excuse carries no weight.

Goffman introduced the term 'total institutions' to describe the totality of mental hospitals and penitentiaries in detaching subjects from social interaction with the larger world outside. He added that the particularity of such institutions is highlighted in the centralizing of activities under one 'single authority'; the uniformity of treatment of all subjects under their influence; and the organization of activities under a supervisory apparatus executing strict rules (1971: 16–17). In order to effect this detachment, symbolic procedures are required. These rituals are called 'trimming' or 'programming', in which the body is adjusted and habituated to 'the administrative machinery' and internal rules of the institution immediately upon admission (1971: 26). In the context of the industrial factory, which has attributes of the total institution, the badge represents the programming of workers' behaviour to conform to the industrial mindset and the 'trimming' of their bodies to fit its industrial obligations. It is a 'summary' of the employment contract between the workers and the employer. While a contract is usually referred to when a dispute occurs, the badge – which has to be worn at all times in the workplace – represents the employee's commitment to abide by workplace regulations within the factory domain. If a worker does not wear her badge, she becomes exposed to the threat that her basic rights as an employee will be ignored.

The presentation of a worker's identity badge to the security guard is not the only ritual that occurs at the factory's front gate. The process of programming is also accomplished through management's efforts to undermine the subject's identity and their 'usual image to others' (Goffman 1971: 30). Within the institution, the principle of uniformity applies to every subordinate individual, and personal image is determined by the definition generated by the authority. This necessitates the stripping of attributes that have an association with subjects' prior existence since those personal attributes are the representation of 'self-identification', which may be in contradiction with the purpose of the institution (Goffman 1971: 26). This is illustrated in the case of Ery, a female migrant worker employed at PT Matra, a South Korean-owned footwear factory, which has a policy of body-searching workers before they enter the plant. The ritual scrutiny of the security guard is repeated at the end of each shift in order to secure the property of the enterprise against those trying to illegally remove it. The workers have to line up again, awaiting their turn to be searched, before they can pass through the gate.

PT Matra exports its products to the United States, Japan and South America. Domestically, its products are only marketed in only a few select outlets, such as in Mal Taman Anggrek, an upper-middle-class shopping mall in West Jakarta, with a retail price of at least Rp. 900,000 (US$100), or nearly twice the government-regulated minimum monthly wage in 2002. The company forbids workers to bring food or drink into the factory compound: only food and drink provided by the company can be consumed in the designated canteen area during the set time for meals. A number of other articles are also subject to exclusion, including *mukena*, the white cloaks covering the body and head for Islamic prayer, which are not permitted on the shop-floor. Ery explained:

We are watched by the security guard from the front gate. The guard checks whether or not we are carrying a *mukena*. It is not allowed to be brought in. It has to be left at the security post. When the call for prayer [from the mosque nearby] is heard, we come back to the post to get the *mukena*, take it to the *musholla* [prayer room], and leave it there afterwards for the next prayer. It takes time to walk such a distance, whereas we have to work out the limited time allocated for prayer. Plenty of running around!

When interviewed, Ery and her colleague, Lely, told me that they had become accustomed to such restrictions and could understand why the company imposes them. Having access to food and drink during work, they said, might prove a distraction from the production process. However, at the same time, they maintained that it was difficult to perform a job that demanded concentration and physical labour with only one meal break in an eight-hour shift.

The normal work hours in this shoe factory end at 3.30 in the afternoon. However, workers from the hand-sewing division often do not return home until 10.30 or 11.00 in the evening. Ery explained that when demand for the company's products was high shop-floor employees were forced to undertake compulsory overtime in order to meet production deadlines. The length of compulsory overtime varied from one division to another. During the peak season, divisions other than hand-sewing would still complete their work as early as 6.00 or 9.00 pm. According to Ery, the use of machines made the work in other divisions more efficient. In addition, those divisions mainly dealt with the production of components that required no correction because of the accuracy of the machines. In the cutting division, for example, once the cutting instrument was set to incise a certain pattern, it would perform the task repetitively at constant intervals with relatively high precision. The same applied to the moulding division, where the leather would take shape following the desired contour once workers put a sheet of patterned leather into a pre-installed mould. In contrast, the tasks required of workers in the hand-sewing division are more complicated than in other stages of production, not least because of their manual nature. Workers are required to finalize two pairs per hour for a simple design with one pattern on each side of the shoe, or one pair per hour for a more complex design involving more patterns. Precision is not assured in the hand-sewing division, especially when the workers become tired and their concentration drops off, creating piles of rejected items to be re-done. This added to the employees' levels of stress and the feeling of being 'chased' (*keteter*) when they already had to meet the target of one or more pairs of shoes an hour.

Most workers acknowledged that adjustment to corporate discipline was difficult given the pressure to meet production deadlines. But they accepted the company's policy of compulsory overtime because it helped boost their earnings so that they could buy items other than daily basic necessities. However, Ery and her colleague, Lely, are reluctant to work until 10.30 pm, spending 15 uninterrupted hours on the production floor, with only short breaks for meal-times and prayers. They argue that prolonged work hours gave the workers little chance to do other things, including their domestic tasks at their lodgings. Ery said:

I do not mind doing overtime, as long as it does not go until 10.30 in the evening. If I work until 10.30, I get fed up [*suntuk*], I get sick of working [*jenuh*], my body gets tired [*capek*]. Working until that late means we don't have enough time to have a good night's rest, because on the following day we have to be in the factory again at 7.30 in the morning. Working until 8.30 in the evening would be quite enough [*pas-pasan*]. When we get home, there would still be time to wash our clothes, do something else and get enough rest.

For most workers, having to stay in the plant until late evening brought a feeling of discomfort. This was not only because the evening was supposed to be a time of respite. Many said that it felt strange to have to work hard after dark. This appeared to be related to the experience migrants brought from their villages, where most activities (particularly economic activities) ceased at dusk or when the air resounded with the early evening call for Islamic prayer (*maghrib*).

Mills (1999: 187) and Roseberry (1994) have described the significance of rural values such as these in shaping marginalized urban subjects' perspective on their existence in the city. In the factories of Tangerang, rural values and images become the source of tension in workers' adaptation to capitalist disciplines, and their encounter with the factory regime becomes a medium through which workers connect with the rural community, using their romanticized pictures of the village to judge the appropriateness (or otherwise) of urban reality. They also become a strategy with which to manage their alienation. Workers imagine the countryside – their place of origin – as a place of natural purity; of rice fields (*sawah*), clean rivers and peace of mind. These images are often invoked when urban migrant workers complain about urban hardship and industrial pressure. The idea of a virgin countryside is essential in the construction of the identity of these urban migrants: amidst their active search for modern advancement in the city, they need a local connection to revisit. These images become what Helsinger terms, speaking of early nineteenth-century Britain, 'portable icons' that allow workers to escape from urban anomalies (cited in Maclean *et al.* 1999:14). The practice of *mudik*, or returning to one's place of origin to mark the end of Islamic fasting month (Antlov 1999: 204; Pemberton 1994: 237), helps keep this idea of rural nature and peace alive, despite the fact that in the countryside itself rural development has diminished people's experience of nature and replaced it with urban-centred themes of modernization.

Women working on the shop-floor

Ery is one worker among a 1,000-strong workforce employed in the PT Matra plant. At 7.30 am sharp, the beginning of the shift, she must be already sitting on her line in the hand-sewing area. There are ten lines in the division, each operated by 24 workers. Here, shoes are finished by manually stitching a design on the unornamented product. The production floor consists of seven divisions. Production begins in the cutting division where plain leather is incised with a particular pattern by a machine-activated sharp instrument. The leather is then shaped in a mould in the moulding division after first being soaked in a chemical solution to soften it. Once it has been contoured, the leather is forwarded to the sewing division, where a plain shoe is constructed by sewing the patterned pieces of moulded leather together. This task, which is mainly performed by female workers, is carried out with specially designed sewing machines. From here, the shoe is passed to Ery's hand-sewing division where it is decorated. The level of complexity of tasks completed in the hand-sewing division depends on the particular design ordered. The more intricate the design, the more time it takes to put the final touches on a pair of shoes. As soon as the hand-sewing is completed, the sole-bottoming division glues the decorated shoe upper and the rubber sole together. The finished shoes are now ready to be packed in the packing division before they are transported out for local market or export. In addition to the principal divisions described above, there is a general division (*bagian umum*), whose task it is to forward the results from one division to the next processing section within the assembly line.

It is no coincidence that the sewing division and the hand-sewing division, to which Ery and her friend Lely are assigned, have a high proportion of female workers. A number of studies have discussed the high level of involvement of females compared to their male counterparts in manufacturing, particularly light industries (Caraway 2007; Mather 1985; Saptari, 1994; Wolf 1992). Indrasari Tjandraningsih's late 1980s study of textile, garment and footwear industries in Majalaya found that female workers were especially dominant in the large-scale export-oriented footwear industries, where women were responsible for two-thirds of the entire production process (2000: 260). In Tangerang, this is true in the textile, garment, and leather industries where women outnumber men by a ratio of more than two to one.

Most female workers from PT Matra factory I spoke to explained that the detailed and intricate character of the work makes this occupation a preserve of women. Diane Elson and Ruth Pearson have been critical of this explanation for the feminization of factory work because it relies on the stereotyping of 'innate capacities and personality traits' of women (1981: 92). Elson and Pearson argue that the prevalence of women in these industries is explained by the assumption that sewing is typically part of a daughter's 'training' within the family and that this training enables girls to develop the 'manual dexterity and capacity for spatial assessment' that is required on the shop-floor. Because it is interwoven with everyday domestic work, sewing is categorized as unskilled labour. From the industrial employer's point of view, this assumption leads to the employment of women for the sake of efficiency or 'profitability', because women become more productive more quickly and do not require training before they are ready to perform the task. Therefore, according to Elson and Pearson, it is not the women who make themselves 'bearers of inferior labour' in the industry, but, the industry that makes 'inferior bearers of labour' of the female recruits (1981: 93–94). However, the declining participation of daughters in domestic work means that sewing no longer an 'innate' attribute. The presence of a private sewing course in Tangerang, whose participants were all young females, indicates that formal training is now required by job-seeking daughters to prepare them to participate in the industry. Moreover, growing exposure to discourses of modernity through cultural flows brought by education and rural modernization provides the basis, and promise, of a modern existence to the move to an urban centre. The increasing proportion of women who manage to complete their secondary education are, in fact, capable of undertaking up-skilled employment such as accounting and typing, and their higher level of education has an impact on their receptiveness to modern discourse, which, in turn, shapes their 'increasing realisation of their role in the urban and urbane world' (Hull 1994: 5).

Susan Joekes, writing on the condition of workers in the Moroccan clothing industry, suggests that another argument employers make for the increasing presence of women in industrial workplaces is their 'docility' (1985: 189). The notion of women's 'subordinate role in domestic and public situations' underscores females' presumed inability to disrupt industrial operations; their 'meekness, passivity, and obedience', combined with 'their youth and lack of experience' in the sector, thus ensuring a less-troubled working environment (Joekes 1985: 189–90). However, she asserts, such a stereotypical view of the subordination of women does not always match reality, since Moroccan women workers have long been involved in labour activism. Experience of worker movements in Tangerang in the mid 1990s indicates that female workers' superior skills of persuasion and communication, as well as their patience in labour organizing work, often placed them in leadership positions in industrial actions. Ironically, the stereotyping of women as being docile provided them with some level of protection – shielding them from arrest, physical threats and intimidation since authorities were unlikely to identify them as ringleaders. This suggests that claims about women's docility and passivity are merely a fiction believed by the company or corporate agencies.

In another South Korean-owned factory, PT PCA, workers are not permitted to take more than one day of sick leave at a time. One of the female workers from the company, Dewi, commented that even in the case of serious illness a letter from the doctor is not sufficient to obtain an extension of sick leave, forcing many to take annual leave when sick. However, annual leave is only granted to workers who had worked a minimum of one year. Dewi, who had joined the company eight months earlier, was not yet eligible for this entitlement. She frequently suffers gastric problems that often last a few days, and finds it difficult to return to work after her single day's sick leave has been used. 'I always feel extremely weak and dizzy,' she said. However, after a few times, she figured out how to deceive the system that she claimed was 'inhuman' (*enggak berperikemanusiaan*). Dewi noticed that the head of division was the only authority on the work floor who recommended sick leave for an ailing worker to the rubber-stamping administration office. Therefore, according to her, once the head of division, a male, could be 'taken in hand' (*kepegang*), things could be 'negotiated' (*bisa diatur*). 'I flirted with him, and attracted his attention,' Dewi explained. After quite some time, the head of division believed that he was intimate enough with Dewi to teasingly ask her to be his girlfriend. Dewi told me:

> I never responded to it. How dare he! But I kept being nice to him. I don't care if he holds my hand, caresses my back or shoulder in the workplace. I'll kick him if he does more than that.

Luckily Dewi never experienced more serious sexual harassment. But more importantly she managed to take her foreman 'in hand', encouraging him to do favours for her, particularly in relation to obtaining sick leave. After that, Dewi could get enough bed rest when she felt unwell. Indeed she could get sick leave even when she just did not feel like going to work. Moreover, when Dewi eventually resigned from the job in order to take a break, the head of division ensured that she could rejoin the company when she was ready to return – a privilege that, under normal circumstances, would be denied a worker who had resigned.

Dewi's case reveals that the stereotype of women's obedience to their employers is a false perception based on the social construction of women's inferiority to men. As Dewi's actions show, the power relations established between the employer – in this case represented by the foreman – and the employee prove to be open to manipulation. By exploiting her sexual attractiveness Dewi elevated her bargaining power in the face of the harsh regime of the industrial workplace. With these kinds of manoeuvres, the subordinate subject is able to turn the domain of others of superior agency into a 'playable' arena in which she stages a tug-of-war in order to drag the playing field, the regulations, down to her level. From the workers' perspective, strict corporate discipline can be a negotiable domain that allows for compromise without the company's knowledge. Other female workers might not be as skilful as Dewi in this regard, and as Tjandraningsih asserts, this relation of power remains susceptible to 'misuse' by the male superior (2000: 264). However, many female workers commented that, when confronted by the stereotyped image of a vulnerable female, male foremen or managers felt obliged to demonstrate their 'gentlemanliness' in order to 'ease' the circumstances of their female subordinate.[2]

In general, company regulations on both sick leave and annual leave are enforced on the shop-floor, without regard for the sex of the worker, the type of task or length of employment. However, these rules particularly affect married female workers, who also have the domestic role of caring for their offspring. Rusilah is an ethnic Javanese who had been employed in the PT Matra factory for about two years. Her husband, whom she met in Tangerang, is a shop-floor worker at a chemical factory in a neighbouring sub-district. One time, the couple's 7-month-old only son, Reza, had diarrhoea and had been admitted to hospital. On normal days, her 18-year-old younger sister, whom Rusilah had brought from the village, looked after the baby. However, Rusilah decided to stay home after the son was discharged from hospital because she was concerned about his condition. Despite a letter from a doctor stating the circumstance of her son's health, the company did not grant her sick leave, which is given only when a worker is herself ill. Accordingly, she was forced to use four days from her annual leave entitlement, which the couple usually used to visit relatives in their home villages.

Unlike Dewi, Rusilah is not good at flirting with her superior to negotiate sick leave; even if she was, she did not think an area manager/supervisor would be attracted to a married woman like herself. She softly told me, while cuddling her baby, and with a bitter expression on her face:

> The remainder of my annual leave won't be enough to return to the countryside. I could [still go], but it's too much hassle to travel with my kid for such a short time. This year I will just have to stay in Tangerang.

She actually could have split the four days' leave she took with her husband, but she felt that it was her responsibility, as a mother, to look after her sick baby. 'Besides, I do not want my husband to sacrifice his work [by taking leave],' she explained, although he only earned as much as she did. It was she who had to take their son to the hospital and take care of him during the recovery process. Her double responsibility as a worker and a mother allowed her little leisure even after her work in the factory was complete (see also Kim 1997; Lee 1998).

In addition, as her medical allowance does not apply to family members, Rusilah had to dig deep to cover the cost of Reza's medical treatment and medicines. This was difficult since the cost of raising a child in the city, which included bringing her younger sister to help with the domestic work, is crippling. Although both husband and wife worked, their situation is exacerbated by the regime of the minimum wage, which remains insensitive to the expenditure associated with child rearing and family maintenance. Furthermore, differentiation between male and female workers still occurs with regard to entitlements. Women are eligible for menstruation leave, maternal leave, miscarriage leave as well as a menstruation allowance under Indonesia's labour legislation, but a married female worker does not receive all the entitlements male workers enjoy. For example, Rusilah was not entitled to receive an accommodation allowance. PT Matra factory provides lodgings for its single employees, but married workers with a family have to find private dwellings for themselves, for which an accommodation allowance is available. However, based on the assumption that the male is the head of the family (*kepala rumah tangga*) and the principal breadwinner, that allowance is only paid to men. Similarly, a maternity allowance is paid to male employees' wives, while a female worker such as Rusilah is not eligible.

Wolf (1992: 118) argues that, in addition to providing a rationalization for the differentiation in benefits, the notion that men's economic duty is more onerous than women's reinforces the practice of 'male superiority' within society at large (see also Elson and Pearson 1981: 92). Rusilah's self-sacrifice in taking full responsibility for her child and using up her annual leave while letting her spouse work and save his leave is a clear illustration of how men are positioned as the main wage earner and superior within the family. Despite her own view of her secondary role, her experience suggests that being female does not make her less dependent on income from her own paid work and, hence, less important in the family economy. The fact that she resumed her factory employment after giving birth suggests that her contribution to the couple's urban survival is as vital as that of her husband. Indeed, all the married female workers I spoke to had been employed in industrial work before their marriage. They met their spouses in Tangerang and returned to the city to recommence their factory work after having a wedding ceremony in the village. 'I had already got used to work,' was a common explanation I heard from these married women workers. In contrast, wives who were brought from the village by their working husbands generally stayed at home and considered themselves housewives whose primary task was to support their spouses and children.

Encountering the system

The direct superior of most shop-floor workers in PT Matra is the head of the group (*ketua regu*) who supervises a line. In the hand-sewing division, there are ten lines whose group heads are predominantly women; these lines rotate at least once every two months. Above the group heads is the line head (*ketua line*), who supervises several lines. There were two line heads in Ery's division, each of whom supervised five lines. The heads of line are accountable to a division head (*ketua bagian*), whose task is to organize the workers in his/her area in order to meet the daily quota of the division based on the instructions of the production manager. The production manager, a South Korean national, oversees the division heads on the production floor. Unlike the newly recruited factory women who are the focus of this study, supervisory roles are usually reserved for those who have been working in the factory for over five years. These women had maintained their positions in the company despite the financial crisis. Only a small proportion of women could enjoy such mobility, which was only available to workers who have demonstrated their loyalty and obedience, and have no record of wrongdoing. Ordinary factory women are usually happy enough to be upgraded from the status of provisional or temporary workers to that of permanent worker, which is only possible after serving the company for at least two years without serious violation of company rules. With more established or permanent status, workers might expect a better leave allowance and a redundancy benefit according to their length of service.

The workers often complain about being reproached by the fretful (*cerewet*) and fault-finding (*bawel*) group heads, their immediate supervisor, when they work too slowly. The hierarchy is also designed to control the physical mobility of the employees with regard to non-production-related activities within the factory premises. When a worker is ill and wants to see a doctor at the health clinic, she has to obtain a referral letter (*surat berobat*) from her group head. Only with the written approval of this supervisor is the ill employee able to leave the line. If a referral letter is issued, the worker takes it to the head of line to have it signed. The head can accept or reject the request, depending on their personal disposition and the reasons provided by the employee. From there, the letter is to be taken by the worker to the administrative officer, who approves it and makes a record for administrative purposes. The worker is permitted to visit the health clinic, located outside the company complex, only after these clearances are obtained and inspected by the security officer at the front gate. The clinic serves a number of manufacturing industries in the sub-district, but it only provides services to workers at the company's expense on production of proof of their identity and a letter of reference from their company. Lely complained that several times when she was dreadfully ill the head of group would not give her permission to leave work to see the doctor or simply to rest at home. She added that, based on her experience, female group heads in particular are often reluctant to give approval; that they are always less ready to believe female workers. Lely stated that, based on her experience with different group heads, she preferred a male supervisor, as they are usually more understanding (*pengertian*).

Contact with the production manager, a South Korean expatriate, occurs on an almost daily basis at PT Matra factory. According to the workers, the production manager is a joint owner of the company. He monitors almost every aspect of production at the plant, checking and controlling the performance of workers on the lines throughout the working day. Many women said that the presence of the manager at the line distresses them, although he never comments on individuals' performance. Commenting on how she feels when the *mister* – the term used to refer to the expatriate manager – is standing behind her and watching her working, one worker observed, 'I feel like I have just committed a wrongdoing (*serba salah*) and I get so nervous (*grogi*).' The production manager has to be consulted if workers wish to leave the production building during their lunch break. First, the worker has to obtain the relevant letter (*surat pengantar istirahat*) from the group head, and then take it to the line head, the head of division, the *mister* and, last of all, to the administration office. Without this letter, the presence of a worker outside the production building, even if still in the factory premises, is against the company rules. Workers' access to restrooms is also heavily controlled. Workers have to carry a card when leaving the line for the lavatory. Each line is allotted one card so that no more than one employee can leave at any one time. According to the workers, the policy was introduced because the company felt that productivity would be affected by the absence of more than one worker from a line.

The strict control over their movements and behaviour of workers during working hours leaves women with little opportunity to take a break outside the officially designated meal and prayer times. A walk to the lavatory is considered an opportunity to meet the need for a short break in the middle of a distressing work session. Waiting outside the toilets, which are inadequate in number, is the only way employees can enjoy a little freedom in the workplace, chatting with others, smoking or eating snacks. Some even try to take a nap or simply close their eyes a little while in the lavatory. However, even that opportunity is limited since company security officers regularly check the lavatory area, sending the crowd back to the line, or knocking on the toilet doors to warn the occupant to hurry.

In addition to the strict, elaborate disciplinary and bureaucratic procedures imposed by manufacturing corporations on their shop-floors, a 'carrot' approach is adopted by companies in order to ensure workers' loyalty. These measures range from the provision of sport facilities and a space for praying to the provision of entertainment facilities. These are intended, according to one company's work agreement, to 'accommodate the advancement of talent and creativity of the workers'. A large corporation like PT GHTG Group provides facilities such as a film-viewing and music room, which are available twice a week. Even outdoor recreation is guaranteed in most work agreements. For example, once a year, PT Matra factory helps to organize a one-day trip for its workers to visit places of interest within three to four hours of Tangerang. The company pays for transportation and logistics but the trips are mostly organized by the workplace union.

According to Ery, joy and laughter are certainly features of these short trips, which allow workers to escape the routine of the industrial town. However, once at their destination, no focused activities are organized by the company or the union.

Instead, the participants are free to do things individually or in small groups, except during the lunch break. In her study of urban industrial migrant workers in Bangkok, Mills (1999) found that extra-firm gatherings like these became a way for unions to promote 'solidarity' in order to endorse 'class-based unity' as a stratagem to counter urban structural impediments. This was missing during the leisure trips of workers of PT Matra. The union appears to get involved in technical matters (ordering buses, arranging catering) without using these events as a means to promote the union agenda. Nor are the events used as an opportunity for the company's officials to relax the barrier between the higher-level staff and production workers, since office personnel do not participate. As a result, though delighted with this firm-funded initiative, the workers do not develop a feeling of obligation to the company in the form of loyalty or emotional attachment.

The transience of factory work

Despite its modern connotations and promises of status and a better income, which conform to factory women's expectations of a certain urban lifestyle, for many women, a factory job is merely transitional. Migrant workers' perceptions of their engagement in industrial activities are shaped by their working environments. Many workers said that abusive labour practices are 'unbearable' (*enggak bikin betah*) and that they want to leave factory employment (*kayaknya mau keluar*). The majority of workers with whom I spoke have already made plans for their future, setting a limit to the period of time they will remain in the sweatshop (usually less than eight years) before quitting. In January 2001, Ery predicted that she would no longer be working in the factory in two years' time:

> I am tired of working in the factory and I want to go back to my home village to help my parents, help my mother at home. Perhaps by next year I'll already have left this work.

About a year after this conversation, I had an opportunity to return to the area for a short visit. I found that Ery was no longer working in the factory. She and three other colleagues from the same footwear factory had resigned from the job three months earlier and had returned to their villages. 'I just want to take a break from factory [work],' she had told friends who were still living and working in the area. Since Ery had left the job, she had revisited Tangerang once and tried to get a job at another manufacturing factory. Having failed, she left again for her village. But Lely, Ery's friend, who had also resigned, had better luck. She had found another factory job in different sub-district in Tangerang after being at home 'doing nothing' (*nggak ngapa-ngapain*) except helping her mother with domestic tasks for about two months.

The decision made by Ery and her colleagues was certainly risky, given the ongoing problems with Indonesia's economy triggered by the 1997 financial crisis. However, the city is a site where fantasies of pleasure can be realized, and the factory is a part of the migrants' urban experience that they may discard when it no longer brings 'pleasure' and contentment. This does not mean that factory work is a one-off experience: women seem happy to re-enter the sector after a taking short break. The fact that urban employment is not always available under difficult macro-economic conditions was probably not foremost in Ery's mind when she decided to resign. As long as the rural economy remains able, through its 'cushion' mechanism (Wolf 1986: 371), to absorb children temporarily unemployed from the urban sector, the problem of scarcity in urban employment is of secondary concern migrant workers like Ery and Lely.

Future expectations enable young migrants to perceive their factory work as temporary. As a result, their loyalty and emotional attachment to their employer is low, as demonstrated by their everyday resistance in the workplace. Basic skills learned in school contribute to their confidence in their ability to achieve upward mobility in urban areas, as women imagine gaining public sector or office work after leaving the manufacturing sector. Whether or not such expectations are realistic remain to be seen. However, their optimism explains their attitude towards their engagement in the industrial sector as something that is not worth fighting for if their current employment is threatened.

Conclusion

In the manner of a total institution, a manufacturing factory uses fortress-like walls, badges, body-searches and the unrelenting control of workers' activities while in the factory to contain workers in a particular reality. Production conditions on the assembly line and the strict rules that intrude on individual habits are sources of pressure and anxiety for the workers. Values brought from past lives, mostly in the countryside, serve as a benchmark by which rural migrants judge work practices as unjust and treatment by the factory regime as degrading. Despite offering a steady income, then, the factory shop-floor remains an alienating reality. This is evident in female factory workers' detachment from their work, and their belief that their industrial employment is not permanent, which in turn suggests that, despite the discipline imposed by the total institution on the workers, the incorporation of rural women into capitalist production is never complete.

Wolf, speaking of manufacturing workers in rural Java, has noted that rural daughters' '*preference* for factory employment' (1992: 136, emphasis in original) as well as their 'limited and constrained options', have contributed to their acceptance of industrial control and discipline. Moreover, she asserts, support from their parents' household economy means that they accept low payment and poor working arrangements without protest. Wolf argues that this degree of compliance is linked to the 'nature of transition' from agriculture to industry experienced by these daughters (1992: 134). Female migrant workers in Tangerang exhibit a similar level of acceptance, albeit for different reasons. As a result of their better education and experience of urban modernity, these workers believe they have the opportunity to work in different kinds of occupations, which in turn contributes to their perception of factory work as transitional. These expectations of post-factory employment serve as a defence mechanism that enables them to respond to the pressure emerging from the regime on the shop-floor.

The processes factory women have to undergo in their integration into the manufacturing regime evoke Turner's notion of liminality to describe a stage in transition between two different realms defined by status, age or place (1967: 93–111). This notion is based on Arnold Van Gennep's 'rite of passage' (cited in Turner 1967: 94; see also Barnard and Spencer 2002: 489), which is divided into three stages: separation, transition and incorporation. Badges and body-searches are examples of rituals that mark the detachment of workers from their pre-factory existence, or separation. Habituation to the factory regime – its work methods, discipline and control – realigns workers' behaviour to the industrial world of work and represents the transition. The everyday, long-term practice of the regimentation of factory work marks the outcome of transition, that is, incorporation. Since workers' integration into the industrial institution is never complete, the stage of transition, or liminality, colours the entirety of their time on the shop-floor. This is because a worker's industrial body, her physical presence in the factory, is constantly overshadowed by her past values and expectations of a post-factory existence. These past shadows and future possibilities make workers' total incorporation problematic. Liminality, therefore, is not merely a stage that marks the arrival of workers at, and adjustment to, the factory. Rather, the difficulties they experience in habituating their selves to the industrial regime – and their lack of attachment to their work – suggest that factory women are continuously in a state of transition; caught between past and future, as imagined in their present factory existence.

Notes

1 Despite my deep involvement in ethnographic fieldwork, I failed to gain access to the factories; requests to the management of a number of companies met with no success. Accordingly, portrayals of women's experiences on the shop-floor depend on the narratives and stories told by the workers. In order to protect those workers, pseudonyms are used for interviewees, the companies where they worked and the name of neighbourhood in which the fieldwork was undertaken.
2 Likewise, to lighten the strain, humorous stories about female workers challenging power on the shop-floor by showing disrespect toward the supervisor were often told. These types of everyday resistance in James Scott's (1986) sense included saying bad things about the supervisor, breaking the no-chat rule and eating while performing tasks on the assembly line, mostly when the supervisor is not present.

References

Antlov, H. (1999) 'The new rich and cultural tensions in rural Indonesia', in M. Pinches (ed.) *Culture and Privilege in Capitalist Asia*, London: Routledge.

Barnard, A. and Spencer, J. (2002) 'Rite of passage', in A. Barnard and J. Spencer (eds) *Encyclopedia of Social and Cultural Anthropology*, London: Routledge.

Braverman, H. (1974) *Labor and Monopoly Capital: The degradation of work in the twentieth century*, New York: Monthly Review Press.

Caraway, T. (2007) *Assembling Women: the feminization of global manufacturing*, Ithaca, NY: Cornell University Press/ILR Press.

Elson, D. and Pearson, R. (1981) 'Nimble fingers make cheap workers: an analysis of women's employment in Third World export manufacturing', *Feminist Review*, spring: 87–107.

Foucault, M. (1991) *Discipline and Punish: the birth of the prison*, Harmonsdworth: Penguin.

Geertz, C. (1973) *The Interpretation of Culture: selected writings*, New York: Basic Books.

Goffman, E. (1971) *Asylums: essays on the social situation of mental patients and other inmates*, Harmondsworth: Penguin.

Hadiz, V. (1997) *Workers and the State in New Order Indonesia*, London: Routledge.

Hull, T. (1994) 'Workers in the shadows: a statistical wayang', in D. Bourchier (ed.) *Indonesia's Emerging Proletariat: workers and their struggles*, Clayton, Vic.: Monash University.

Joekes, S. (1985) 'Working for lipstick? Male and female labour in the clothing industry in Morocco', in H. Afshar (ed.) *Women, Work, and Ideology in the Third World*, New York: Tavistock Publications.

Kim, S. (1997) *Class Struggle or Family Struggle? The lives of women factory workers in South Korea*, Cambridge: Cambridge University Press.

Lee, C. K. (1998) *Gender and the South China Miracle: two worlds of factory women*, Berkeley: University of California Press.

Maclean, G., Landry, D. and Ward, J. (1999) *The Country and the City Revisited: England and the politics of culture 1550–1850*, Melbourne: Cambridge University Press.

Mather, C. (1985) 'Rather than make trouble, it's better just to leave: behind the lack of industrial strife in the Tangerang region of West Java', in H. Afshar (ed.) *Women, Work, and Ideology in the Third World*, New York: Tavistock Publications.

Mills, M. B. (1999) 'Enacting solidarity: unions and migrant youth in Thailand', *Critique of Anthropology*, 19 (2): 175–92.

Ong, A. (1987) *Spirits of Resistance and Capitalist Discipline: factory women in Malaysia*, Albany: State University of New York Press.

Pemberton, J. (1994) *On the Subject of "Java"*, Ithaca, NY: Cornell University Press.

Roseberry, W. (1994) *Anthropologies and Histories: essays in culture, history, and political economy*, New Brunswick, NJ: Rutgers University Press.

Saptari, R. (1994) 'Gender at work and the dynamics of the workplace: Indonesia's *kretek* cigarette industry in the 1980s', in D. Bourchier (ed.) *Indonesia's Emerging Proletariat: workers and their struggles*, Clayton, Vic.: Monash University.

Scott, J. (1986) 'Everyday forms of peasant resistance', in J. Scott and B. J. T. Kerkvliet (eds) *Everyday Forms of Peasant Resistance in South-East Asia*, London: Frank Cass.

Thompson, E. P. (1967) 'Time, work-discipline, and industrial capitalism', *Past and Present* 38: 56–97.

Tjandraningsih, I. (2000) 'Gendered work and labour factory control: women factory workers in Indonesia', *Asian Studies Review*, 24 (2): 257–68.

Turner, V. (1967) *The Forest of Symbols: aspects of Ndembu ritual*, Ithaca, NY: Cornell University Press.

Wolf, D. L. (1986) 'Factory daughters, their families, and rural industrialization in Central Java', unpublished PhD thesis, Cornell University.

—— (1992) *Factory Daughters: gender, household dynamics, and rural industrialization in Java*, Berkeley: University of California Press.

Young, K. (1994) 'A new political context: the urbanisation of the rural', in D. Bourchier and J. Legge (eds) *Democracy in Indonesia: 1950s and 1990s*, Clayton, Vic.: Centre of Southeast Asian Studies, Monash University.

6 Bodies in contest
Gender difference and equity in a coal mine

Kuntala Lahiri-Dutt and Kathryn Robinson

Feminist theory has lurched between consideration of women's specificity or difference, usually with regard to biologically based attributes and capacities, and women's 'sameness' with men in terms of demands for gender equity. This ambiguity is exemplified in the area of work, and the constitution of women's economic citizenship. The global movement for protection of women workers in the second half of the nineteenth century exemplified the concern with women's specific difference while ensuring women's rights to be part of the paid labour force. The contrary positions were reflected in the division between women's groups that wanted the state to protect women from excessive exploitation and those that felt that protective legislation was a form of discrimination against women workers. Much of the protection debate was bogged down by the equation of equality with sameness: an inability to recognize equality under conditions of difference, as is now at the core of Equal Employment Opportunity legislation. In her landmark essay on gender difference and equality, Joan Scott enjoins us to:

> ... reconcile theories of equal rights with cultural concepts of sex difference, to question the validity of normative constructions of gender in the light of the existence of behaviours and qualities that contradict the rules, to point up rather than resolve conditions of contradiction, to articulate a political identity for women without conforming to existing stereotypes about them.

> (Scott 1988: 48)[1]

Internationally, the most intense action around the question of protection occurred in the second decade of the twentieth century, coinciding with the period in which young Indonesian nationalists were articulating their anti-colonial struggle. A leading intellectual figure in the protection debates was the German socialist Clara Zetkin (Kessler-Harris *et al.* 1995: 14), who was later an important influence on women in the left-leaning Indonesian women's organization Gerwani, which was formed in 1950. In Indonesia, labour law has overwhelmingly constituted women's rights in terms of sexual difference, inconsistent with the terms of women's political citizenship, which is framed by the Constitution in terms of equal rights. The first labour law enacted by the new Republic, Law No. 12 of 1948/1951, contained clauses protecting women workers. This law incorporated protection provisions from Dutch law enacted in the colonial Netherlands East Indies (Staatsblad No. 647 of 1925 and Staatsblad No. 45 of 1941), in particular a ban on night work between 6.00 pm and 6.00 am, and limitations on work deemed to present moral danger.[2] Law No. 12 further prohibited women working in mining, but female workers were given special leave for menstruation (two days per cycle), paid maternity leave and the right to breastfeeding breaks. An International Labour Organization (ILO) publication asserts that the 'original intention of the provision was to protect women working in unsatisfactory work environments' (Olney *et al.* 2002: 16). The Minister for Labour, S. K. Trimurti, who enacted the labour law for the new republic, was a major female figure in the Indonesian independence struggle, and had also been a leading figure in the left-wing women's organization Gerwani and the Labour Party (Partai Buruh Indonesia). On this basis, she was invited to become Indonesia's first Minister for Labour in 1947–8. She oversaw the drafting of Law No. 12 1948/1951, including the protection clauses for female workers.[3]

In 1958, the infant Indonesian Republic ratified ILO Convention 100 on equal pay for equal work (Law No. 10 1958) in a further embrace of the international labour agenda. Until the 1980s, when new foreign investment regulations in Indonesia resulted in the opening of the economy to foreign investors, around two-thirds of the female labour force was employed in agriculture (Sumbang 1985: 324). For this reason, in this period, the legal provisions surrounding the formal labour market had little impact on most women's work conditions. During the 1980s, the growing light manufacturing sector (as in other parts of the world) came to be dominated by young women workers. In addition, the affluence generated for the middle classes in the New Order economy created a group of middle-class women, whose class position derived from their own white-collar occupations (Sen 1998). As women have moved increasingly into the formal economy, the gender-specific provisions of labour legislation have become controversial.

The New Order developed a state ideology defining women's citizenship primarily in terms of maternal and domestic responsibilities, justified in terms of her *kodrat* or biological predestination (see Nilan and Utami ch. 7 of this volume). From 1978, in response to the UN-sponsored world conferences on women, Indonesia included a section on women in the GBHN or Broad Outlines of State Policy enacted every five years to accompany each new development plan. The revisions of GBHN over the next 20 years show a gradual embracing of women's role in employment outside the home. From an initial acknowledgement of women's *peran ganda* (dual role) within the home and in the wider economy, government rhetoric shifted over the years to stress the importance of both men and women as 'human resources' for development, consistent with state emphasis on growth-driven development (see Berkovitch 1999) and the commitments that the Indonesian state made in international fora (such as becoming a signatory to CEDAW [the UN Convention on the Elimination of All Forms of Discrimination against Women] in 1984). Since the fall of Suharto, ILO conventions concerning gender equality in employment have been incorporated into a number of post-New Order government regulations concerning labour relations.[4]

Most recently, women's rights at work were revisited with the revision of labour law in Indonesia, first in Law No. 25/1997 and then in Law No. 13/2003. This was a time of political transition, with the fall of the authoritarian Suharto regime and a period of democratization. The revised statute replaced many existing laws and regulations, but retained clauses providing special protection for women, in spite of demands to exclude them. Article 81 (1) states that:

> Female workers/labourers who feel pain during their menstruation period and notify the manager are not obliged to come to work on the first and second day of menstruation. (2) The implementation of what is stipulated under subsection (1) shall be regulated in work agreements, the company regulations or collective labour agreements.

Night work is no longer banned in the 2003 law, except for pregnant women, although employers are obliged to meet regulations concerning transport, refreshments and morality (Article 77). In the public debate surrounding the new law, unions supported the continued provision of menstruation leave, in spite of the criticisms noted above that it could contribute to discrimination against women in the workforce. The labour activist Dita Sari commented that it was supported because it was not sensible to give up a right that had already been won.[5]

The move from the paternalistic and exploitative system of labour relations since the fall of the Suharto regime has had contradictory effects. The new system allows greater unionization, but shifts much of the regulation of labour relations and remuneration from centralized standard setting to local bargaining (Ford 2004). The revised protection clauses in the 2003 labour law leave intact the right to menstruation leave but the specific provisions are dependent on company regulation and enterprise agreements, rather than being set out in the law. The conditions under which women receive the leave have become less transparent – not that they were ever fully enforced by the state. The fact that rights to menstruation leave need to be negotiated in enterprise agreements has the potential to cause conflict with male workmates. The case of women mine-operators described below illustrates the potential of such provisions to adversely affect women's earnings relative to those of men in a setting where otherwise there is no difference in remuneration for male and female workers.

The critiques of protection clauses in late twentieth-century Indonesia mirror international debates: that they potentially discriminate against women and can serve to exclude women from the (usually higher-paid) areas of the workforce where men predominate. How to achieve gender equity while recognizing gender difference has been a contentious matter for feminism everywhere.[6] Writing in 1975, Suwarni Salyo of the Komisi Nasional Kedudukan Wanita Indonesia (National Commission on the Position of Women) commented that these rights often resulted in employers excluding women from employment, or excluding married women from managerial positions (1975: 449). In the mid 1980s it was noted that protective labour laws 'are frequently disregarded or cited as reasons for hiring men' (Morgan 1985: 316). By the early 1990s, different class interests emerged in regard to the protection clauses. IWAPI, the Association of Indonesian Businesswomen, argued that menstruation leave under the legislation was 'contradictory to the aims of women's emancipation ... [because] the large numbers of women who make use of this right only serve to lower the productivity of the companies in which they work and, as a result, many companies are reluctant to employ women' (Kacasungkana cited in Sen 1998: 46). IWAPI succeeded in having a proposal to repeal the clause put before parliament in 1992, but the proposal was not passed.

Middle-class women in white-collar employment no longer make use of this provision – to them it is 'old-fashioned' and discriminatory. They also represent a management point of view, that such leave reduces productivity. The view put by the middle-class female opponents of menstruation leave echoes the point made by Ester Boserup (1970: 113, cited in Elliott 1994), that they perceive menstruation leave as 'a serious impediment (particularly where multiple shifts work has been introduced) to the employment of women in large-scale industries'. It is often argued that there is a danger that women, once excluded from particular occupations, are forced to work in alternative and dangerous occupations (Elliott 1994). For women's work in an arena such as mining, which is commonly viewed as masculine, protective legislation brings to the fore the gender differences within the category of 'women'. However, Kacasungkana argued in 1992 that the majority of blue-collar workers continued to make use of the provision, especially because of poor nutrition and health among working women (cited in Sen 1998: 46).

Protection clauses in Indonesian labour law have delivered benefits to women but have also contributed to a segmented labour market in which women on the whole labour for lower wages. However, menstruation leave has had utility for the growing number of women factory employees whose work often includes compulsory overtime that can stretch the working day to 10 or 12 hours and may often involve either standing or some other form of physical work. Women factory workers described by Warouw (2004) in the industrial region of Tangerang (in the period 2000–1) struggle to survive on the minimum wage, and rely not only on overtime but also allowances to survive. All women workers were deemed 'single' by employers and did not receive the allowances awarded to men as the presumed breadwinners. Women who opted to work during the mandated two days' menstruation leave could claim an extra allowance. In the example provided by Warouw (2004: 233), a woman worker received Rp. 8,000 menstruation allowance to complement her base wage of Rp. 426,500 and overtime of Rp. 1,035, 500. Electing to work through menstruation leave also gives women an increased opportunity to benefit from routinely worked overtime. Workers in Tangerang have commonly been required to seek the supervisor's permission to visit the toilet during the long working day and this can be embarrassing for women. This is similar to the situation described by Lee and Cho (2005) in Korea, where most women workers do not take the menstruation leave and receive a special compensation (50 per cent of premium wages) for working on a legal day off. Female workers' wage levels are on an average lower than male workers' earnings by about 40 per cent, and, as in Tangerang, the menstruation leave is one way of compensating for wage discrimination.

The new labour law in Indonesia makes the precise form of entitlement to menstruation leave subject to negotiation between the employers and the enterprise union in businesses with more than 100 employees. In the increased climate of political contestation since 1998, there have been a number of studies of work conditions that have noted the poor enforcement of protection legislation. A 2003 report (SMERU 2003), produced after the reform government ratified the 1948 ILO Convention on Freedom of Association and Protection of the Right to Organize in 1998, noted that failure to receive menstruation leave entitlements was one of the common reasons for industrial disputes. Eva Komandjaja (2004), from the women's organization Yayasan Jurnal Perempuan, noted:

> ... most companies are also lax about granting time off for menstruating workers. According to Law No. 13/2003, a company is required to grant two days of paid menstruation leave to all women workers each month. Of the 10 companies surveyed in Jakarta, Tangerang, Bandung and Solo, only one is abiding by the menstruation leave regulation appropriately. Seven other companies stated that they would grant the two days only if the worker actually felt too ill to work. However, in such cases, the woman must be examined by her supervisor before the leave is granted.

Some companies provided medication (such as pain relief) in the company clinic, so the women could continue working. In many cases, employers compensated workers choosing to attend on leave days; a representative of one company stated that only 5 per cent of women workers took the leave, the rest preferring the bonus. Another company defended the practice of checking the women claiming the leave because, in many cases, women abused the right and took leave near the weekend (Komandjaja 2004). The factories discouraged women from exercising this right in order to keep the assembly line fully staffed. Women feel they attract the hostility of supervisors if they take menstruation leave. Blecher (2004: 483) noted that:

> In Indonesia, women are routinely asked to drop their pants and prove they are menstruating in order to obtain the legally mandated menstruation leave. As a result, many women choose to forgo their right to this leave rather than submit themselves to humiliation.

The NGO Clean Clothes Campaign (CCC) activists, Keady and Kretzu (2003), reported that the 'procedure to take menstruation leave in Nike's subcontracted factories is plagued with a degree of fear and humiliation that is so severe, most women would rather suffer than take the days off'. Under the new post-2003 procedures, a woman must speak to her line-chief and visit the factory clinic to prove that she is menstruating. The toilets are inadequate, in number and standard, to enable women to appropriately manage their bleeding. Workers commonly had to queue in their two allotted toilet breaks per day, and toilets often were broken or had no water.

In a global context, protection legislation today is more likely to relate to pregnancy and childbirth.[7] Menstruation leave is not common, and is a right for women workers only in a number of East Asian countries and Indonesia. Korea, like Indonesia, legislated menstruation leave, breastfeeding breaks, the prohibition of women's work at night and in mine pits or dangerous and harmful work in the 1953 Labour Standard Act (Kim 2001). Japan has a well-established system of 'maternal protection' of women workers which extends to paid menstruation leave (Nohara and Kagawa 2000: 582). Taiwan's Gender Equality in Employment Law (2002) provides for paid maternity leave and breastfeeding breaks, and allows women to take a day's menstruation leave per month as part of their annual entitlement of 30 sick days at half pay, and this is now enjoyed by almost one-third of women workers (Taiwan Headlines 2007). These countries are unique in the world in legislating menstruation leave (Lee and Cho 2005), but the difference between them is that whereas Korean and Taiwanese employers are obliged to provide paid menstruation leave once a month, Japanese and Indonesian employers are not. The original provision in the 1948 Indonesian law did require employers to pay for two days' leave, but in the 2003 revised legislation, the conditions surrounding menstruation leave are subject to negotiation between employers and unions, and unlike maternity leave, payment is not obligatory (Article 84). It is now commonly reported that employees are required to undergo a medical examination to prove that they are indeed menstruating. The case study below shows how the changes in the provisions of the 2003 law open up space for contestation, which is particularly significant in a modern mining company where women are moving into traditionally male occupations in which additional incomes and promotions are tied to productivity that is directly associated with attendance.

Mining as gendered work

'Mining ... is imbued with notions of masculinity, where men are assumed the "natural" workers, forcing the reluctant feminine of nature to yield its hidden secrets' (Robinson 1996: 137). Ore bodies tend to be located in remote places, and the frontier nature of mining creates a hard-nosed style of doing things (Burke 1995). Workers in mines are represented as undertaking dangerous, dirty and hazardous work, characterized by a form of masculinity suitable for heroes. Pit life is perceived as a uniquely male world where the sharing of risks contributes to the formation of male solidarity (see Eveline 1995). The hard and rough work of mining creates a common view that mining is difficult work, unsuitable for women: 'Images of mining as human endeavour incorporate the imperatives of physical strength, endurance and filth, all characteristics of masculinized work.' Indeed the body effects of such male endeavours are 'one of the main ways in which the power of men becomes "naturalized", i.e. seen as part of the order of nature' Connell (1987: 85). Mine workers are invariably 'pit men', 'a man from the picks' or 'labouring men', and male miners create a 'proletarian solidarity'[8] (Lahiri-Dutt and Macintyre 2006). It is not surprising, then, that until the 2003 revisions of the labour law, Indonesia, like many other countries, banned women from working in the mines, especially in underground mining. The imperative to 'protect' women from this 'dangerous and dirty' work originated in modern Europe and North America in the early modern period, and although today large-scale mining is a safe, mechanized, well-paid and attractive area of labour, such views have salience still and help to keep mining as a masculine area of work. In modern mining towns the mine is usually no longer an underground pit, but the dominance of men in operational and managerial positions is still evident,[9] and the women of the community are principally miners' wives or workers in service industries including prostitution (Robinson 1996).

Many of the 'protective bans' on women's work underground or in the mines can be traced to late nineteenth-century Britain. The results of such bans were not always positive for women, as they continued to work in mines but as unauthorized workers, hence liable to other forms of exploitation. The emphasis on the masculine nature of mining work has devalued women's work in mines and rendered them invisible. Artisanal mining has a long history in Indonesia, as elsewhere in the world, and it is always a form of household production, involving men and women. However, the mine in this case study is an example of a more recent phenomenon, of transnational mining companies moving into remote areas of developing countries. Therefore, it is significant that a large-scale operation such as the one under study is hiring women, not only in the offices as secretaries and assistants, but also in the mine pits as operators of heavy machinery. The employment of women as mine-operators has the potential to change notions of gendered work in Indonesia.

This masculinized world of the mine pit is the setting for our study of menstruation leave for women working as operators in the Kaltim Prima Coal mine (hereafter KPC) in Sangatta, East Kalimantan. The data were collected in 2004 when Lahiri-Dutt undertook a survey of women employees, with the objective of developing a gender policy for the company. The research was undertaken at a time when national labour legislation, including protection clauses, was under review and subject to public discussion. While the numbers of women involved in this mining project are small, the issue of menstruation leave has been contentious, perhaps surprisingly, even among female employees.

KPC was established in 1987 and the mine began operation in the early 1990s. In terms of production, it is one of the largest mining companies in the world.[10] It had a presence in Sangatta before government services reached the remote forest-covered tract some 50 kilometres north of the equator. Consequently its relations with the local community operate on a patron–client model (Kunanayagam 1995), with the company becoming a major provider of services to the community that has sprung up around the mine site. In its 17 years of operation in Indonesia, about 308 women have entered the company workforce and at the time of the study there were 147 female employees. In recent years, there has been a slight decrease in the proportion of women from a high of 7.6 per cent in 1994 to 5 per cent in 2002. Just over half (56 per cent) of the women workers are in the 'white-collar' or administration section of the company – almost all in lower-level jobs. There is only one woman in the senior managerial level in the operations area of the company. Female office staff are usually typists, secretaries or clerks. The remainder of women work in operations-related areas. The proportion of females in mining operations is lower than in other/office job areas. Operators' jobs entail driving trucks and other heavy machines such as mechanized shovels in the pits. The female operators comprise only 3 per cent of all workers in mining operations; the figure seems small but is significant in absolute terms because of the large number of employees in mining operations. Indeed, operators represent 34 per cent of the total female workforce, and this is the largest concentration of women in any single division. Women workers face subtle prejudices. A senior manager in the Human Resources department articulated a common misogynist view: 'Women are made of 60 per cent emotion and 40 per cent reason; they are not good as leaders in positions of responsibility.'

Expatriate company managers explained their commitment to hiring women operators in the following terms:

> Women are more careful in their jobs and as a result not one of them has had any accidents. They can also cope better with repetitive and tedious jobs, are easier to deal with, and tend to have a steadying impact on men. Above all, women do not take time off for prayers, interrupting work schedules in the field, and cope well with colleagues at the workplace.

A senior Indonesian manager added that 'women create less trouble than men', referencing industrial disputes, which he saw as mostly originating with men. A (male) supervisor noted that, 'Women are easier to give instructions to.' Another Indonesian manager commented that it is commonly perceived that women operators are more careful – no woman driver had so far had a collision.

The average woman worker at KPC is young – about 33 years old[11] – and married (56 per cent of them to a spouse within the company); has minimal educational achievement (at most, senior high school); and works in a low-level job. The available statistics for women currently employed by KPC in terms of length of employment show that roughly one-third have been employed for 0–6 years, another third for 6–12 years and the final third for 12–18 years. Women commonly leave their job after about four years of service. This pattern is very often linked to difficulties for married women combining child care and shift work responsibilities. Child care, in particular, is a major issue for all women working outside of home in Sangatta because most of the company employees are migrants from other islands like Sulawesi and Java. Because of the lack of locally available family support, families need to employ domestic help. Women who overcome the problems of child care seem to remain in the job for about 8–9 years. Among women employees, the operators start at a younger age, 18–20 years, than the female clerical staff, who start at around 22–24 years and have higher levels of education (Lahiri-Dutt 2004). Although at the lowest rank in the company hierarchy and with limited promotion opportunities, the operators are able to earn more than the clerical staff. At best, operators can advance to the level of 'trainer'; so far only one woman has been promoted to this position.

In spite of the odds, the notable fact is that some women do remain for many years in their jobs as operators. This does not necessarily indicate a strong commitment to building a career in the mining industry. Working outside of home may even appear as something that was forced upon them. Nurmaliyah commented that a woman stays on in her job as an operator 'if her husband is in a similar level as hers or is in a lower rank. If the husband is much higher in rank, then she prefers to stay at home.' Women's dual role or *peran ganda* recognized in government policy is a reality for the truck operators. Gender roles do not change quickly in a closed mining community where the most common role and status for women is as housewives. This conflict becomes apparent after the birth of a child or two, especially since most workers lack family support. Several women operators were forced to apply for 'unfit termination' of the job after having children, for lack of child care. The 1974 Indonesian Marriage Law enshrines the notion of the male as head of the household and principal breadwinner and the wife as the primary housekeeper. The model of the stay-at-home housewife is exaggerated in the work and housing conditions established by the mining company. However, many of the women expressed pride in their ability to perform as well or better than men in this traditional male occupation. Nengseh, a local Kutai woman with little education expressed her feelings of power on her first day on the job:

> When I came to work in the field, it was better than the idea I had about it. In my mind, I had imagined it to be a dirty place. In my imagination, I had also visualized the truck to be very hot, but I found that it was quite comfortable.... I was not sure of my ability to drive such huge trucks and kept thinking, 'Will I be able to drive such gigantic trucks? I cannot even drive a car, how will I drive this huge truck?' It was bigger than anything I had ever seen before. When I was all by myself, I was delighted and very proud too to be sitting in the cabin of the truck by myself. All my fear had vanished, and a confidence overtook me. Holding the steering wheel of the truck, I felt a surge of power coming on to me.

Figure 8 Female mine worker.

The delight and pride she felt with her job, being alone in the cabin of the truck, driving it around the mine pit, and the vanishing of her fears created a new confidence. She repeated: 'I still feel a sense of power, holding the steering wheel of the truck.'

The job of an operator is a radical break from the usual occupations these women are likely to have pursued. They drive trucks around in the pit, carrying overburden material (i.e. the rock and soil overlaying the ore body) or spraying water to reduce dust, and (more rarely for women) operate the shovel at the coalface. The high level of mechanization means that the job does not involve heavy physical work. In spite of this, the more skilled shovelling operations at the coal seams remain reserved for male operators. The work in the pits is done in shifts and the company had to seek special permission from the local government to hire women to work at night in the mine pits, because women's night work is still restricted under the 2003 legislation. The trucks are 'state of the art': gigantic machines, with air-conditioned cabins, often fitted with radio communication and GPS that enable management to monitor their movements from the pit office. If anything, the work is monotonous: for example, Diana complained about the repetitiveness of the movements and said that boredom was the most tiring aspect of the work. The nightshift is disruptive of family life for both men and women, but for women with young children, it can mean lack of sleep and fatigue leading to increased risks. Yet, no woman had had an accident in the history of the mine, and as a rule, women operators have the reputation of being careful in the pit. (However, the numbers of women are not large enough to test the claim that women work more safely than men.)

Women accept multiple discomforts at work. Lower back pain is common among all workers as they have difficulty reaching equipment fitted in modern shovels and trucks that are ergonomically unsuited to small Indonesian bodies. There is a lack of toilets close to the pits for both men and women. Whereas men can cope with this, especially on nightshifts, women find it more difficult. The toilets are inconveniently located, usually in the dumping area, which can be quite a distance from the handling point, especially difficult for women during menstruation. Several female operators complained about the lack of adequate lighting in the toilets at night and raised the need for the provision of culturally appropriate squat toilets rather than the Western-style toilets installed. Hafsah is a 29-year-old woman from Sulawesi, now married with a small child, who works as an operator. Hafsah feels that she must not be too demanding,

> Otherwise men in the field would think I am not up to my job. They will say, 'If you can't work like us, don't try to work here in the mines.' Even when I am at home, I behave like any other housewife, so that my neighbours think that I am just like them, not different. My friend said, 'this is a man's job', but I have now proven that I can do it.

Menstruation leave created a stir among women operators because their remuneration is attached to a sizeable performance-related cash bonus directly related to attendance and productivity. This economic incentive, introduced by the company primarily to ensure regular attendance to increase productivity, can amount to almost six months' additional pay in a year. If women operators take the menstruation leave to which they are entitled, their income is dramatically reduced relative to that of their male co-workers. The various unions in the company are aware of the issue, and in general supportive of the women, although they are yet to take an official stand on the subject. One union leader commented that 'A woman operator should be eligible to get the bonus even if she stays at home, because this facility was granted to her by the law set by the highest authority in the country.' Another union leader argued strongly that 'Female operators must have the same bonus rate even if they are unable to work during their heavy period days.'

However, the question of the 'right' to take the leave has divided employees. Notably, it has inserted a wedge between the female employees: the office staff are less inclined to stay at home for two days whilst the operators are keen to take the leave. Women take on the stereotype of mining as men's work, as difficult, dirty and dangerous. For example, Yosephina, a young Buginese girl, said: 'I am working at a man's job in the field; I am driving heavy trucks and cutting the coal with machines. Tell me, how will I be able to work during my periods?' Some women operators do feel that they are not capable of performing their duties while menstruating. Perhaps relevant here is another fact that divides the women: operators wear a uniform of close-fitting blue jeans, while office workers are more likely to wear skirts. Therefore, when the expatriate office manager challenged Lahiri-Dutt: 'Do you take two days off in a month?' his question glossed over significant issues of difference. Lahiri-Dutt's answer to him would have been, 'No, I do not', but if she were working in a mine pit dominated by men and where toilets are inadequate, in a job that is still highly gendered, the confusion of categories might have forced her to feel that she should take leave for the two days that are granted under the law of the country as her gender right. The female office workers differ from the operators in their felt need for menstruation leave. Office-based women staff have generally failed to express support for the operators when the unions argue that when the woman's productivity is counted for bonus, the two days' leave should not be factored in. The operators want the leave because of their different work conditions (relative to the office staff) and their different bodies (relative to male operators), but they experience high economic costs from exercising their right.

Whereas women's menstruation and associated constructs of gender have been the subject matter of intense anthropological scrutiny (see, among others, van de Walle and Renne 2001; Classen 1992 for other countries; and Hoskins 2002 and Pederson 2002 for Indonesia), the objective of some Western feminists has been to break the taboos associated with this natural sexual marker. Each culture has its own 'laws' surrounding menstruation. Islam, for example, views menstruation as a state of being unclean, but also a time of cleansing. For the majority of Muslim women of Indonesia, for example, menstruation marks them as ritually impure and they are unable to pray or to fast in Ramadan.[12] These prevailing attitudes to menstruation and the gendered nature of mining work become relevant in the workplace and many women operators choose to take the two-day leave as their birthright. In all cultures, however, menstruation marks women as different from men. In Anglo-Saxon cultures, menstruation has tended to be hidden, but in some Asian countries laws providing menstruation leave bring this aspect of feminine physical reality into public discourse, as a natural condition that is to be 'protected' in defining women's economic citizenship. However, it remains difficult for a woman worker in an Indonesian mine pit to go to her '*ledihan*' (leading hand, operators' term for 'leading hand' or supervisor – usually a man) with complaints of pain and discomfort. It is this '*ledihan*' who would permit her to go to the clinic for a check-up to ascertain whether or not she has periods and is thereby entitled to paid leave. In the mining company this medical check process is perfunctory, and does not involve the extreme invasive practices described in the Clean Clothes Campaign report cited above, where women were expected to 'drop their pants', but the woman must go to a supervisor of the opposite sex to tell him of her 'condition' and this is embarrassing for her.

The question is, then, is menstruation a legitimate marker of difference in the workplace? In a traditionally male workplace such as the mine pits, this unresolved debate results in a contestation of discourses around gender equity versus gender difference over female bodies at work. The everyday presence and participation of women in work at the mine pit has not disrupted stereotypes about 'men's and women's work': in the minds of the company management, the trade unions and the truck drivers themselves, the gender stereotypes prevail. Because she is 'out there in the field', an operator feels that she is in a masculinized blue-collar job, although she may in fact be sitting in an air-conditioned cabin in a truck. Intangibles such as the sense of risk, the heavy work (albeit performed by machines), shift work and, above all, the masculine representations of mining in popular and official discourse contribute to the feeling that 'this is a man's job'. With regard to working during menstruation, one of the woman operators argued that the working conditions in the mine pits should be more clearly explained in the employee recruitment and induction processes. Some female operators commented that they had not had an accurate picture of the working conditions in the field before commencing employment. A union leader proposed that job advertisements should mention general working conditions, such as night shifts and the provision of facilities such as toilets – matters of concern to prospective female employees. This would more adequately prepare female workers for work conditions in the pits. The continued provision of menstruation leave in the revised labour legislation, despite attempts to have it removed, perhaps indicates the continued significance of menstruation as a marker of gender difference in Indonesia.

Conclusion

Menstruation leave for women workers reveals the tension between claims for gender equity and gender difference. Indonesian law is contradictory, with women being guaranteed formal political equality but also subjected to regulatory regimens that emphasize difference. In particular, the gender ideology of the Indonesian government has valorized women's biological specificity (*kodrat*) as the basis of their social participation. Whether or not menstruation physically compromises women's ability to perform the same tasks as male co-workers is not clear. The impediments to workplace participation that the operators describe, however, do not relate to their physical limitations so much as to the practical obstacles they face in their specific work conditions and their primary responsibility for domestic affairs. This gendered division of labour is exaggerated in the context of a mining town, and in the Indonesian context, by the continuing circulation of state-promulgated gender ideologies emphasizing women's *kodrat* and the provisions of the 1974 Marriage Law. For women workers, the maternal stereotype undermines the possibility of equal pay and permanent employment status. Protection clauses such as maternity, breastfeeding and menstruation leave help to address some of the tensions between domestic and work responsibilities, and bonuses associated with menstruation leave can help address women's wage disadvantage. While issues like a lack of proper toilets have elsewhere been used as excuses to exclude women from male-dominated workplaces, the question of menstruation leave in the pit illuminates some of the practical problems that women face in male-dominated workplaces.

At the Sangatta mine, women from poor rural families have been introduced to new forms of disciplined, shift-based and well-paid work, in an occupation which they perceive as being conventionally male. Although the job itself no longer requires physical strength,[13] women operators continue to see it as hard and dirty work and therefore as suitable for men. This view is held widely not only by the women operators who choose the 'male' job of working heavy machinery at the mine site, but also by trade unionists and female office workers. At the mine, women are notionally remunerated at the same rate as men, but menstruation leave has the potential to disadvantage women in their take-home pay. Paradoxically, because working in the pit is perceived as a 'dirty and dangerous' male occupation, women actually *want to* take the leave rather than have it paid out, like many factory workers, or ignore it like the office workers. In Sangatta, many male trade union leaders have supported women's right to take menstruation leave without discrimination in pay. Menstruation leave opens, in the words of the Human Resources manager in Sangatta, 'a can of worms'. To feminists, it raises complex questions of gender equity, difference and women workers' rights. To the workplace health professional, menstruation may raise the question of women worker's health, safety and productivity. The Indonesian state regards the protection clauses in the labour law as a measure to protect women from the harshness of working life. This attitude is linked to an official valorization of woman's reproductive duties as primary. However, seen as a celebration of the distinctive nature of women, menstruation leave raises the question of whether women indeed require 'special' protection in the workplace (or indeed in other spheres of life, including quotas in representative political bodies). If the leave is seen as part of the 'rights package' of a woman as a worker, who is responsible for the fulfilment of that right? Is it the responsibility of the state to ensure that women can elect to take the leave without financial or other forms of discrimination, or should it be left to corporate social responsibility? The requirement of 'proof' in many enterprise agreements puts a burden on the woman worker which may make her reluctant to claim her rights.

Gender-specific leave may lead to discrimination against women in the job market and it is up to the state to prevent that disadvantage and facilitate women's free participation in the job market.

Notes

1 The authors would like to acknowledge the kind help provided by PT Kaltim Prima Coal (KPC), particularly the initiatives of Mr Evan Ball, the managing director, and Dr Harry Miarsono, the general manager of the Community Empowerment and External Relations Division. They are also grateful to Professor Ann Curthoys for her advice and Ms Fritha Jones for assisting in locating relevant literature and producing the figures.
2 Night work for female workers had been banned in the Netherlands in 1899 and 1919, and by the 1920s, when it was debated in the Netherlands East Indies, it was banned in the Netherlands Antilles (Locher-Scholten 1987: 99 n.2).
3 Whereas in most parts of the world, protection legislation such as prohibitions on night work fell away as the climate for labour regulation moved more towards equal treatment of men and women in a 'human resources' framework, in Indonesia, Article 76 of Law 13, 2003 retains protection clauses, for example restrictions on night work (11 pm to 7 am) for pregnant women, and an obligation on employers to provide transport, food and drink and a decent and safe workplace for women engaged in night work (11 pm to 5 am).
4 These guidelines are implemented in the sets of Circulars of National Guidelines in Indonesia, Ministry of Manpower, concerning prohibition of discrimination against women workers in company regulations or Collective Labour Agreements (URL: http://www.ilo.org/public/english/employment/gems/eeo/guide/indonesi/mmp.htm, accessed 8 August 2005).
5 In her view, in general the new law did not provide adequate protection for women and children.
6 In the context of the Indonesian women's movement, from the early years of the twentieth century there was a strong demand for the state to intervene to protect women's rights, especially in regard to marriage and divorce, while arguing that the instruments of the state should guarantee equity.
7 Forty countries ratified the ILO Maternity Protection Convention (revised) 1952, and eleven have ratified the Maternity Protection Convention 2000. One hundred and twenty countries provide some kind of maternity leave.
8 This solidarity is expressed not only in strong traditions of unionism but also a 'marraship' or mateship among co-workers, identification with a particular seam, and cavilling or grouping.
9 Garza (2005) interviewed young women who migrated to Sangatta, East Kalimantan, in search of husbands – miners are desirable spouses because of their high wages and pensions.
10 The company has a good record in terms of some of the common complaints against resource-based industries. It is an ISO 14001 company, with exemplary records of care for the environment and one of those against which civil society organizations such as JATAM had the least number of complaints.
11 The range is 22 years to 49 years.
12 A woman politician from the new Islamist party, PKS, informed Robinson (pers. comm. 2006) that she had campaigned on the issue of menstruation leave in the 2004 elections. In her view, the prohibition on performance of daily prayers and fasting while menstruating indicated concern for increased risk to women's reproductive health at this time, and, by implication, similar protection should be given to women's bodies in the workplace.
13 Unlike early mining by women – see Gier and Mercier (2006) for a global review.

References

Berkovitch, N. (1999) *From Motherhood to Citizenship: women's rights and international organizations*, Baltimore, MD: Johns Hopkins University Press.

Blecher, L. (2004) 'Above and beyond the law', *Business and Society Review*, 109 (4): 479–82.

Burke, G. (1995) 'The Confucian collier? Labour relations in mining in the Asia-Pacific region', paper presented at the AIRAANZ Annual Conference, University of Melbourne, February.

Classen, C. (1992) 'The odor of the other: olfactory symbolism and cultural categories', *Ethos*, 20 (2): 133–66.

Connell, R. W. (1987) *Gender and Power: society, the person and sexual politics*, Cambridge: Polity Press.

Elliott, J. (1994) 'Labour legislation and gender in Indonesia', *Asian Studies Review*, 17 (3): 33–42.

Eveline, J. (1995) *Stories of Heavy, Dirty and Limp: protecting the institution of men's work*, Canberra: Administration, Compliance and Governability Program, Research School of Social Sciences, Australian National University.

Ford, M. (2004) 'A challenge for business? Developments in Indonesian trade unionism after Soeharto', in M. Chatib Basri and P. van der Eng (eds) *Business in Indonesia: new challenges, old problems*, Singapore: ISEAS.

Garza, J. (2005) 'Yearning for community: ethnography of a settlement adjacent to a multinational mining company in east Borneo', unpublished PhD thesis, Monash University.

Gier, J. J. and Mercier, L. (eds) (2006) *Mining Women: gender in the development of a global industry, 1670 to 2005*, New York: Palgrave.

Hoskins, J. (ed.) (2002) *Blood Mysteries: beyond menstruation as pollution*, Pittsburgh: University of Pittsburgh.

Keady, J. and Leslie, K. (2003) 'Labour rights in Indonesia: what is menstruation leave?', *Newsletter*, 13 November, Amsterdam: Clean Clothes Campaign. Online: http://www.cleanclothes.org/news/newsletter13-indon.htm (accessed 8 August 2005).

Kessler-Harris, A., Lewis, J. and Wikander, E. (1995) 'Introduction', in U. Wikander, A. Kessler-Harriss and J. Lewis (eds) *Protecting Women: labour legislation in Europe, the United States and Australia, 1880–1920*, Urbana and Chicago: University of Illinois Press.

Kim, E. (2001) *The History of Korean Women's Human Rights Legislation in the 20th Century*, Research Report 210–19, Seoul: Korean Women's Development Institute.

Komandjaja, E. (2004) 'Most employers neglect women's rights', *Jakarta Post*, 24 January, Jakarta. Online: http://www.thejakartapost.com (accessed 9 August 2005).

Kunanayagam, R. (1995) 'In the shadow of the company', unpublished MA thesis, Monash University.

Lahiri-Dutt, K. (2004) *KPC Gender Survey*, Consultancy Report No. 1 to PT Kaltim Prima Coal, Sangatta: Kaltim Prima Coal.

Lahiri-Dutt, K. and MacIntyre, M. (eds) (2006) 'Introduction', in *Women Miners in Developing Countries: Pit Women and Others*, Aldershot: Ashgate.

Lee, K. W. and Cho, K. (2005) 'Female labour force participation during economic crises in Argentina and Korea', *International Labour Review*, 144 (4): 423–52.

Locher-Scholten, E. (1987) 'Female labour in twentieth century Java: European notions – Indonesian practice', in E. Locher-Scholten and A. Niehof (eds) *Indonesian Women in Focus*, Dordrecht: Foris Publications.

Morgan, R. (ed.) (1985) *Sisterhood is Global*, Harmondsworth: Penguin.

Nohara, M. and Kagawa, J. (2000) 'The health care system for female workers and its current status in Japan', *International Archives of Occupational and Environmental Health*, 73 (8): 581–6.

Olney, S., Goodson, E. Maloba-Caines, K. and O'Neill, F. (2002) *Working Conditions, Gender Equality: a guide to collective bargaining*, Booklet 2, Geneva: International Labour Office. Online: http://www.itcilo.it/actrav/english/library/socdiag/v07201.htm (accessed 27 October 2005).

Pederson, L. (2002) 'Ambiguous bleeding: purity and sacrifice in Bali', in J. Hoskins (ed.) *Blood Mysteries: beyond menstruation as pollution*, Pittsburgh: University of Pittsburgh.

Robinson, K. (1996) 'Women, mining and development', in R. Howitt, J. Connell and P. Hirsch (eds) *Resources, Nations and Indigenous Peoples*, Melbourne: Oxford University Press.

Salyo, S. (1975) 'Tentang pengertian tenaga kerja', in *Peranan Wanita Indonesia dalam Pembangunan*, Jakarta: P.T. Norindo Pratama.

Scott, J. W. (1988) 'Deconstructing equity-versus-difference: or, the uses of poststructuralist theory for feminism', *Feminist Studies*, 14 (1): 32–50.

Sen, K. (1998) 'Indonesian women at work: reframing the subject', in K. Sen and M. Stevens (eds) Gender and Power in Affluent Asia, London: Routledge.

SMERU Research Institute (2003) *The Practice of Industrial Relations in Indonesia*, Jakarta: SMERU Research Institute.

Sumbang, T. (1985) 'Indonesia', in R. Morgan (ed.) *Sisterhood is Global*, Harmondsworth: Penguin.

Taiwan Headlines (2007) 'Gender equality law helps remove employment barriers for women: poll', 3 June. Online: http://www.taiwanheadlines.gov.tw/fp.asp?xItem=64865 &ctNode+47 (accessed 17 May 2007).

van de Walle, E. and Renne, E. P. (eds) (2001) *Regulating Menstruation: beliefs, practices, interpretation*, Chicago: Chicago University Press.

Warouw, J. N. (2004) 'Assuming modernity: migrant workers in Tangerang, Indonesia', unpublished PhD thesis, Australian National University.

7 Meanings of work for female media and communication workers

Pam Nilan and Prahastiwi Utari

For a number of years in Indonesia, young women have been enrolling in, and graduating from, media and communications degrees at university in much larger numbers than young men. However, women still constitute only a relatively small minority of workers, and very few women hold managerial positions in the media and communications industries. The gendered disjunction between training and employment in this field of work is somewhat unusual. For the most part, male-dominated professional occupations are served by professional degree programmes that are equally male-dominated – for example, engineering. It certainly seems that there is something compelling about work in the media and communication industries that draws the interest of women yet marginalizes them at the job appointment and workplace levels.

In this chapter we explore the various meanings of work for Indonesian women who have jobs in the sector of media and communications. We are using data gathered in Java by the second author as part of her doctoral research between June 2001 and March 2002. Data were collected using a survey of 180 female communication studies undergraduates from first to final semester at a state university in Central Java, interviews with 40 of those female students; interviews with 40 sets of parents of those students, a focus group with 10 sets of parents of female communications students, and interviews with 15 communications lecturers from the same university. Individual interviews and a focus group were also conducted with established female media workers in Solo, and interviews were conducted with media industry bosses in Solo and Yogyakarta. Further interviews and a focus group were conducted with female media workers and media industry bosses in Jakarta. In total, 23 media employers or managers were interviewed: 5 were from newspapers, 3 from radio, 5 from television, 4 from advertising, 3 from public relations and 3 from online media. In addition, 46 female media workers were interviewed, of whom 13 worked for newspapers, 9 for radio stations, 7 for television stations, 6 for public relations firms, 6 for online media companies and 5 for advertising agencies. In interpreting this data, the second author of this chapter drew upon her own extensive experience as a lecturer in communications and practising radio journalist and broadcaster in Indonesia.[1]

Our aim is to explore the meaning of work in the media and communication industries for women employed in the field. To this end, we look first at the discursive context for the lived experience of Indonesian female media workers. In the second part of the chapter the personal meanings of their work are explored through an examination of interview accounts, which tell a complex story about the mismatch between demand for communications courses and the number of women employed in the field. Young women enthusiastically enrol in the degree, usually with parental support, because it matches their career ideal of rather glamorous, office-based work for women: presenting the news, meeting people, writing journalistic articles on interesting topics. Over the four years of degree study, however, female students and their parents come to realize that most work in media and communication industries is very different from this ideal. For many, the nature of this work constitutes an indefensible challenge to *kodrat wanita* – the modest, self-effacing, 'god-given' domestic role of Indonesian women.

In particular, experiences during practicum (workplace experience) seem to convince many female students to seek other kinds of work after graduation. Those who do get jobs in the industry express dissatisfaction with many aspects of their working lives: irregular work schedules, constant deadlines, discriminatory workplace practices, sexual harassment and public censure. Yet they also appear to gain satisfaction from making a career in the field for which they were trained. We conclude that although it is an attractive and rewarding area of employment in some ways, media work poses many difficulties for Indonesian women as they grapple personally with traditional gender roles for women and structurally with entrenched gender discrimination in the workplace.

Kodrat wanita and *wanita karier*

In middle-class conservative Indonesian discourse about women and work, which still reflects many elements of New Order ideology, women should ideally be 'in the home'. Oey-Gardiner argues that the New Order re-invented tradition regarding 'women's inherent nature', to emphasize domestic responsibilities (2002). The Indonesian Marriage Law No. 1/1974 (Republic of Indonesia 1974), as well as a whole range of regulated and unregulated employment practices, enshrine the discourse of *kodrat wanita* (divinely assigned female gender role). *Kodrat wanita* encodes both the ideal of *ibu* (symbolic or actual mother) and *peran ganda wanita* (the dual role of women) (Sullivan 1994: 133), to implicitly limit the employment and career options of Indonesian women (Setyawati 2001). It seems 'natural' that women should place their responsibilities as wives and mothers above everything else in their lives. One second-year communications student in our study made this clear:

> The most important thing for me in finding a future media job is that it should not burden me. As long as I can carry out my home duties appropriately, I will take it. However, if it interferes with my family life in the future, I will forget it. For me, taking care of the family is more important than work.
>
> (Zulfiani, second-year communications student, July 2001)

The religious discourse that 'marriage is morally required of all Muslims and a woman's role is officially centred on the home and her family's well-being' (Davies 2005: 234) further limits the participation of Indonesian women in the public domain. Meanwhile, over 46 per cent of Indonesian women undertake formal paid work every day (CIRCLE 2002: 3). We note that middle-class, well-educated Indonesian women seem to prefer to work (in moral safety) in female-dominated work places and occupational sectors. Here, the kinds of work they do, the positions in the hierarchy they occupy, the hours they work, and the salaries they earn, can be justified as appropriate for a 'good' woman. In that sense they occupy the contemporary subject position of *wanita karier* within the wider conservative discourse of *kodrat wanita*.

For the younger generation of women, Sen (1998: 35) argues that the glamorous young career woman is one of the icons around which Indonesia's position as a modern nation in a global economy and culture is established, especially in advertising and media products. When young women contemplate a career in media and communications, it is probable that they imagine a future working life that combines office glamour with 'suitable' working conditions for respectable women. However, this is not the reality of careers in this professional sector. Workplaces are male-dominated, technological expertise is demanded, there is little job security, and, while wages are high, working hours are irregular. These working conditions are typical of media and communications industries – which include print media, television, radio, film, satellite linking and upload franchises, advertising, public relations and online media – worldwide. In Indonesia these industries have not only expanded in the last ten years but also changed significantly (Widiadana 2005), particularly as far as high technology is concerned (see Hill and Sen 2005). For example, while the output of print media (newspapers, magazines and tabloids) has declined, the number of online media providers has grown exponentially. There are now twelve free-to-air national television channels and another two major cable providers. Clients and consumers expect professional standards in media and communication products (Widiadana 2005), which places workers in this (mainly private) labour force sector under more and more performance pressure.

Workers in the media and communications sector in Indonesia are journalists, presenters, public relations advisors, photographers, camera operators, sound engineers, production staff, printing workers, ICT (information and communication technology) and digital media technicians, graphic artists, managers and technical, secretarial and clerical support staff. Following the worldwide pattern, this is an intensely male-dominated occupational field. In Indonesia, as elsewhere, women constitute the majority of workers only in low-paid, non-professional and non-technical support areas, even though, in keeping with global trends, they constitute the majority of enrolments in university-level media and communications programmes. In the professional area of journalism, for example, *Jawa Pos*, the newspaper with the largest circulation in East Java, only recruited eleven female journalists in seven years (1991–7). *Suara Merdeka*, which has the widest coverage in Central Java, had only twelve female journalists from a total of 113 in 1998 (Siregar *et al.* 1999: 19). In 1998, female journalists numbered only 755 of 5,532 members of Persatuan Wartawan Indonesia (PWI, Association of Indonesian Journalists) (Soemandoyo 1999: 127). More recent research by Hanitzsch (2005: 493) indicates that this gender imbalance in journalism has changed little. Over two-thirds of Indonesian journalists in 2004 were men.

As tertiary-qualified professionals, journalists and other media workers enjoy relatively high wages and good career prospects. Yet, because employment contracts are the norm, job security is not assured. Workers can expect high mobility and high turnover. Competition for advertised jobs is keen. Candidates are expected to have expertise in using ICT equipment, and must show willingness to travel, relocate and work irregular hours. Our study found that these working conditions did not appeal to female graduates. Despite many more females than males graduating from the degree, far fewer women than men applied for jobs: 'It is rare to find women working in this company, since in the recruitment process so few apply, which means we only appoint a few' (Ibu Desy, director of an advertising agency, January 2002). It appeared that female communications graduates were reluctant to apply for jobs as journalists and reporters because they would not only be expected to create news items, but also to gather news in all kinds of places, and at all times of the day or night. Even as public relations officers and advertising account managers they would be expected to deal with all kinds of clients, and would be obliged to sometimes meet them outside working hours. So, although journalism, public relations and advertising were popular majors for women in the communications degree, working conditions that so explicitly challenged the ideals of female modesty proved a career disincentive for some.

It is perhaps not surprising, then, that women are significantly under-represented at management level in the field of media and communications, except in certain niches like women's magazines. The first reason is that there is only a very small number of senior female workers at the apex of the promotional pyramid. Most are married with children, or perhaps even grandchildren, by this stage of life, and have been unable to capitalize on advancement opportunities at key career points. The second reason is the still-active opposition to women becoming managers and leaders in Indonesia. Just a few years ago one major objection to Megawati Soekarnoputri becoming president was the claim that a woman could not become the leader of a Muslim country (Sen 2002: 14). Certainly within New Order gender ideology, it was imagined of 'good' women workers that they would give freely of their labour power 'without expectation of prestige or power' (Suryakusuma 1996: 102). Such ideas continue to impact negatively upon the promotion of women. We note that women are significantly under-represented at management level throughout the Indonesian labour force, and it would simply be unlikely to find any kind of reversal in strongly male-dominated media and communications industries.

These workplace realities are not evident to those commencing the *komunikasi* degree. We found that the 'masculine' nature of most media and communications work was not apparent to the majority of first-year female communications students. Many had enrolled believing it would realize for them the glamorous *wanita karier* discourse:

> I am interested in communication studies because when I finish, I can find a job such as a journalist, TV news presenter and so on. My job will enable me to get acquainted, to talk with, and even be close to famous people. Imagine that!
>
> (Lanny, first-year student, July 2000)

Through obtaining her degree, Lanny sees a future for herself in TV journalism interviewing famous people and presenting the news. Yet Lanny's imagined future is very much the exception in this field of work, and the pathway to it is not usually just through degree study, but through other channels of selection, usually on the basis of appearance and voice. The *komunikasi* degree does not offer a major in news presentation, so journalism might seem a logical choice for Lanny. Yet journalism *per se* entails daily work practices located within the career domain (and *kodrat*) of men. One female student at the end of her degree expressed this directly:

> I remember the first time I tried tracking down news. My mum looked so unhappy. She was worried, because in her perception it is unusual for girls to take photos and travel everywhere. It is a man's job, not for a woman.
>
> (Suriya, fourth-year student, July 2000)

Suriya's mother's perception is correct in one sense. Writing about Indonesian journalism, Hanitzsch observes that 'the "typical" Indonesian journalist is young, *male*, well-educated and earns an above-average salary' (2005: 493, our emphasis).

As middle-class professional workers, female media and communication workers in Indonesia do enjoy high occupational status and high income. So in one way it seems odd that many female media and communications graduates do not seek work in the profession they trained for, but look for lower-status work as receptionists and shop assistants. Yet, this is not strange at all when we consider how media and communications work is viewed through the lens of *kodrat wanita*. Not only are the working conditions unappealing to women, the work itself is morally at odds with the prevalent middle-class discourse of genteel, respectable femininity. One father was infuriated by his daughter's job choice:

> I can't understand my daughter Ayu's decision to work in television media after graduation. Why would she seek work as a journalist? Will she be proud of herself for coming home late or hanging around in the street all day? It is better for her to get a job such as an *orang kantoran* (office worker). Working as a journalist is not suitable for her as a woman.
>
> (Pak Kusuma, father of a fourth-year student, August 2001)

A female media worker in Jakarta admitted that the irregular working hours of her job meant that neighbours who observed her coming and going at night were likely to regard her as a *perempuan bawaan* (prostitute), so she rented an apartment in an executive block. Many bosses in the study stated outright that media work was not suitable for women, making comments like: 'It is better for women not to choose a job as a media worker.' They often implied 'risks' in their explanations, for example:

It is a job that demands we are outside the home with unlimited working hours and high-risk practices. It is difficult for women to do this given their limitations.

(Pak Budiono, radio coordinator, March 2002)

Coming up to deadlines, our volume of work increases 180 per cent. It means we must be prepared to work all night until the job is finished. This is a daily reality for some media workers. Physically, it is difficult for this work to be done by women.

(Pak Mahidin, newspaper editor, September 2001)

Some of the obvious 'risks' for all reporters in Indonesia include the threat of violence in street disorder and demonstrations, seeking out known criminals and dealing with the police. Pak Budiono seems to be alluding to this kind of risk in his assessment of the unsuitability of women doing this kind of work, although he also mentions 'unlimited working hours', which constitute a different kind of risk. Working at night, presumably in teams of men, signifies moral peril. Indeed, the 1925 law prohibiting women from working at night was only repealed in 2003 (see Lahiri-Dutt and Robinson ch. 6 of this volume; Locher-Scholten 1987). The expectation of night work is the main point in Pak Mahidin's explanation of why women are unsuited to the job, although he also alludes to the presumed inability of women to handle deadline pressures. Both bosses – who were older men running long-established businesses – refer to naturalized ideas about femininity in their comments. In public rhetoric, *kodrat wanita* means having an 'essential' feminine nature of *lemah lembut* (soft and weak). In this discourse, women do not speak loudly and certainly not in their own interests; they do not push their own interests against those of husbands and fathers. Instead, they are docile wives and mothers and dutiful daughters (Wieringa 1993: 26). Women are ideologically regarded as weak, emotional and incapable of overcoming challenges. By this definition they must be regarded as categorically unfit for work as journalists, and for most other kinds of demanding, high-pressure media work.

Many bosses stressed the need for media workers to be 'tough', assertive, able to face deadline pressures, to be competitive and handle criticism, to survive disagreements and rough language. These, they felt, were naturally qualities that men possessed. Women would simply be unhappy in such jobs. In their workplaces, they said they tried to allocate to women tasks that women would feel comfortable and happy to undertake. This was also a common experience for female students during the practicum, for example:

I was aiming to apply in practice what I had learned. And yes, I did get a realistic picture of the tasks of a PR person, and I became acquainted with real working life. However, my activities were only performing ordinary, conventional tasks such as answering the phone, typing, welcoming visitors and showing them the workplace.

(Rosdiana, fourth-year student, July 2001)

While this young woman felt belittled by the allocation of typically 'feminine' media workplace duties during her practicum, it is likely that the workplace managers would have more or less automatically assigned her these low-level duties, while assigning a male intern more challenging ('hard and risky') tasks that utilized his professional degree skills. Our data contained many stories about the routine gendered delegation of tasks in media and communications workplaces.

The strength of the naturalized discourse of women's role (Oey-Gardiner and Sulastri 2000) is such that employers in this study usually did not show any recognition that their gender-biased employment policies and delegation of lesser duties to female workers, were actually discriminatory practices. They seemed to think they were being kind. In Indonesia, gender discrimination in professional fields across the workforce begins at recruitment, when male applicants are implicitly preferred over females, and is then reflected in lower pay, marginalization from decision making, and, at the end of careers, gender-differentiated ages for retirement. Indonesia has enacted laws to address discrimination, but they seem to be having little effect.

For example, not only does Indonesia have labour laws protecting the rights of workers in general, there is also a law which rules specifically against discrimination on the basis of gender. After ratifying the United Nations Convention on the Elimination of All Forms of Discrimination against Women (CEDAW), Indonesia passed Law No. 7/1984 (Republic of Indonesia 1984). Yet it seems little has really changed on the ground. Female media workers in this study indicated that their bosses showed little awareness of laws that protect the rights of female workers. Often the women themselves were poorly informed about their rights (Nilan and Utari 2005: 28). Even five years ago, discrimination against women was identified as a significant problem in Indonesia by the International Labour Organization (2002: 9; see also Mariani *et al.* 2000: 75). Gardner claims that in 2002 female workers in Indonesia were paid on average about 68 per cent of men's wages (2003: 7). In Indonesia, female workers are still implicitly defined as single, even if they are married – 'the underlying assumption being that married women do not work and that the husband is the primary income earner' (Gardner 2003: 7).

While these kinds of naturalized beliefs about the proper roles of men and women continue to adversely affect the working lives of women in many countries (including Australia), in Indonesia a number of contradictory regulatory provisions directly subvert the intentions of laws protecting the rights of female workers. For example, the tax rates of female workers are higher than those of men regardless of marital or household support status, and where employers offer them, women are not paid family allowances. One of the biggest employers – the public service – does not, by definition, pay *any* female public servants the rice allowance for family members, only men. However, far from attracting much attention, these gendered work practices tend to be seen by all parties as a 'natural' state of affairs (Oey-Gardiner and Sulastri 2000). In conservative rhetoric, to challenge such provisions is to seek to undermine the cultural basis of Indonesian life, and even to emulate immoral Western practices.

As an example of the highly naturalized discriminatory employment and workplace practices against which female media workers must construct a sense of their work as meaningful, we offer the following story told through our data. When employers in Central Java were interviewed, one manager was initially sympathetic about the *rintangan* (barriers) women faced in their media careers:

We choose workers more for their work capabilities than for their sex. Nevertheless, from experience I have seen that men survive better than women in their careers. Women quit easily from positions. I think it is natural because women face more barriers in their careers than men.

(Pak Iskandar, radio station director, September 2001)

However, further probing during the interview revealed that Pak Iskandar routinely implemented what he called a *ketentuan tugasnya* (unwritten rule of the job). In his radio station, only unmarried women could be live-to-air DJs, or undertake music programming. If they got married they were shifted to support positions away from broadcasting altogether where performance bonuses were no longer paid. A central assumption of the discourse of *kodrat wanita* is that a girl will marry. Marriage is an almost universal practice, and (with motherhood) more or less defines adult status for women (Blackburn 2001). Once married, it is assumed a woman will either be in the home (unemployed) or undertake a less demanding form of paid work. We gained a personal view of this naturalized gender convention from one of the female DJs at the same workplace:

When I was interviewed for my current job as a DJ in this radio station, Pak Iskandar asked me when I wanted to get married. I had to tell him beforehand because he would prepare someone to take over my duties. It seemed like a tradition in this company that if a female DJ married, another girl would take over the job. However, this warning was not given to men who applied for the same position.

(Diah, radio DJ, September 2001)

In fact, it is Pak Iskandar himself who constructs and maintains this significant barrier for female radio workers in their careers at his radio station. He is in principle contravening Article 2(b) of the Indonesian Human Rights Law No. 39/1999 (Republic of Indonesia 1999), by discriminating against female workers on the basis of marital status. Yet, he is also acting within the spirit of those clauses of the Indonesian marriage law that implicitly limit married women's career options (Setyawati 2001). Several older male employers and managers in this study styled themselves as the moral guardians of their female workers, and protectors of the institution of the family. To this end, they practised a highly gender-differentiated delegation of tasks, for example:

I feel that *tidak tega* (I cannot bring myself) to assign female journalists to cover hard news such as crime. Psychologically we know that women have certain limitations in their capacity to do this work. I feel *kasihan* (sorry for them) if they become frightened, worried or stressed on the job. As an editor I must demonstrate *perasaan tenggang rasa* (sensitivity/consideration) and avoid assigning women to cover hard news stories.

(Pak Mahidin, newspaper editor, September 2001)

Of course it is precisely the practice of regularly covering top news stories – often involving crime – that establishes a journalist's reputation and leads to career advancement. Pak Mahadin's paternalism only reinforces the naturalized routine discrimination against women in media and communications workplaces. This example supports the recent claim by Arivia (2006: 1) that the 'protection' of women in Indonesia is a guise for continued 'domination' by men (but see also Lahiri-Dutt and Robinson ch. 6, this volume, on 'protection' of women workers). She adds that 'women and men are segregated on the job, each assigned tasks considered "appropriate" for their gender' – to the detriment of women's well-being.

In our study there were many bosses who said they preferred female employees for some frontline tasks (especially presenting jobs) because they were *cantik* (pretty) or *molek* (cute/attractive). In private media and communications industries, where increased sales, ratings, new accounts, website hits and public interest boost profits, attractive young women are obviously a drawcard. Some media bosses also commented positively on the specific qualities they thought women brought to bear on other key tasks, for example:

To conduct an in-depth interview with a challenging information source, I prefer to send a female reporter. They are more flexible. Although there is a lot of talking and exploring information, they don't get bored. And if I send male reporters, because they look *sangar* (menacing) I feel sure that the information source will turn out to be uncooperative.

(Ibu Any, chief editor of a women's tabloid, September 2002)

When facing a difficult information source, I find female reporters show tougher spirit than male reporters. They don't despair or give up so easily. Even if the information source either does not want to give any information, or ignores them at first, female reporters still find ways – begging, bargaining, giving alternatives – to make sources of information talk. They are *ulet dan gigih* (persevering).

(Pak Wulandari, online media editor, March 2001)

Several others mentioned that what they valued in their female employees was the quality of *kesabaran* (patience). While one could certainly argue that qualities of flexibility, perseverance and patience perpetuate the feminine gender stereotype, these are also qualities of a good news reporter. In this sense, some media bosses see female reporters as better suited to the job than males, implicitly contradicting the perceptions of some other employers in the study.[2]

Reading this data another way, we may note that in the case of Ibu Any's claim, the media organization in question is a woman's tabloid, with a female editor-in-chief. This may constitute a more 'feminized' workplace culture than mainstream newspapers and journals, allowing women to be more readily recognized for their skills. In the second case we note that Pak Wulandari is an online media editor. Online media in Indonesia is for the most part a post-1998 media industry.[3] Accordingly, the workplace culture in this second example might well be more youthful and diverse – less traditional and therefore less intractably masculinized – permitting more open recognition of merit. The strongest discriminatory attitudes towards the presence of females as professional workers in the media and communications workplace were expressed by older males, whether they were parents, university lecturers or bosses. While this observation should not be understood as implying that conservative ideas of *kodrat wanita* are in retreat, it does suggest that ideas about women and paid work seem to be evolving in some contemporary professional workplaces, at least as far as unmarried women are concerned.

An alternative discourse?

The idea of having a professional or business career is appealing to young women from higher socio-economic backgrounds. In a pilot research survey conducted by the authors in 2004, of 52 17-year-olds in a *sekolah unggulan* (preferred government secondary school) in Central Java, 3 out of 26 girls (unprompted) wrote down *wanita karier* as their life ambition, while more than half the girls gave detailed descriptions of their future careers, including terms like 'business woman' and 'professional'. Yet it should not be imagined that these aims are entirely socially acceptable. Tension around the discourse of *wanita karier* is not only concerned with working conditions, but also with the idea of paid work taking priority over women's domestic responsibilities.

Many of the female media workers in our study were keen to balance their lives so that they fulfilled obligations in both directions. They were structurally located within the modernist work discourse of *wanita karier*, since they all embarked on careers in media and communications industries, yet in the focus groups and interviews they actively supported the discourse of *kodrat wanita* in the private domain – feeling it defined them as Indonesian women. These discourses inflect the meanings that female media workers construct and negotiate around their own work. In their accounts and discussions they moved between defence of themselves as good wives and mothers (either in the present or the future), and expressions of desire for personal fulfilment through their careers. While money was rarely mentioned, we take it as given that they were unlikely to give up paid work altogether, since the material well-being of their middle-class affluent households depended on it. The question then, was how much of their time and effort would be sacrificed in either direction. The most frequent solution to the dilemma was to avoid promotion or higher duties after marriage, since this demanded longer hours and periods outside the home. Young unmarried women on the other hand, seemed keen to get a variety of media work experiences, perhaps before such opportunities were implicitly closed off.

Loving the job

In accounts by female media workers of their work, rising to challenges and job satisfaction stood out:

> Since I first became a reporter for this women's tabloid, I felt I was getting challenges. I don't come from Jakarta, so I didn't know the places here. When they [the editors] gave me news-gathering assignments, I was really excited about going to new places and meeting new people. Finding them by using buses, taxis, even *ojeg* [motorcycle transport] gave me really interesting experiences.[4]
>
> (Iin, tabloid reporter, February 2002)

Opportunities for travel and meeting all kinds of different people were two common reasons given by students in the interviews for choosing the media and communications degree. Yet Iin's account points to some job practices which parents in the study would have found objectionable. For example, it is not considered modest behaviour for a young middle-class woman to take *ojeg* transport, which involves riding behind a male stranger on the back of a motorcycle. Not only does *ojeg* transport pose moral dangers, *ojeg* drivers often drive recklessly and at high speed. In short, the kind of work Iin undertakes as a reporter carries all kinds of risks particularly unsuitable for a respectable, middle-class woman. The actual daily work of reporters and journalists really is hard and demanding. The reality of this could come as something of a shock to new female reporters. For example:

> This is the craziest work you can imagine. I had just come back from Pontianak after a week of reporting when they sent me off again to cover another news story in Semarang. It meant that just one day after I arrived home I went away again. There is no tradition here that I could refuse the task because I was tired. Yeah ... to be a *kuli tinta* [ink coolie] is to be a super woman.
>
> (Hasuna, tabloid reporter, January 2002)

Pontianak in West Kalimantan province is around 1,000 kilometres from Jakarta. It is a one-and-a-half-hour flight, or two days by ship. Hasuna said she worked not only in Pontianak but also in the Mempawah, Singkawang and Ketapang areas. After flying back to Jakarta, Hasuna had to then go and cover news in Semarang – about 600 kilometres from Jakarta. The journey takes eight hours by train. Yet Hasuna said she loved her work.

Many of the young female journalists in the focus group seemed proud of their achievements as reporters, despite the risks. For example:

> I did *jagongan* [sitting down to wait for someone] until two o'clock in the morning in front of the Cipinang jail waiting for Tommy's wife to come.[5] We [the press] were convinced she would come because the next day he was going to be moved out to Nusakambangan jail. Although his wife didn't come until then, we did not give up. It was great news, so waiting until early morning was not a problem.
>
> (Tika, tabloid reporter, March 2002)

We sense here the challenge and satisfaction a reporter like Tika gains in chasing down 'big news'. Yet at the same time we can see how transgressive this kind of work is for women in relation to the discourse of *kodrat wanita*. Tika does not work regular hours in a nice office but, when the work situation demands, will stay out all night in a largely male group of journalists to collect news.

Female media workers as working mothers

If this kind of work is transgressive for single female journalists and reporters, it is even more so for married women. Yuli was a newspaper reporter with a young family. In continuing to work, and perhaps even undertake assignments similar to the one described by Tika just above, she had to negotiate family pressure:

> I still remember what my mother-in-law said: what do you gain from your job now Yuli? You just leave your family and get nothing! She thought it was better for me to stay at home with my kids and it was enough just to live on my husband's salary. Uh, she thought I should be satisfied just with that.
>
> (Yuli, newspaper reporter, February 2002)

There is much we can read here about the meanings of paid work for married women in this field. Yuli alludes to pressure from a powerfully positioned female relative by marriage who doesn't think she should be working at all, let alone the presumably irregular hours of a newspaper reporter. Her mother-in-law thinks Yuli gets 'nothing' from the job and is damaging her children. In refuting this argument Yuli indicates that she would not be 'satisfied' by giving up her job and staying home. This claim distances her, as a woman intent on her career in journalism, from the traditional discourse of womanhood expressed by her mother-in-law. Yet it is the mother-in-law who articulates the majority viewpoint. An International Labour Organization (ILO)-funded study found that in Indonesia still 'a majority of men and women disapprove of women who continue working after giving birth to a child' (Sziraczki and Reerink 2003: 48).

This legacy continues to affect not only the way married female media workers are judged by others, but also how they view themselves. As Davies (2005: 233) emphasizes, the New Order 'focus[ed] on women as wives and mothers, clearly defined borders and highlighted transgression and marginality; there were no legitimate official models available for women outside' that of *Ibu*. Contemporary professional working mothers like Yuli struggle for legitimacy by assuming full financial responsibility for their children's care, for example. She stressed her maternal responsibility, repeating phrases like 'I must take care of my children', and describing how her entire salary goes to pay for child care and domestic help:[6]

> Nearly all of my salary goes to the care of my two children. I hire two *pembantu* (domestic workers) and one babysitter. One house girl specifically takes care of my older son and the other does the housework. The babysitter looks after my younger son who is only eleven months old.
>
> (Yuli, newspaper reporter, February 2002)

Despite family tensions and the moral pressure of working motherhood, Yuli seemed intent on her career as a newspaper reporter. Earlier in the interview, she emphasized how she had to overcome frustration when she began her job:

> I remember how I felt frustrated when much of the news I collected did not get printed by my editor on the grounds that such news had low status. If they did print it, they just put it in as second-class news in the later pages.
>
> (Yuli, newspaper reporter, February 2002)

Romano's study of Indonesian journalism recounts how many *wartawati baru* (junior female reporters), keen to find exciting news, find they are engaged in much less satisfying work due to the gendered construction of media work and rewards (2002).[7] It seems probable that Yuli has worked hard to gain seniority since those early days in her career and has overcome some of the gender bias described by Romano. If she is now reporting front-page news then both the professional and economic rewards would be compelling. It is no wonder that she would not want to give up her job.

We may conclude that, for Yuli, working as a qualified media professional gives her a strong sense of who she is as a person in the world, beyond her role as wife, mother and daughter-in-law. Williams, writing about returned female work migrants in Eastern Indonesia, argues that migration for work signifies struggle for a new subjectivity, a repositioning of self (2005: 401). For Yuli, resigning from her job to devote herself to her family would mean moving back into the 'old' subjectivity of *kodrat wanita*, and away from the newer subjectivity of *wanita karier* – which is clearly where she currently positions herself. As a news reporter, however, she does not just carry out typical white-collar, day-time, office work. She must work long shifts and odd hours – all night in some cases – in teams composed mostly of men, and deal with a variety of physical and moral risks. In this way, her transgression of the discourse of *kodrat wanita* is greater than that of a married woman with small children who works in a white-collar job. As another working mother explained:

> I felt sometimes my husband was cranky if I came home late or I had to meet my clients in the night and outside. He suggested I should finish my job in work time and avoid taking it home. It is very hard for me to do, because sometimes I work overtime due to meetings or client appointments. In the first years of my marriage, my husband accepted my working lifestyle. However, now because we have a child, he accuses me if I come home late of not being responsible for our child.
>
> (Asiyah, advertising account manager, September 2001)

It seems that married female media workers must struggle constantly against the judgement – from all sides – that there is something unnatural about their work. However, there was quite some variation in the accounts given in interviews. For example, although Asiyah complained about her husband's attitude, she seemed to survive the juggling of domestic and career responsibilities with the support of her husband and extended family:

> Fortunately I live not far from my parents, so every morning before work we entrust Deni [her son] to my parents and pick him up again after we finish work. This is Deni's routine five days a week. People call him *anak eyang* [child of the grandparents], but we don't care. This is the best way for me as a media worker to raise my son.

> (Asiyah, advertising account manager, August 2001)

Dealing with sexual harassment

In male-dominated media and communications workplaces, the relatively few female professional workers stand out. Sexual harassment of various kinds is a common experience, judging by our focus group data. While the women agreed that most male colleagues were respectful, helpful and showed good manners, they also described male colleagues with 'discriminatory' attitudes towards women. These men whistled when they entered the office, came up behind and embraced them, even squeezed their waist or buttock. Some young female media workers claimed these behaviours were *keisengan* (just for fun) and not worthy of attention. This certainly represents one technique for workplace adaptation and survival, but it also connotes a certain degree of acceptance and passivity. Others felt strongly that these behaviours constituted harassment and had developed ways of stopping them:

> If we just keep silent, they will do it all the time. I do not hesitate to tell them off about those behaviours. I don't care if they regard me as *judes* [vicious], *cerewet* [sharp-tongued] or even like a *nenek sihir* [witch]. I always scold them if they are behaving badly.

> (Sharifa, newspaper reporter, March 2002)

Sharifa comments on how she may be judged – as *judes*, *cerewet* and like a *nenek sihir* – because she takes male colleagues to task over sexual harassment. This constitutes further evidence of workplace-modified behaviour. Female media workers in Indonesia are subject to sexual harassment because they are women working in a place where women do not 'naturally' work. Male colleagues may well believe they can get away with it because such women are presumed to have loose morals, or not care (unlike other women in more traditional jobs). To stop sexual harassment, some female media workers develop practices of scolding and criticizing male colleagues. Such 'harsh' practices further distance them from the discourse of traditional femininity in which women exhibit pleasant, quiet and modest behaviour.

Modifying the presentation of femininity

Analysing the professional career trajectories of women in the West, Katila and Merilainen (2002: 339) describe one strategy employed by women in male-dominated workplaces: the adoption of surface-level characteristics of the dominant culture in order to gain legitimacy. This implies that the worker develops a kind of dual or split identity. Female workers gradually re-fashion their 'public face' and connote a kind of 'masculine identity' that can command authority, since everything is played by masculine game rules. In the interviews and focus groups, we found that quite a number of the female media workers talked about modifying their appearance and behaviour to suit the job. For the most part, this referred to behaving more like a man, for example:

> As a woman journalist I must downplay my femininity. The demands of media work lead to me to be more masculine. In chasing down news stories for example, I must be smart and quick – even take risks at times. If I conducted my work *klemar-klemer* (slowly and modestly), I would get left behind and have no news to report.
>
> (Rosmah, newspaper reporter, February 2002)

Rosmah's account categorizes certain characteristics – being 'smart and quick', taking 'risks' – as belonging to the discourse of masculinity, while *klemar-klemer* – acting in a slow and modest way – belongs to the discourse of femininity. She implies that effectively tracking down news stories is incompatible with the gendered behavioural practices encoded in the discourse of femininity. To succeed in this job she has to do the opposite and behave like a man.

It seems that not only is most media and communications work 'masculine' in nature, but so also is the workplace culture. Female media workers described how they had to adapt to becoming 'one of the boys' in workplace teams. In editorial or programming discussions under deadline pressure it is common for a heated exchange of views to take place, often involving rough language. When assignments are handed out it is also common for media workers to argue with managers and between themselves. Female employees in this male-dominated work environment have to learn how to deal with such interactions. One of them commented:

> Comradeship with male colleagues taught me how to take the noise and pressure, especially rough language in the meeting room, without showing disapproval or breaking into tears, especially under the strain of tough criticism. I learned to take responsibility for my own work, asking for no help and making no excuses.
>
> (Nadia, newspaper reporter, January 2002)

Other female media workers gave accounts of learning to deal with workplace situations rationally rather than emotionally, and commented that this meant they had become more like men. We note how these examples of women learning to adapt to workplace deadlines and pressures underline the gender essentialism of media bosses in the study. They claimed that women were fundamentally unsuited to demanding media work. It also illustrates that female media workers can and do acquire these workplace capabilities if they are exposed to the full range of job responsibilities, not just allocated low-level tasks deemed suitable for women.

For some female media workers it was not just a matter of altering discursively 'feminine' behaviour. They felt they had to adapt in appearance. In the focus group in Central Java in September 2001, a participant claimed that one of her colleagues was already a *tomboi* (gender-nonconformist girl). In her daily work she always dressed like a man; she cut her hair short; she wore jeans and a T-shirt. She wore sports shoes and even a denim jacket. 'It is a practical thing for her to do, you know. We have to be mobile women in this job,' the young reporter explained. Another reporter in the same focus group supported the claim about women dressing down:

> In my daily work, I don't perfect my appearance. For example when it comes to make-up, I just put on thin powder and no lipstick. Sometimes the information sources are reluctant to give up their information if the reporter is *menor* [gaudy] in dress or make-up. Maybe they already have the idea in their heads that reporters [usually men] present themselves as *dekil* [caked with dirt] and *nyentrik* [eccentric].

> (Lini, newspaper reporter in focus group, September 2001)

We may note that this appears to be the very opposite practice to that of bosses employing female graduates because they are *molek*. But what the young women are talking about above is a different kind of 'frontline' work, seeking information rather than presenting information or representing the industry. The logic here is that the informant should not be distracted by the appearance of the reporter. For female reporters this means dressing down to look more like male reporters who usually dress casually.[8] This demonstrates again the masculine normativity of journalism, since it implies the informant expects to be interviewed by a male rather than a female reporter.

Conclusion

Our analysis of some meanings of work for female media workers reveals not only the attractions and challenges of media work, but also the difficulties experienced both on the job and beyond it. Anecdotal evidence suggests that, of the minority of female graduates who do get media and communications jobs, quite a few will move on after a few years to less demanding positions outside the field, especially when they marry and have children, or they will remain at lower promotional levels within organizations. The discursive opposition between media and communications work and the ideal conduct of a married woman appeared to be very strong. For example, one young female media worker implied that the job was ruining her marriage prospects. In the focus group she quipped:

> With this job lifestyle I would probably be divorced by a husband as soon as possible. Yeah! Because I always come home late – in the middle of the night – unlike those women who work in 'normal' jobs. And then I imagine that my

husband will have already fallen asleep when I come in, or still be waiting up for me with a glum face. So how would I be able to serve him sexually as a wife?

(Tika, tabloid reporter, September 2001)

Our data on the experiences of female media and communications workers indicate that there is almost no aspect of their daily work practices which does not implicitly contradict the conservative discourse of *kodrat wanita*. Such workers appear to understand themselves as women doing a man's job who need to become more like men in order to do the job successfully. The glamorous image of *wanita karier* in media and communications industries – reading the news in an attractive outfit, meeting famous people, writing articles in a nice air-conditioned office – is matched by only a tiny handful of positions. All other women entering the field quickly find themselves undertaking work practices categorically unlike the white-collar office work usually undertaken by tertiary-educated Indonesian women. On the basis of their gender they may be given less demanding (and less career-building) assignments and responsibilities than male recruits. They will almost certainly be expected to show mastery of ICTs.[9] They will have to quickly adapt to working in male-dominated teams, and in a masculinized workplace culture. They will have to deal not only with paternalistic and discriminatory treatment from bosses and managers, but also censure from their families and society at large. Self-doubt and even moral guilt about their own life priorities will also plague them, and may determine whether they stay in the job, seek promotion, or resign. Certainly the moral discourse of femininity comes down particularly harshly on married women with children who continue in a 'masculine' work lifestyle such as journalism. Yet our data also suggest that the relatively few women who graduate from a media and communications degree and go on to make a career in the field, thrive on the challenges and rewards of the job even though their work does not fit with conventional notions of Indonesian femininity.

Notes

1 All tape-recorded material was transcribed and translated from Indonesian to English by the two authors. Pseudonyms are used in the quotations.
2 Moreover, these qualities constitute elements of the discourse of *wanita karier* to some extent, given the forbearance and dedication Indonesian women must demonstrate to create a career against the odds.
3 Under the New Order, news media were strictly controlled and licences were hard to obtain. After the fall of Soeharto, there was a proliferation of new media products, especially tabloids and online media (Hill and Sen 2005).
4 *Ojeg* transport means paying for a pillion ride on a motorcycle. Young men wait with their motorcycles at key public transport locations such as bus stations to pick up customers.
5 Tommy (Hutomo MP) is the youngest son of Indonesian former president Soeharto. Tommy was jailed due to his involvement in a murder case.
6 She did not mention her husband's paternal responsibility or salary at all.
7 The Indonesian word *wartawan* means journalist, but like many English terms like

'nurse' and 'policeman', *wartawan* is actually inherently gendered as a male occupation. Any gender transgression for such terms must be linguistically marked as a sub-category (such as policewoman or male nurse in English). The Indonesian term *wartawati* signifies a female journalist; there is no sub-category term for male journalists – they are *wartawan*, the generic term for journalist.

8 Female graduates wearing the *jilbab* (Islamic headscarf) are likely to find this adaptation towards a 'masculine' appearance difficult to achieve. However, this does not mean they will necessarily be unemployed. For example, there is rapid growth of Islamic media in Indonesia (Nilan 2006), where they would presumably be favoured for jobs.

9 The current demand for workers to demonstrate mastery of sophisticated ICTs in Indonesian media and communications industries plays out negatively against the deficiency of professional training in ICTs in Indonesian universities, and impacts negatively on women entering these jobs, since they are marginalized in ICT training in universities. For a detailed discussion, see Nilan and Utari (2006).

References

Arivia, G. (2006) 'Feminism an alternative to women under patriarchy', *Jakarta Post*, 11 April. Online: http:www.thejakartapost.com/Outlook2006/pol04b.asp (accessed 11 April 2006).

Blackburn, S. (2001) 'Gender relations in Indonesia: what women want', in G. Lloyd and S. Smith (eds) *Indonesia Today: challenges of history*, Singapore: Institute of Southeast Asian Studies.

CIRCLE (2002) 'Labour market conditions in Indonesia', CIRCLE-Indonesia – Center for Industrial Relations Research and Labour Education, Global Policy Network website. Online: http://www.GlobalPolicyNetwork.org (accessed 2 April 2006).

Davies, S. G. (2005) 'Women in politics in Indonesia in the decade post-Beijing', *International Social Science Journal*, 57 (184): 231–42.

Gardner, S. (2003) 'Women in trade unions: no big gains for women workers', *Inside Indonesia*, 76: 7–8.

Hanitzsch, T. (2005) 'Journalists in Indonesia: educated but timid watchdogs', *Journalism Studies*, 6 (4): 493–508.

Hill, D. and Sen, K. (2005) *The Internet in Indonesia's New Democracy*, London: Routledge.

ILO (2002) Indonesia tripartite action plan for decent work 2002–2005, International Labour Organization. Online: http://www.ilo-jakarta.org.id/download/decentwork.pdf (accessed 3 April 2006).

Katila, S. and Merilainen, S. (2002) 'Metamorphosis from nice girls to nice bitches: resisting patriarchal articulations of professional identity', *Gender, Work and Organization*, 9: 336–54.

Locher-Scholten, E. (1987) 'Female labour in twentieth-century Java: European notions, Indonesian practice', in E. Locher-Scholten and A. Niehof (eds) *Indonesian Women in Focus: past and present notions*, Leiden: KITLV Press.

Mariani, I. R., Armando, A., Hasyim, H. H., Mutmainnah, N. and Ilyas, N. (2000) 'Hope for the future', in I. Joshi (ed.) *Asian Women in the Information Age: new communication, technology, democracy and women*, Singapore: Asian Media Information and Communication Center.

Nilan, P. (2006) 'The reflexive youth culture of devout young Muslims in Indonesia', in P. Nilan and C. Feixa (eds) *Global Youth? Hybrid identities, plural worlds*, London: Routledge.

Nilan, P. and Utari, P. (2005) 'When there is no equal opportunity legislation: women as media workers in Indonesia', *Pandora's Box*: Special Issue – Women of the World, Annual Academic Journal of Women and Law Society, University of Queensland.

—— and —— (2006) 'Media and communications work in Indonesia: transformations and challenges for women', in J. Connell and J. Burgess (eds) *Globalisation and Work in Asia*, Oxford: Chandos Publishing.

Oey-Gardiner, Mayling (2002) 'And the winner is ... Indonesian women in public life', in K. Robinson and S. Bessell (eds) *Women in Indonesia: gender, equity and development*, Singapore: ISEAS.

Oey-Gardiner, Mayling and Sulastri (2000) 'Continuity, change and women in a man's world', in M. Oey-Gardiner and C. Bianpoen (eds) *Indonesian Women: the journey continues*, Canberra: Australian National University.

Republic of Indonesia (1974) *Undang-Undang Nomor 1 1974*, Jakarta: Government of Indonesia.

—— (1984) *Undang-Undang Republik Indonesia, Nomor 7 1984*, Jakarta: Government of Indonesia.

—— (1999) *Undang-Undang Republik Indonesia Nomor 39 1999*, Articles 31–38 (Human Rights), Jakarta: Government of Indonesia.

Romano, A. (2002) *Politics and the Press in Indonesia*, London: Routledge/Curzon.

Sen, K. (1998) 'Indonesian women at work: reframing the subject', in K. Sen and M. Stivens (eds) *Gender and Power in Affluent Asia*, London: Routledge.

—— (2002) 'The Mega factor in Indonesian politics: a new president or a new kind of presidency?', in K. Robinson and S. Bessell (eds) Women in Indonesia: gender, equity and development, Singapore: ISEAS.

Setyawati, L. (2001) 'State and womanhood: the reconstruction of womanhood in the Indonesian New Order and its implication in family planning', *Masyarakat Jurnal Sosiologi*, 9: 26–36.

Siregar, A., Pasaribu, R. and Prihastuti, I. (1999) *Perspektif Gender atas Industri Surat Kabar Indonesia*, Yogyakarta: LP3Y and Ford Foundation.

Soemandoyo, P. (1999) *Wacana Gender dan Layar Televisi: studi perempuan dalam pemberitaan televisi swasta*, Yogyakarta : LP3Y & Ford Foundation.

Sullivan, N. (1994) *Masters and Managers: a study of gender relations in urban Java*, Sydney: Allen and Unwin.

Suryakusuma, J. (1996) 'The state and sexuality in New Order Indonesia', in L. J. Sears (ed.) *Fantasizing the Feminine in Indonesia*, Durham, NC: Duke University Press.

Sziraczki, G. and Reerink, A. (2003) *Report of Survey on the School to Work Transition in Indonesia*, GENPROM Working Paper No. 14, Geneva: Gender Promotion Programme, ILO.

Widiadana, R. (2005) 'First Asia Pacific media forum opens in Bali', *Jakarta Post*, 14 March. Online: http://www.asiamedia.ucla.edu/article.asp?parentid=21710 (accessed 4 April 2006).

Wieringa, S. (1993) 'Two Indonesian women's organizations: Gerwani and the PKK', *Bulletin of Concerned Asian Scholars*, 25 (2): 17–30.

Williams, C. P. (2005) ' "Knowing one's place": gender, mobility and shifting subjectivity in Eastern Indonesia', *Global Networks: A Journal of Transnational Affairs*, 5 (4): 401–17.

8 *Makkunrai passimokolo'*

Bugis migrant women workers in Malaysia

Nurul Ilmi Idrus

Bone is a regency located about 173 kilometres to the east of Makassar, the capital city of South Sulawesi, which has a population of 686,986 (BPS-Sulsel 2005). Most people in the villages of Bone – as in other Bugis areas[1] – remain engaged in agriculture, and many of them live in poverty. This can be observed, for example, from the potholed streets to the village, the poor houses, sanitary facilities, living conditions, and insecure employment. Considering such poverty, it is not surprising that many people leave their villages. According to the Head of the sub-district of Lappo'asé, in Bone, 90 per cent of adults have at some time worked in Malaysia as migrants, many of them illegally.[2] However, both males and females refuse to be called or to call themselves illegal TKW (I. *Tenaga Kerja Wanita*, female workers) or illegal TKI (I. *Tenaga Kerja Indonesia*, Indonesian workers) because such terms have negative connotations.[3] Instead, illegal migrants – males as well as females – call themselves *passimokolo'*.[4] *Passimokolo'* originally comes from the Dutch word for 'smuggle', and is pronounced by Bugis as '*smokol'*, referring to a boat. Thus, the term *passimokolo'* refers to those who enter Malaysia by boat in the middle of the night in order to avoid Malaysian officials; *makkunrai passimokolo'* are women workers – *makkunrai* means women – who smuggle themselves into Malaysia under the cover of night.

This chapter discusses the meanings of and the motivations for illegal migration for women from Bone. The data were collected via interviews and field notes based on observations conducted in Bone regency in South Sulawesi, the origin of many illegal migrant workers. The fieldwork was conducted between August and December 2005, assisted by two of my graduate students who originally come from Bone. I interviewed 20 married and unmarried Bugis women, aged between their 30s and their 60s, whose educational experiences varied between not completing primary school to having a senior high school diploma. The discussion below is divided into four sections. I begin by examining modes of migration for illegal Bugis women migrants, before exploring the Bugis ethos of searching for brighter futures (B. *massappa' dallé*), paying particular attention to how women articulate this idiom.[5] This is followed by an analysis of how women perceive their work and how the worlds of work at home and abroad are articulated. Finally, I discuss the kinds of work women are involved in and how women migrants construct their identity once they return to Bone.

Modes of migration and escort negotiation

The Bugis are well known for their mobility, which is seen to result from the conjunction of the hierarchical nature of the society, the urge to secure a brighter future, the ethos of competition in social life, and belief in reward for merit and hard work (see for example, Acciaioli 2000, 2004; Pelras 1996: 319–34, 1998). The Robinson (1991: 34) observes that for the seafaring Bugis from South Sulawesi, long-term absence from their native villages in favour of travel to far-flung regions of the archipelago is generally considered a basic cultural trait. Lineton (1975: 179) argues, based on her research on peasant migrants in Wajo in South Sulawesi, that the primary reason people migrate is to bring 'increased wealth to the area – and perhaps most important of all – [to spread] ... knowledge of economic opportunities offered by other lands'. Their propensity for mobility may be based on a philosophy that 'whenever there is fruit, we will be there to search' (B. *tégi-tégi maéga bua-bua, kogitu taué lao massappa'*). Such cultural expressions make it acceptable – indeed, almost incumbent upon – the Bugis to leave their place of origin in search of a better life. Thus, we can find Bugis settlements in other parts of Indonesia and abroad.

Sobieszczyk (2000: 397) identifies three basic types of recruitment for migrants in Thailand: formal recruitment through authorized agents; informal recruitment through unlicensed agents, in which migration fees are paid directly by migrants at the time of migration; and 'debt bondage', a type of informal migration in which migration fees are paid to agents by migrants after arriving at a destination country by working off their 'debt'. In her study of legal female migrant workers from Nusa Tenggara Timur (Eastern Indonesia), Williams (2003: 89–91) shows that the boundary between women recruited formally or informally was blurred. In Bone, I found that although the Indonesian government had established a Badan Koordinasi Penempatan Tenaga Kerja Indonesia (BKPTKI, Coordinating Body for the Placement of Overseas Migrants)[6] – *passimokolo'* are unaccustomed to formal recruitment and usually enter Malaysia without legal documents (B. *massimokolo'*).

Decisions about status

From Pare-Pare, the nearest harbour on the west coast of Sulawesi, they travel by ship to Nunukan in north-east Kalimantan for Rp. 250,000 (US$27). Then, from Nunukan to Tawau in Sabah, Malaysia, the ticket varies depending on whether or not they have a travel 'document' (usually a *surat lintas*).[7] Those who have a 'document' only pay RM 30 (about US$7); 'undocumented' migrants have to pay RM 50 (about US$12). Once the passage is purchased, everything will be taken care of by the 'organizer' (*pengurus*).[8] If they are found by the Malaysian police on the way to Tawau (i.e. at sea), they are never asked to go home. Instead, they are hidden by the *pengurus* or he negotiates with the police. Negotiations never occur directly between migrants and the police. Thus, migrants, organizers and police are all involved, such that there is a mutual, illegal collaboration. There is a Bugis saying related to this that if you want to search for a brighter future, go to a place where many human footprints are found. Since it was common for Bugis to cross the border without major problems, this practice was followed by others.

The legal or illegal status of female migrants is not about whether or not they are ignorant of the law, but about a calculation of 'profit and loss'. This comes from the idea that if one is an illegal migrant, one maximizes the profit by keeping expenses to a minimum. I heard this point made a number of times. In response to such an idea, an ex-illegal female migrant, for example, told me that:

> Virtually every woman in Bone who travels to Malaysia in search of work is *passimokolo'*. The most we have is *surat lintas* (I. crossing letter). They cross without a working visa, working contracts or any job training. This is risky, but it's much easier than going with legal procedures. We just go.

> (Asma, 35 years)

This implies that they become *passimokolo'* not because they cannot be legal, but because being illegal has the potential to yield more profit and also requires less financial investment.[9] For those who want to legalize their status as foreign workers, the costs are much higher: the recruitment company takes care of them and pays for their documentation when they get a job. The workers pay their debt back in monthly instalments through their salary, but the total amount paid is much greater than the initial cost to the company. Ironically, in most cases, the legal workers are never told how much of their salary is taken every month (nor for how long) since no details of the monthly salary are received. Even when they are given the details, they cannot complain as the cost of the documentation is paid in advance by the company. Furthermore, they cannot keep the document as it is used as surety for their debt. One woman said, 'We Indonesian workers were fooled by the Malaysian company,' implying their awareness of their powerlessness since their 'legal status' was under the control of the company. In this sense, whether they like it or not, they are 'trapped' by the company for an unknown period. Accordingly, many women prefer to stay undocumented.

This suggests that being *passimokolo'* is considered preferable to being legal, even though it causes psychological stress. The undocumented workers have to 'play cat and mouse' with the Malaysian police. They are afraid of being discovered, of imprisonment and of arbitrary punishment, especially since the enactment of Immigration Act No. 1154A/2002, in which the Malaysian government, through its Operasi Tegas (M. Firm Operation), chased Indonesian *passimokolo'* away from Malaysia.[10] Many of them returned to Indonesia; some tried to legalize their status at the border between Malaysia and Indonesia (at Nunukan), since returning home as a result of deportation is considered a source of shame; and some ran to the forest in order to avoid being chased by police.[11] However, there are also cases in which once-legal workers become illegal because of the complexity of the legalization. This is because legal recruitment is not just more complicated and expensive, but also tiring and time-consuming (physically and psychologically).

Protection of female modesty

Passimokolo' women generally go to Malaysia without any promise of a job. They are usually accompanied by or follow their 'relatives' (that is, participate in family migration), or they are involved in marital migration or independent migration. The first refers to women who migrate in a group, which consists of family members (e.g. parents, brothers/sisters and/or other members of the family). The second type of migration consists of a woman, her husband and children. In this form of migration, the husband is usually the first migrant of the family, and is later followed by other members of his family. The third is when women migrate individually. Single males mostly migrate by themselves. In contrast, single women are usually accompanied by a female relative or a friend who is already regarded as a sibling (B. *silessureng*) and who has already been in Malaysia for some time and has a job.[12] For example, many informants I interviewed went to Malaysia for the first time to visit their family using a visitor passport (M. *paspor pelawat*). However, this 'visiting' varies according to their circumstances when they get there. Some stay because they find a job. Some companies take care of their documentation while they are working, but mostly they stay without documents. Others visit their relatives and bring goods to sell. These might include items such as clothes, shoes, food (e.g. *dempo'*, half-dried fish, a speciality from Bone), cigarettes, palm sugar, batik sarongs, fabrics, etc. to sell to Bugis people in Malaysia.[13] Later they become commuting small traders – those who travel back and forth between Malaysia and Indonesia and call themselves *pa'bisnis* (B. trader).

The Bugis are greatly concerned with female modesty (B. *malebbi'*), and link this to notions of family honour (B. *siri'*).[14] The majority of Bugis are also fervent Muslims, and their everyday life is inseparable from religious beliefs and practice as well as local *adat* (I. custom).[15] I heard a number of times from my informants that working abroad is not prohibited by either religion or *adat* as long as women can guard their virtue, and are escorted by their *muhrim* (A. father, uncle, husband, brother, or other male relatives),[16] since women are not allowed to go far away from their home alone. This is in contradiction with the common idea in some Muslim societies that women should stay at home and not venture into the public sphere. In addition, there seems to be room for negotiation in relation to who can be a *muhrim* for a *passimokolo'*. In a number of cases I heard that women went to Malaysia with female relatives (female cousins, mother, aunt or other distant female relative), who are clearly not included in the term *muhrim*. This implies that their migration is acceptable to the community as long as women go with one of their family members (or those regarded as family members) – particularly those who already have experience in Malaysia.[17] In this sense, *passimokolo'* create a space around the notion of *muhrim* and female mobility, resisting the common perception of women's immobility in some Muslim societies (and supported by the Majelis Ulama Indonesia, the Muslim Scholar's Council).

Despite the fact that the identity of *muhrim* can be negotiated, while some males go to Malaysia with informal job recruiters (I. *calo'*), women do not. *Calo'* are usually male Bugis who have already had plenty of experience working in Malaysia and have a relationship with one or more companies under informal contract for worker recruitment. *Calo'* profit from this recruiting by taking the first month of the worker's salary, with the consent of the company. A number of times I was told that women never go with a *calo'* unless he is a close relative because they are afraid of being deceived, especially if the *calo'* is not known personally, not to mention if he is a stranger.[18] This also shows that it is better for women to go with female relatives, though they are not included in the term *muhrim*, rather than with *calo'*, who are males, but clearly not related to them.

A single woman, Ramlah, for example, went to Malaysia with her mother, who had become a *passimokolo'* years before. Since Ramlah failed to become a civil servant after graduating from high school, she responded to her mother's offer to help her go to Malaysia in order to work in the plywood industry. Even though there was no guarantee that she would find a job when she arrived in Tawau, she dared to go because of her mother's encouragement and the lack of alternative opportunities in her village. Further, if she wanted to become a civil servant later, having had experience in Malaysia potentially provides a channel (B. *dékkéng*) and money for bribery (see next section). Thus, working in Malaysia, in spite of a small wage, is better than nothing or better than being unemployed in the village. There is a Bugis saying related to this: *'namu céddé', assala' engka pallapi' kompé'-kompé''*, meaning that 'even a little money is okay provided that there is still something that can be put in the wallet'. In other instances, I found that female commuting small traders – both married and unmarried – usually went to Malaysia in female groups, without their *muhrim*, even though there were other males, who were not their *muhrim*, from the same village or regency in the same boat, but without any consultation between the female groups and the males. Even though the group of women and the men in the boat did not know each other, the women 'felt secure' during the journey from Bone to Tawau because their fellow passengers were Bugis or even just from South Sulawesi, reflecting the Bugis term *pessé* (social solidarity).[19] These practices imply that women do not passively accept conservative notions of restricted mobility for women and of female honour and modesty. They negotiate the requirement to travel with *muhrim* in such a way that they can be reasonably flexible about the identity of their escort. Clearly they are redefining notions of female modesty, respectable company and honour, pragmatically extending respectable female space to include even the international workplace. Sometimes, too, they create 'space' in which they socialize with others away from their place of origin.

Articulating *massappa' dallé'*

I went to Malaysia in search of a brighter future. If I could not find a job, at least I would find a husband. If I could not continue to work, at least I would get married. If women stay single, they are called *barang kembali* (I. returned goods). I didn't want to be *barang kembali*, I wanted to get married, and here I am, I am married!

(Nursiah, 35 years)

Nursiah made this declaration proudly. Such sentiments are very common among women in Bone. Her statement indicates the importance of marital status and the broad meaning of searching for brighter futures (B. *massappa' dallé'*) for women. This indicates that marrying 'out' (in terms of kinship, geography and local identity, i.e. village, and perhaps even ethnicity) is permissible, though presumably only if the man is a Muslim.[20] From this emerges the question: what actually is the meaning of searching for brighter futures for female migrants?

Generally speaking, when people talk about *massappa dallé'*, they are talking about material 'fortune' – that is, it is an economics-driven notion.[21] Among female illegal migrants, however, there are differences between single and married women in perceptions of 'fortune'. For single women, searching for brighter futures is not solely about the need for remunerated labour, it is also about searching for a prospective husband. Women are simultaneously looking for a job and a marital partner. However, there are variations to this pattern. There are women who become *passimokolo'*, but stay unmarried because no one proposes to them. But this is rarely the case. In most cases, women work and find a partner, get married, stay and work. But there are also those who go to Malaysia looking for a job, but later quit when they get married. This implies that even though economic motivation is important for *passimokolo'*, this is not the most important point and the sole concern, since marriage might override economic intention.

A single *passimokolo'* who goes to Malaysia is expected to find a prospective marriage partner before returning to the village. There is a local saying, *pergi bujangan, pulang sudah laku* (I. going with a single status, returning with a marital status). Otherwise, she will be called *barang kembali* (I. returned goods), or an 'unmarketable' woman. Such a woman will be cited as an example of an unsuccessful and unlucky woman because no one was interested in marrying her overseas. Thus, there is a dichotomy of *barang laku* (I. single women who return with marital status) and *barang kembali* (single women who remain unmarried) for *passimokolo'*. Many women marry while in Malaysia, while others return to the village because they did not want to marry away from their parents and/or want to get married in their own village. Such women are not stigmatized as *barang kembali* since they would then be married soon after arriving home. Men also hope to marry when they migrate, but since men are the ones who propose to women, the social stigma of *barang kembali* is not attached to male migrants.[22] From this point of view, the success of single *passimokolo'* is determined not just in terms of the success of collecting money or other goods from Malaysia, but also the success of finding at least a prospective husband. Most single women who go to Malaysia return home married; *barang kembali* are rare.

A woman who becomes prosperous as a result of migration but does not marry or at least find a prospective husband will be considered to be not fully successful. I met Nur one afternoon. She was a young and beautiful ex-*passimokolo'*, who became *barang kembali* when she returned to Bone. Nur defended herself by saying:

> It is not that I didn't want to get married, it is because I didn't want to marry a blue-collar migrant worker. I wanted to marry someone who has a better job. I

quit my job because I could not stand the Malaysian police who can be hunting for *passimokolo'* at any time. In Bone, I got married to a white-collar official who works at a telecommunication company. See, I found my Mr Right.

Thus, becoming a *passimokolo'* gives women some room to move when it comes to their choice of marital partner. Those who are still single when they return may negotiate their single status more effectively in their family household as a consequence of their contribution to the family income.

The first point is illustrated through Hadijah's case. Hadijah went to Tawau (Sabah, Malaysia) under the cover of night (*massimokolo'*) with her cousin. The cousin, who was also *passimokolo'*, worked at a plantation, but there was no guarantee that he would be able to find her a job.[23] Two months after her arrival, Hadijah found a job as a plantation worker. A year later, she met a man, a Makassarese from Bulukumba, another regency in South Sulawesi, at her workplace, who became her husband. The courtship was short since Hadijah was warned by her sister back home to get married soon not just to avoid gossip about their relationship, but also because Hadijah was in Malaysia only with her cousin, and no male relative could watch over her. Most importantly, she had to forestall complaints about her prospective husband, who was not a Bugis, though he is a Muslim. Hadijah did not return to her village to get married partly because her parents already passed away. Her sister gave her consent for Hadijah's marriage, but she could not afford to come to Malaysia for the wedding. Hadijah was married in the presence of other people from Bone working in Malaysia. However, many single women are married in Malaysia because their family are also in Malaysia. Women who meet their husbands in Malaysia and whose parents are in the village generally return to the village to marry.

Neni's case illustrates the second point. Initially, Neni just went to visit her family in Malaysia. Before returning to Bone, a number of people ordered some goods from Bone via Neni, which prompted her to become a commuting trader (B. *pa'bisnis*) between Tawau and Bone through *massimokolo'* (B. under the cover of night). She is still unmarried, and hence *barang kembali*. In spite of the fact that she is less fortunate than those women who return home married, she does at least have some bargaining position in her natal family on account of her contribution to her parents' household income. As a female small commuting trader, to some extent she enjoys the freedom of not always being under the scrutiny of village people because almost every other fortnight she is in Tawau.

What, then, is the 'fortune' (B. *dallé'*) sought by women like Hadijah and Neni? Hadijah's 'fortune' consists of success in finding both job and husband. The marriage was the primary success; hence, quitting her job after becoming pregnant was not perceived as a social problem (though it might have been an economic one). Despite the fact that Neni has not realized her desire to become a married woman, commuting between Bone and Tawau as a *pa'bisnis* has increased her personal autonomy as a single woman because of her significant contribution to the family, and has also lessened social scrutiny of her marital status and her socializing. As this suggests, the notion of *barang kembali* (I. returned goods) implies that if a girl goes away and returns unmarried, she will still bring benefit for the family (e.g. through her income). Hence, the maxim which states that 'leaving bald headed, returning with luxuriant hair' (*makkellu' peppé'ko mulao, mabbulu rombékko lésu*) for single women refers to accumulating money or goods, to finding at least a prospective husband, and/or to achieving some individual freedom away from home. The first two are socially sanctioned and the latter is the young women's perception of their situation. In fact, it is considered more successful for a woman to find a husband (or at least a prospective husband) than to find a job. Thus, marital status is perceived as more important than working status for women.

For men, although marriage is important, success in finding a job and collecting money is more important than marital status. This is because males are considered the income earners and the ones who propose to women. Thus, as long as a man has a job, it is not difficult for him to find a wife. This is not the case for *makkunrai passimokolo'* because they are the ones who are chosen, and working is not a guarantee that a young woman will find a husband. This indicates the difference between the value of working for men and women. This difference is related to the state-defined dichotomy of husband as the head of the household and wife as the housewife, as stated in the Indonesian Marriage Law No. 1 of 1974 (Article 31: 3). Thus, when a Bugis woman heads the household, her identity as household head is commonly denied. Local statistics show that no women head households not because there are no widows or no women-headed households, but because the image of head of the household is attached to men rather than to women. As a result, women who head households are not registered as heads. The usual head of the household is the oldest male in the house, whether or not a woman is the breadwinner. A woman only becomes registered as a household head if there is no adult man in the house and the woman is the only income earner.

For a married woman, 'searching for a brighter future' is about helping her husband to earn money for the family. No matter how significant their income, married women consider themselves to be 'following their husband'. As a woman states, '*kalau suami pergi, istri ikut saja*' (I. if a husband goes, the wife just follows). Yet, in spite of the fact that there are women who migrate solely as dependants of their husbands, most 'follow' their husbands because they think Malaysia offers better employment opportunities than the village and they think that working in Malaysia is better than working in Indonesian towns because of the type of work on offer and the disparities in monthly salary. Hamidah, for example, told me that she never worked when she was in Malaysia, not because she had no interest in working or no opportunity to work, but because she was not allowed to work by her husband since they had a baby. From this example we can see that there need to be complex analyses that take into account not only marital and economic motivations for women, but also gender ideologies and women's reproductive status. In this case, the gender ideology assigned an at-home parenting role to the woman, and, despite her willingness to work and the availability of work in her new place of residence, this ideology prevailed. In this case, migration did not automatically open up 'new space' or autonomy. However, it is a mistake to say that women's migration is solely social migration without economic interest because, in fact, marital migration includes economic aspects as well. Piper and Roces (2003), for example, point out that international marriage migration indicates that work and marriage are not necessarily discrete.[24]

When married *passimokolo'* are found by the police, they usually negotiate by saying that their documents are with their husbands. As Sabariah, an ex-*passimokolo'*, told me, it is easier for married women to negotiate with the police than for unmarried women, especially if those women are with their children. Not every married woman, however, goes to Malaysia for work; some just accompany their husbands and take care of their children (marital migration), even though work is available for them, as in the case of Hamidah above. Yet, women's status as workers is often blurred, not least because of Indonesian state perceptions of men as the providers, as we shall see in the following section.

Defining work

What is the meaning of work for *passimokolo'*? They often think of working as 'going to the office' or 'going to the office in uniform'. It usually refers to being a *pegawai negeri* (I. civil servant) – a favoured occupation in the village – not just because of the monthly salary, pension and other financial advantages (e.g. bank loans), but also because of the pride in wearing the light brown uniform of the Indonesian nation-state and the status of a permanent, secure, white-collar job. Broadly speaking, any kind of job beyond this framework is not considered as 'working', especially if their job is done at home and does not require a uniform. The terms used to describe their work in Malaysia include terms such as *bantu-bantu suami* (I. helping their husbands) and *mengunjungi keluarga* (I. visiting the family), particularly for commuting traders. The following case illustrates the problematic definition of work.

When I interviewed, Syamsiah, a former female migrant worker in her 40s, she said that she had had no work experience in Malaysia. But as the interview went on, she stated that she used to work as both a tailor and a domestic helper for a Bugis family in Tawau. After two months in Tawau, a mature Bugis man named Anwar, who was also from Bone, became interested in marrying her. He had been in Tawau for over 20 years, working as a small itinerant trader from one market to another, selling kids' toys and accessories. Anwar already had his Malaysian IC (Identity Card). I was told that a person holding an IC can be treated as a Malaysian citizen. As a *passimokolo'*, Syamsiah realized that marrying a Bugis Malaysian 'citizen' gave her some benefits, which was one of the reasons why she finally decided to marry Anwar. Her marriage to Anwar afforded her protection. Her primary purpose in going to Malaysia had been to make enough money for a bribe so that she could apply for a job as a civil servant in Bone, but when Syamsiah got married, she quit her job and stayed with her husband in a rented house. Then she opened a small shop at home, selling accessories, cosmetics and kids' toys, trying to forget her aspiration to become a civil servant – a high-status job in her village. Despite the fact that she did not achieve her aspiration, she was considered *barang laku*

(I. saleable goods) because she was married, had a nice husband and four children. Syamsiah and her nuclear family returned to Bone in 1997 because Anwar was sick and did not want to die in Malaysia. Since all of Syamsiah's jobs were conducted at home, she did not consider them as 'work', even though all of them made money.[25] Now widowed, Syamsiah continues working in a market in Bone, selling the same things in order to survive. She considers this 'working', not just because she does it at the market, but also because now she is the only income-earner in the family, playing stand-in in the husband's role.

It is interesting to note that even though Syamsiah only earned RM 100 (US$24) a month as both a tailor and a domestic helper when she worked in Malaysia, she enjoyed the work because her boss treated her as a part of the family (B. *tennia to laing*), and all her expenses (food, room and other expenses) were covered, as she lived at the workplace. We can infer from this that Syamsiah did not consider that the low pay at these jobs was problematic. This is particularly because, as a *passimokolo'*, she felt that working in that place gave her security. 'Security' came from the fact that her boss was Bugis, but also because of the way she was treated (as a family member). She considers that such feeling and treatment cannot be reckoned with money (I. *tidak dapat diukur dengan uang*). Thus, money is not necessarily the main concern of *passimokolo'*: security is also important. As she stated:

> If I worked on a plantation, for example, I would probably make more money, maybe twice as much, but I would feel threatened because I have heard that overseers like to threaten *passimokolo'*. I want to live peacefully. Earning little but feeling secure is better than earning more but feeling insecure.

Those who work as domestic helpers are usually employed by successful Bugis families who have been in Malaysia for a long time, or by Malay households. This is not just for their security – as in the case of Syamsiah – but also because working with non-Muslims usually involves cooking pork. Malaysian regulations dictate that only Malay households (which are by definition Muslim) can employ Muslim (Indonesian) domestic helpers. Indonesians are cheaper than Filipinas, who work for the more affluent and pork-eating Chinese (Chin 1998: 89). Even though working as a domestic helper with a Bugis family is not well remunerated, as in the case of Syamsiah above, these workers feel that the security provided by their Bugis or Malay employers is much more valuable than that provided by the non-Bugis, especially the Chinese. They have heard – especially from television – that many *passimokolo'* have become the subject of inhuman treatment, including physical and sexual abuse. Hence, in considering where to work, the amount of money is not the sole concern. They consider that, as women and as *passimokolo'*, they are vulnerable to exploitation.

In Eastern Malaysia, Indonesian migrants are typically employed in the construction, plantation and manufacturing industries. This kind of work requires that workers go outside of their houses. Women are also involved in such work. However, women are paid less than men. This is not seen by women themselves as problematic: they say that men are stronger than women, so men are more productive. Consequently, they consider it reasonable that men's basic payment is higher (RM 800/month, or US$192) than that of women (RM 500/month, or US$120). It would be a mistake, however, to divide women into two mutually exclusive categories of those who work outside the house and those who work and stay home. Rather, women, wherever they are, are always ideally connected to the house. They are identified as *pangngonro bola* (B. housekeeper) and as income spenders rather than as income providers.[26] However, the clear-cut division of domestic women and public men is not a rigid dichotomy, as women as well as men can cross into each other's sphere.[27]

Those women who work as *pa'bisnis*, or commuting traders, between Bone and Malaysia seem not to consider themselves as workers, as they see their work as only *jalan-jalan* (wandering around) in the sense of having fun and visiting relatives in Malaysia. In fact, they sell various goods, depending on orders from Malaysia and vice versa, either by cash or credit, but mostly by credit. Rida, for instance, is a single woman in her early 30s. At this age she is already labelled '*isyani*' (B. evening prayer), implying that she is 'late' and at risk of not finding a husband, since women in her village usually get married in their 20s. A single woman at this age is considered close to being an unsaleable woman (B. *makkunrai lado'*).[28] Rida does not consider herself a worker because of the way she does this work and because of the quantity of things she sells. She does not sell things in the market; rather, she goes from one house to another in Tawau, bringing whatever Bugis people in Tawau have ordered, or they come to the house where she stays in order to get their order. The quantities are always small. Similarly, when she goes back to Bone, she brings people's orders from Tawau. Thus, earning money as a small commuting trader is not perceived as working, since working is also related to how and where one does the work, and whether the business is big or small. Rida's work as a commuting small trader, who is half a month in the village and half a month away in Malaysia, gives her space from social scrutiny in terms of her marital status, on the one hand, and a better position in her family for negotiating her behaviour, on the other. However, she still considers herself a woman who is dependent on her parents because, as she said, 'I still eat and live in my parents' house.' Thus, female income – despite her central contribution to the family's income-generating activities – is not seen as independent earning, as long as she is still 'attached' to the family, especially as a single or unmarried woman.

Types of work and reconstructing identity

Even though *passimokolo'* see themselves as people searching for brighter futures in Malaysia, they are proletarians who have no option other than to sell their labour power.[29] Many times I heard that the work ethos (I. *etos kerja*) of Bone people is better when they are in Malaysia rather than in the village. Later I came to understand that they are more receptive to doing different kinds of (lowly) work when in Malaysia than they are when they are at home. In Malaysia, Bugis migrants commonly work in plantations, but they also hold other kinds of blue-collar jobs, like construction work, shop keeping, and working as commuting traders, waitresses, nannies and domestic workers.[30] Some of these occupations probably would not be acceptable if practised in the village (e.g. domestic helper, waitress). However, such jobs can be acceptable when people are away from home, especially as *passimokolo'*, and therefore need to protect themselves. This is one reason why they avoid being called TKI or TKW since either term is usually identified as domestic helper (I. *pembantu rumah tangga*), a lowly status job, rather than as migrant workers in general.

Since domestic work is an unacceptable job for village people, this inconsistency when away from home is rarely mentioned or is ignored. One informant, for example, stated:

> No Bugis women who intends to become a domestic helper in Malaysia, mentions this in Indonesia. We mostly work in plantations or in making plywood. If we want to work as domestic helpers, it is better to stay at home rather than to become domestic helpers, we don't want to become helpers for others. Torajanese, Javanese and those who come from the Philippines usually work as domestic helpers or become prostitutes in Malaysia.[31]

> (Norma, 30s)

For Bugis women, working as a domestic helper is considered to be shameful, and would lower one's social status. Most of those who work as domestic helpers, for example, in Makassar, the capital city of South Sulawesi, are Torajanese and Javanese. This is consistent with Robinson's findings: she notes that in the context of internal migration from the villages to the cities of South Sulawesi, 'household servants (maid, cooks, nannies and gardeners) were almost exclusively Torajan' (1991: 39). This is not to say that none of the *passimokolo'* from Bone works as a domestic helper in Malaysia; rather, it is that such work is not respected.

One of the attractions of working in Malaysia, despite the stigma of working as a house-maid, is the variety of work available; another is the monthly earnings. The following statement illustrates the advantages:

> Despite the fact that life is hard in Malaysia, we like working there because we get a monthly wage. In our village we only get money once a year from the paddy harvest. Most of the time we are moneyless (B. *marakko*). We want something more. Besides, there are various types of work we can do, not just in the construction and manufacturing industries, but also other types of work that we are reluctant to do in our village.

> (Rennu, 38 years)

One other aspect of the construction of women's work was revealed during an interview with an old woman in her 60s, named Rohani. She told me that she used to work as a nanny in a plantation district, while in the village most women of that age just stay at home. Child care was provided by the company for their women workers with children. When I expressed my concern because working as a nanny needs a great deal of energy, she said that child care work is dominated by senior women on low wages, such as RM 200 (US$48) per month, because the company considers that they are not strong enough to work in the plantations. Hence, instead of being unemployed, they are employed as nannies. Rohani said, the wage is *pangngelli sabummi* (B. only enough for buying detergent or soap). This reflects that it is senior women (not men) that provide child care. Furthermore, women's work is seen as 'easier' than men's work, and so, as mentioned earlier, women get paid less. Thus, women's work is constructed as less valuable than men's work, implying a gendered construction of work.

Work is not about earning and saving, but rather about earning and consuming. Most of the money earned from working in Malaysia is spent there. One woman, for example, said to me: 'It is good to work in Malaysia. We can buy lots of things, since we know for sure that money is coming every month. We want to enjoy our money.' They differentiate themselves from Javanese workers in Malaysia, whom they consider to be poorer and to suffer more, and more likely to send money back to their home village. Bugis people, in contrast, seem to like to spend their money on consumables. I rarely found *passimokolo'* who had brick houses or who had invested in land. Most are relatively poor, as evidenced by the condition of their houses (unfinished brick or timber houses) and their lifestyle. Apparently the money runs out as soon as they get it, as expressed in the phrase: *habis gajian habis uang* (once there's no wage, there's no money). Usually they have run up debts in surrounding shops (M. *kedai*) between paydays, and have to pay off their debts each time they are paid. However, they tend to buy 'luxurious' foodstuffs or fruits that they can rarely or never eat in the village (e.g. grapes, chocolate milk). All of these goods can be found in Indonesia, but the women cannot afford to buy them even if they are working, let alone if they are not.

Passimokolo' who have returned to their villages also reconstruct their identity through language. They communicate using the Malaysian dialect and using some English Malaysian words with a Bugis pronunciation (e.g. driver becomes *daréba*, levy becomes *lébi*, smuggle becomes *smokol*, Philippine becomes *Flipin*, slipper becomes *seliper*) or using Malaysian words, such as *budak* for children, *penjaga budak* for nanny. This vocabulary shows their imported identity. I was told by a village woman (Nurasma, 40s) that such a way of communicating indicates that they have been in Malaysia, as *passimokolo'*. People in the village who have become accustomed to such language will also respond in the same way in order to show that they also understand the vernacular. The possession of Malaysian goods (e.g. sets of cooking pots, a water dispenser, Milo chocolate milk) is another marker of social identity for *passimokolo'*. Even though similar Malaysian goods can be bought in Bone regency, these goods have special status – Malaysian cooking pots are shown in the living room, Milo is served to guests. Many times I heard expressions like: 'Malaysian pots are different from ours, so is Milo chocolate milk; the taste is different' (I. *rasanya lain*). Thus, buying such goods locally is less valuable than buying them in Malaysia since the locals can differentiate between Malaysian and Indonesian goods.[32] Thus, by communicating with 'foreign language' and possessing Malaysian goods, *passimokolo'* identify themselves as those who live between Malaysia and Indonesia. Crossing the borders of the two countries in search of good fortune is considered to be something 'luxurious' for common people in the village, despite its low cost, the 'under cover' nature of the passage, and the fact that they never reach the big cities such as Kuala Lumpur. *Makkunrai passimokolo'* show to village people that they are 'brave' and 'capable' of going abroad, especially if they go without their authentic *muhrim*. This reflects women's new mobility, character and control.[33]

Conclusion

Searching for brighter futures (*massappa'dallé'*) for *passimokolo'* carries not only a sense of economic purpose (as labour migrants), but also, for single women, the non-economic intention of finding a husband. This second connotation is constructed in the dichotomous idiom of *barang laku* and *barang kembali*, and broadens the usual meaning of *massappa'dallé'*. Migration influences many aspects of women's life, especially the ways single women construct their selves (e.g. migration often brings increasing autonomy and lessens social scrutiny of those who are *barang kembali*). For women, being *passimokolo'* in Malaysia is considered to be easier and less expensive than being fully 'legal'. Even though security is questionable, illegal status is thought to be more beneficial than the reverse. Illegality of status, however, does affect women's working conditions – which are usually nomadic and temporary – making them more dependent on their employer for daily needs and management of debts, limiting their communication, and making them vulnerable to raids and capture.

Defining work is problematic in terms of how and where women do the work, and whether or not they are the sole provider of the family. These problems are related to the construction of women's work and the payment they receive, which differentiates between men and women. This disparity is not seen as problematic by women since they see themselves as weaker than men and consequently as less productive. The small income (B. *céddé*) that results from being *passimokolo'* in Malaysia has added value, which is expressed in the aphorism 'little but luxurious'. Working in Malaysia is about earning and consuming, not about saving or sending money home. Migrating to Malaysia also opens a chance to do various types of jobs, including work that is considered unacceptable back home. But women's vulnerable status affects their decisions about the kind of work they can be involved with on account of their security. Migration also enables women to develop flexibility and enhanced personal autonomy (e.g. in choice of marriage partner), social identity (e.g. in modes of communication, consumption and as a brave new character), and social control (new mobility and new definition of *muhrim*). To conclude, *passimokolo'* live between two worlds, as Malaysians as well as Indonesians. When they are in Malaysia, they feel that they are still in Indonesia because there are so many Indonesians, and when they are in Indonesia they feel as if they are in Malaysia given that an imported status may be shown to others in the village through Malaysian goods, ways of communication, etc.

Notes

1 The population of South Sulawesi consists mainly of people from four ethnic groups: Bugis (*To-Ugi'*), Makassar (*To-Mangkasa'*), Toraja (*To-Raja*), and Mandar (*To-Menre'*). The Bugis represent about 42 per cent of the population in South Sulawesi (BPS-Sulsel 2002). In 2003, the areas of Majene and Mamuju, where the Mandar people predominate, separated and became West Sulawesi.

2 Hugo (2002) indicates that the primary destination for undocumented workers from Indonesia is Malaysia. Anecdotal evidence indicates that the numbers of semi-legal and illegal international labour migrants in Malaysia have increased significantly since 1998, even though one of Malaysia's main strategies in the face of the Asian economic crisis was to force out undocumented Indonesian labour migrants (see Ford 2006).

3 In the text, terms in languages other than English are rendered in italics and tagged with an indication of their language. Most of these words are Bugis (B.) or Indonesian (I.), but some are Malay (M.) and Arabic (A.). While there is no specific term for men (e.g. *Tenaga Kerja Laki-laki*, male workers), TKW is used to specify female workers. TKI refers to both male and female workers, and both – TKW and TKI – are legal terms. In general, when Indonesians mention undocumented workers, either term is followed by the word *ilegal*, such as TKW *ilegal* or TKI *ilegal*.

4 There are a number of terms used for migrants in South Sulawesi (for example, Lineton 1975; Pelras 1998; also Kesuma 2004 offers *passompe'*), but *pattawao* and *pammalésia* are two Bugis terms used for those who work in Malaysia. Bugis migrants typically head for Nunukan (a regency in north-east Kalimantan) first. Since the first destination from Nunukan is Tawau, over the border in Sabah, Malaysia, these migrants are called *pattawao* (B. those who search for a brighter future in Tawau). Some stay in Tawau, others move to other places in East Malaysia, such as Kinabalu, Sandakan and Keningau in Sabah, depending on where their relatives are. The broader term for migrant is *pammalésia* (I. those who search for a brighter future in Malaysia). However, the specific term for illegal migrants is *passimokolo'* (I. *penyelundup*).

5 Pseudonyms have been used throughout this chapter.

6 BKPTKI was instituted on the basis of Presidential Decrees No. 29/1999 and No. 49/2000.

7 *Surat lintas* is a type of passport (M. *Pas Lintas Batas*) that can be used to enter Tawau (Malaysia). The range of this letter's validity is limited to 15 kilometres from Tawau (Malaysia). It is usually valid for a month and is not for working. Hence, one should extend its period of validity (B. *cop*) in Nunukan every time one wants to stay longer.

8 A *pengurus* can be a boat pilot and/or boat owner.

9 Most of the literature on undocumented migration assumes that undocumented migrants have no choice in how they proceed on matters like this (see, for example, Solidaritas Perempuan and Komnas Perempuan 2003).

10 For an account of the deportations see Ford (2006). The amnesty deadline was December 2004.

11 Early in February 2005, a local newspaper, *Fajar*, announced that for those who were ex-Malaysian Amnesty Program and intended to return to Malaysia for work, the Indonesian government would provide a one-stop service for migrant workers. In South Sulawesi, such a service is located in Pare-Pare (150 kilometres to the north of Makassar), where the local harbour is situated. The legal cost is Rp. 2,990,000 (about US$332), plus the cost of local transport (*Fajar*, 7 February 2005). A later announcement stated that the cost had been changed and would be classified in two ways: by aeroplane for Rp. 1,273,000 (US$141) and by ship for Rp. 1,188,000 (US$132) (*Fajar*, 15 March 2005). These are cheaper than the charges previously announced, but are still considered expensive by my informants because additional costs during travel are certain.

12 Here family refers to whoever feels part of the family. In Bugis, a family does not solely involve *sianang* (B. nuclear family). 'Family' might include extended family based on

blood, marriage and *passilessurengeng* (siblinghood, even beyond family or village of origin). This relatedness is called *assiwolongpolongeng* and unites people who share one *siri'* (B. shame, honour). This sharing of *siri'* is a marker that differentiates between family and *to laing*, literally meaning 'other people', but carrying the sense of outsider.

13 Even though cigarettes, palm sugar and batik sarongs are prohibited imports according to Malaysian law, Bugis often try their luck, depending on the kindness of the police who check on them on the way to Malaysia.

14 For a discussion of gender and *siri'*, see Idrus (2003: ch. 2).

15 In Bone, 99.7 per cent of the population are Muslims (BPS-Sulsel 2002).

16 *Muhrim* is an Arabic term that is used in the Qur'an and the Hadith and throughout the Islamic world. It indicates a degree of consanguinity between a man and a woman that renders marriage impossible, but gives them the right of association.

17 Following a number of problems related to female migrant workers, the conservative Indonesian Council of Religious Scholars (MUI) announced an instruction (I. *fatwa*) which prohibits women from working overseas without their *muhrim*. An Indonesian feminist, Anshor (2005), counter-argued that working overseas for women has become a struggle against the state, which does not provide a prosperous life to the people. Thus, according to Anshor, the lack of *muhrim* is irrelevant for female migrant workers, but they must be protected by the state.

18 There have been cases of women becoming the victims of such recruiting. Reports from a women's NGO in Bone, Lembaga Pemberdayaan Perempuan (I. Organization for Women's Empowerment, LPP), indicate that not only were women treated unfairly by their employer, but also they become the object of exploitation by officials. The women in these circumstances said that they try to act calmly and confidently in order not to attract the officials' attention, otherwise they will be arrested and exploited by the police.

19 For detailed discussion of *siri'* and *pessé* see, for example, Andaya (1979); Marzuki (1995).

20 There were a number of cases in which *makkunrai passimokolo'* married men who came from a neighbouring region (though still Bugis, e.g. Pinrang, Pare-Pare) or men who are Makassarese (e.g. from Bulukumba). See, for example, Hadijah's case below.

21 See, for example, Acciaioli (1989 and 2004) and Pelras (1998), who translate *massappa dallé* as 'searching for good fortune'.

22 The stigma attached to unmarried men is related to sexual potency rather than to commodified marital value, which is usually attached to women. For a discussion of stigma to men and women in relation to their marital status, see Idrus (2004: 3).

23 But, as Pelras states:

> `[the Bugis] are economically minded people who are quick to see economic gaps, quick to jump at them and quick at adapting themselves to the particulars of any activity still new to them. This, in turn, makes them receptive to any innovation they need to use to achieve their economic goals.

> (Pelras 1998: 24)

Accordingly, it is believed that as long as one makes an effort (B. *assala' élo' mui makkaréso*), there is always a way to find a job or to survive.

24 Ware (1981: 142–82) states that in the 1970s, the study of migration was generally considered the study of male migration. She indicates that this view was based on the assumption that women almost never practised labour migration, and only practised marital migration and family migration in which men (husbands/fathers) were the heads of the family and main income providers, and wives and children were considered dependents of the husbands/fathers. As a result, marital migration or family migration by women was viewed as economically insignificant. However, Sharma (1986: 42), in her study of Shimla (North India), argues that the idea that female migration is due to marriage or 'other non-economic factors' means that the rural–urban migration of women

remains unanalysed because it is seen as 'belonging to the domestic sphere rather than to the sphere of production and the economy'.

25 Similar findings have been shown by a number of researchers, for example, Astuti (2000).

26 For detailed discussion on this point, see Idrus (2003: ch. 4).

27 See Pelras (1996: 160–65) for his discussion on gender and gender roles in Bugis society.

28 For details on marriage and social stigma among the Bugis, see Idrus (2004: 13–17).

29 See Moore (1988: 93–7) for discussion of migration and proletarianization.

30 The term '*pembantu*', once translated as 'servant', is now often translated as 'worker' or 'helper'. For more information on the working conditions and nuances of the term and occupation see, for example, Robinson (1991).

31 In August, the local daily newspaper in Makassar, *Fajar*, reported that 18 young Torajan girls had been found in a Sandakan karaoke bar without their passports because the passports were being held by their boss. They had been promised work as domestic helpers or nannies, but the work had turned out to be prostitution (*Fajar* 3 August 2005).

32 Smuggled goods from Malaysia can be found at the market in the capital city of Bone. In the main street of Pare-Pare (a neighbouring regency), a number of shops also sell such goods.

33 This has changed somewhat since the enactment of the Malaysian Immigration Act No. 1154A/2002. This Act has limited women's mobility to Malaysia, especially for married women and women with children, because of the cost and the complexity of legalizing their status and of educating the children in Malaysia. The exception is the commuting traders who can still use their *surat lintas* (with its limited period and restricted geographic boundary) to cross into Malaysia. Other ex-*passimokolo'*, who used to work, for example, in plantations, said that married women, especially those with children, now tend to stay in the village and let their husbands go to Malaysia alone because the prospect of moving a whole family is very daunting, not only because all members of the family have to be documented, which is complicated and unaffordable, but also because education for children in Malaysia is no longer free.

References

Acciaioli, G. (1989) 'Searching for good fortune: the making of a Bugis shore community at Lake Lindu, Central Sulawesi', unpublished PhD thesis, Australian National University.

—— (2000) 'Kinship and debt: the social organization of Bugis migration and fish marketing at Lake Lindu, Central Sulawesi', in R. Tall, K. van Dijk and G. Acciaioli (eds) *Authority and Enterprise among the Peoples of South Sulawesi*, Leiden: KITLV Press.

—— (2004) 'From economic actor to moral agent: knowledge, fate and hierarchy among the Bugis of Sulawesi', *Indonesia*, 78: 147–80.

Andaya, L. Y. (1979) 'A village perception of Arung Palakka and the Makassar War 1666–1669', in A. Reid and D. Marr (eds), *Perception of the Past in Southeast Asia*, Kuala Lumpur: Heinemann Educational.

Anshor, M. U. (2005) 'Memaknai fatwa TKI perempuan', *Kompas*, 21 February.

Astuti, T. M. P. (2000) 'Gerakan tandingan perempuan: kasus migrasi perempuan kelas bawah di Grobongan, Jawa Tengah', in E. K. Poerwandari and R. S. Hidayat (eds) *Perempuan Indonesia dalam Masyarakat yang Tengah Berubah*, Jakarta: Program Studi Kajian Wanita, PPS–UI.

BPS-Sulsel (2002) *Karakteristik Penduduk Sulawesi Selatan, Hasil Sensus Penduduk 2000*, Makassar: Badan Pusat Statistik Propinsi Sulawesi Selatan.

—— (2005) *Sulawesi Selatan dalam Angka 2004/2005*, Makassar: Badan Pusat Statistik Propinsi Sulawesi Selatan.

Chin, C. B. N. (1998) *In Service and Servitude: foreign female domestic workers and the Malaysian 'modernity' project*, New York: Zed Books.

Fajar (2005) 'Nama diubah, paspor ditangan sindikat', 3 August.

Ford, M. (2006) 'After Nunukan: the regulation of Indonesian migration to Malaysia', in A. Kaur and I. Metcalfe (eds) *Divided We Move: mobility, labour migration and border controls in Asia*, New York: Palgrave MacMillan.

Hugo, G. (2002) 'Women's international labour migration', in K. Robinson and S. Bessell (eds) *Women in Indonesia: gender, equity and development*, Singapore: ISEAS.

Idrus, N. I. (2003) '"To take each other:" Bugis practices of gender, sexuality and marriage', unpublished PhD thesis, Canberra: The Australian National University.

—— (2004) 'Behind the notion of *siala*: marriage, *adat* and Islam among the Bugis in South Sulawesi', *Intersections*, 10 (August). Online: http://wwwsshe.murdoch.edu.au/intersections/issue10/idrus.html (accessed January 2006).

Kesuma, I. (2004) *Migrasi dan Orang Bugis: penelusuran kehadiran opu daeng rilakka pada abad XVIII di Johor*, Yogyakarta: Ombak.

Lineton, J. (1975) '"*Passompe' ugi*'": Bugis migrants and wanderers', *Archipel*, 11: 173–204.

Marzuki, L. (1995) *Siri', bagian kesadaran hukum rakyat Bugis-Makassar: sebuah telaah filsafat hukum*, Ujung Pandang: Hasanuddin University Press.

Moore, H. L. (1988) *Feminism and Anthropology*, Cambridge: Polity Press.

Pelras, C. (1996) *The Bugis*, Cambridge: Blackwell Publishers.

—— (1998) 'Bugis culture: a tradition of modernity', in K. Robinson and M. Paeni (eds) *Living Through Histories: culture, history and social life in South Sulawesi*, Canberra: Department of Anthropology, RSPAS–ANU in association with National Archives of Indonesia.

Piper, N. and Roces, M. (eds) (2003) *Wife or Worker? Women and migration*, Lanham, MD: Rowman and Littlefield.

Robinson, K. (1991) 'Housemaids: the effects of gender and culture on the internal and inter-national migration of Indonesian women', in G. Bottomley, M. de Lepervanche and J. Martin (eds) *Intersexions: gender/class/culture/ethnicity*, Sydney: Allen and Unwin.

Sharma, U. (1986) *Women's Work, Class and the Urban Household*, London, Tavistock.

Sobieszczyk, T. (2000) 'Pathway abroad: gender and international migration recruitment choices in Northern Thailand', *Asian and Pacific Migration Journal*, 9 (4): 391–421.

Solidaritas Perempuan and Komnas Perempuan (2003) 'Indonesian migrant domestic work-ers: notes on its [sic] vulnerability and new initiatives for the protection of their rights', Indonesian country report to the UN Special Rapporteur on the Human Rights of Migrants. Unpublished draft report.

Ware, H. (1981) *Women, Demography and Development*, Canberra: Australian National University Press.

Williams, C. P. (2003) 'Eastern Indonesian women on the move: domestic work in global cities', *Antropologi Indonesia*, 72: 83–100.

9 Making the best of what you've got
Sex work and class mobility in the Riau Islands

Michele Ford and Lenore Lyons

Tanjung Balai Karimun is a town of approximately 95,000 people in the Riau Archipelago.[1] Together with the islands of Batam and Bintan, Karimun has became part of a Special Economic Zone proposed in 2006 with the aim of enhancing economic development by capitalizing on the islands' close proximity to Singapore.[2] Karimun's development has not been limited to the export of raw materials such as tin, rubber, timber and copra, and more recently sand and granite; like Batam and Bintan, it has an extensive sex industry which caters predominantly to working-class Singaporeans and Malaysians. This chapter examines the place of 'sex as work' for women in the town of Tanjung Balai Karimun, and the impact of women's engagement in the sex industry on other parts of their lives.[3] In particular, it focuses on the life histories of Lia and Ani,[4] two former commercial sex workers who have since left the industry as a result of their marriages to foreign men. Like many of their peers in the Riau Islands, these women have managed to *mencari kesempatan dalam kesempitan* (to find opportunities in hardship), and turn their exposure to foreign clients in the brothels of Tanjung Balai Karimun into a chance to move into the lower middle class.[5]

The Riau Islands' location just kilometres from the much wealthier Singapore and Malaysia provides sex workers like Lia and Ani with access to social and economic capital (cf. Bourdieu 1977) not available to their counterparts in other places in Indonesia. We argue that the opportunities available to these women are the product of the Riau Islands' particular spatiality, and a pattern of migration which has seen large numbers of temporary and long-term migrants from throughout the Indonesian archipelago move in and out of the islands in search of work. Our analysis draws on the writings of Kamala Kempadoo (1999), who argues that the structure and significance of sex work is locally and historically specific and is determined by patterns of economic development, histories of colonialism, and normative constructions of sexuality and gender. Attention to these specificities allows us to see that neither 'sex workers' nor 'clients' are fixed, universal or transhistorical; in other words, 'prostitution is not a single thing' (Nussbaum cited in Schotten 2005: 212). Such an approach allows us to pay attention to the culturally embedded meanings associated with commercialized sexual behaviour in particular local settings, and to recognize that not all sex workers are 'the same'. Many women succeed in making the transition from brothel-based sex worker to Batam wife, but the different modalities of sex work in the islands demonstrate that not all women are able to take full advantage of opportunities for social and economic advancement presented by the particular socio-economic conditions found there.[6] The incompleteness of these strategies suggests that framing sex work within either an empowered or coerced model overlooks the complex realities of women's lives.

In the literature on sex work in Southeast Asia, a structure/agency binary is often used to describe the choices that sex workers face (Law 2000). This binary, based on a forced/voluntary dichotomy, operates between those who privilege free will (women freely choose to enter prostitution) versus those who emphasize the constraints on women's choices (the structural factors that make prostitution a job opportunity for women) (Law 2000: 97). For example, in her brief account of freelance sex workers working in nightclubs and discotheques in Jakarta in the mid 1980s, Alison Murray (1991: 125) describes sex work as a 'rational choice in response to the economic prospects of the city, and in selling their bodies as commodities [the women] are exploiting the capitalist system for their own purposes'. In the absence of a more detailed study of these women, however, Murray risks overstating the extent to which these sex workers are able to turn the tables and take control of their situation. As Rebecca Surtees (2004: 50) notes, it is important not to falsely dichotomize the ways that women experience sex work because 'sex workers do not conceive of their lives and experiences only in oppressive or empowered terms'. Our study supports this view and shows that some sex workers may shift between oppressed and empowered narratives of their entry into – and experiences of – sex work, depending on the audience.

Regardless of the extent of agency or choice involved in the way in which they entered the sex industry, the women we interviewed in Tanjung Balai Karimun describe the provision of paid sexual services as a form of 'work'. In adopting the language of 'sex work' to describe the commercial sexual exchanges that take place in Tanjung Balai Karimun, we are both using the women's own terminology and explicitly engaging with Western feminist debates about prostitution. Crudely summarized, the debate is marked by a continuum between two polar positions: the radical feminist position, which views prostitution as a manifestation of male domination and women's oppression; and the 'sex as work' position, which sees prostitution as a form of labour under capitalism. Radical feminists view prostitution as the ultimate expression of male dominance – as Kathleen Barry (1996: 9) states, 'prostitution [is] the cornerstone of all sexual exploitation'. According to this argument, there is no place for sex workers to claim that commercialized sexual activity is not always entirely harmful or alienating. Radical feminists thus deny the possibility of women's agency in relation to sex work. In contrast, the 'sex as work' position claims that prostitution is a form of income-generating labour, which allows feminist activists to focus on the criminal and legal dimensions of women's labour (e.g. pushing for decriminalization or legalization, and for recognition under international labour conventions); and to attend to the working conditions under which women labour (e.g. health conditions, safety standards, hours of work).

As a discursive strategy it also 'opens up a space for the formation of new identities not based on passivity, or sexual exploitation and sexual victimhood' (Sullivan 2003: 78).

We begin this chapter with an overview of our case study site. We draw on our visits to brothel complexes and hotels in Tanjung Balai Karimun, and in-depth interviews with sex workers, hotel and karaoke bar owners, public officials and non-governmental organization (NGO) activists who deal with sex workers, and members of the general community, to describe the social, economic and cultural contexts in which the sex industry operates. We then turn to the stories of Ani and Lia to explore women's experiences of sex work. Both women have worked in brothels, while Lia also worked as a freelance sex worker.[7] Through their narratives we explore the working conditions of brothel-based sex workers, and the ways that ethnicity, class and nationality shape their interactions with their clients. We also examine the women's feelings about sex work and the role that dominant community attitudes towards prostitution play in shaping their management of working life and home life. Our research shows that, regardless of how women enter the sex industry, their experience of sex work is, as Lia observes, ultimately shaped by their ability to 'make the best of what you've got'.

Sex Work in Tanjung Balai Karimun

Girls and women engaged in the sex industry almost always come to the Riau Islands from other parts of Indonesia – from Sumatra, Kalimantan and Sulawesi, but mainly from Java.[8] As is the case for the informal sector more generally, it is notoriously difficult to determine the actual numbers of women who provide commercial sexual services, or the economic value of their work. The inherent problems of studying the informal economy are further compounded in the case of sex work because of the ambiguous legal status of prostitution in Indonesia, the strong moral proscriptions that surround sex work, the temporary nature of this work for many women and the diversity of forms that it takes.[9] Although exact figures on the numbers of sex workers in the Riau Islands are difficult to obtain, in 2004 one NGO that deals with sex workers on Batam had over 3,500 sex workers on its books, while an NGO in Tanjung Balai Karimun dealt with almost 1,000 women.

The Riau Islands are considered to be a key hub in human trafficking activities in Southeast Asia. The close proximity of Singapore and Malaysia means that the islands play a strategic role in both domestic and international trafficking of women and girls for commercial sex work and domestic work (Agustinanto 2003: 178). Accounts of the local sex industry suggests that women who are trafficked to the Riau Islands from all over Indonesia, but particularly from Indramayu in West Java, are tricked into sex work by promises of good jobs in factories or restaurants (Agustinanto 2003: 179). Irwan, an activist from a Batam NGO, argues, however, that many of the women who end up in the industry have previous experience as sex workers. His theory is that if girls are under-age, they are very likely to have been tricked into entering the industry, but most of those above

18 already have experience as sex workers elsewhere, especially those from Indramayu and Karawang:[10]

> If you go to the entertainment venues in Batam, Tanjung Balai or wherever you're sure to find women from Indramayu, Subang and Karawang. You can tell from the way they talk – they use Sundanese, but their accent is a bit different. In the *lokalisasi* [localized brothel complex] they're commonly referred to as *barang baru stok lama* [new goods, old stock]. What this means is that they've just arrived in Batam as new sex workers, but they've been sex workers in Jakarta for a long time. When we ask them where they come from, they say they used to work in Jakarta, but got moved on. When *lokalisasi* were torn down to make room for housing estates, they decided to try their luck in the islands. Some came on their own, while others were invited to come to Batam or Tanjung Balai or Tanjung Batu or Tanjung Pinang by women already working here. That's generally the case.[11]
>
> (Interview, December 2004)

The sex industry in the islands relies heavily on Singaporean clients. According to a survey conducted by the NGO for which Irwan worked, almost half of all sex workers' clients were from Singapore.[12] Almost all of these men are over 30 years of age, and the majority are well over 40. Whereas Indonesian sex workers charge approximately S$50 per night, Singaporean prostitutes may charge the same amount for one hour (*The Straits Times* 2004).[13] The islands are located a short distance away from Singapore by high-speed ferry, with journeys lasting between 45 and 105 minutes, depending on the destination. Singaporean passport holders can enter Indonesia without a visa and stay for up to 30 days on a tourist pass. These men also enjoy the added benefits of cheap food, gambling, shopping and other forms of entertainment during their visits to the islands, but the main attraction for them is sex. As Irwan notes, the profile of the client base is broadly similar throughout the islands:

> The old men from Singapore – who we call *apek-apek Singapur* [old Singaporean Chinese men] – come to Batam, Tanjung Balai and Tanjung Pinang for gambling or for sex. There's nothing else that draws them here ... there's no nature tourism like in Bali or Bandung, or other places in Indonesia like Lombok. The reality is that the only attraction Batam, Tanjung Balai and Tanjung Pinang has for Singaporeans is sex.[14]
>
> (Interview, December 2004)

Indonesia's national criminal code does not prohibit sex work. It is illegal, however, to participate in the trade of women or under-age males, or to earn a profit from the prostitution of women (Sulistyaningsih 2002: 43–4).[15] Although the national criminal code is silent on the issue of sex work, Islamic laws on fornication (*zina*) could presumably be used against married prostitutes and clients, but the burden of evidence is usually too difficult in such cases to enable prosecution

(Jones *et al.* 1995: 12).[16] In the absence of national criminal laws to prohibit commercial sex, provincial and sub-district governments have introduced a range of regulations aimed at monitoring and restricting the sale of sexual services. However, in many places, local authorities have stopped short of banning prostitution, choosing instead to implement a regime of semi-legal control and surveillance. This *de facto* regulation of prostitution has driven many sex workers into brothel complexes (*lokalisasi*) where, according to Jones *et al.* (1995: 13), 'they are controlled by pimps, procurers and the local government and police, but generally tolerated by the society'. *Lokalisasi* began to emerge in the 1960s and 1970s throughout Indonesia. These centres were modelled on similar centres established by the Dutch colonial government (Sulistyaningsih 2002).[17] Formally described as Rehabilitation Centres for Immoral Women (Panti Rehabilitasi Wanita Tuna Susila), *lokalisasi* are usually established as gated or closed communities consisting of multiple brothels each run by a different pimp (*germo*) or madam (*mamasan* or *mami*).[18] Each brothel houses a number of women, who live full-time on the premises. In addition to the *lokalisasi*, sex work also occurs in unofficial brothels (*rumah bordel*), such as the one in which Lia worked before becoming a freelancer, which have less stringent rules and regulations governing the behaviour of workers and clients.

Lokalisasi are often regulated by local police and/or army officials, and the industry is managed by financial interests that involve members of the Indonesian military, local government, and local and foreign business. In contrast, unofficial brothels are often subject to police harassment and official clamp-downs (Sedyaningsih-Mamahit 1999: 1102).[19] In the islands, the local authorities and the military have been active players in all parts of the industry. As Ali, the former manager of a large karaoke bar financed by Singaporean interests in Tanjung Pinang, observed:

> In the Riau Islands, prostitution is considered *halal* but *haram*.[20] Prostitution is banned by the government under national law, but because we're close to the border, Singaporeans kept coming here looking for sex, and we made the best we could of the opportunity. As a result, the economy started growing, and taxi-drivers, the guides themselves and even the supermarkets prospered. But the government kept causing problems because there was no certainty in their approach. You'd think if prostitution really was beneficial then they'd work out the best way to deal with it, through a licensing system or whatever. But instead the prostitutes are persecuted, and every month the prostitution bosses have to pay off government officials.... The industry is considered *haram*, but if we *mengantar upeti* [pay tribute] we become *halal*. For example when an official comes we have to provide women and money. If we don't want to be disturbed, we need to *mengantar upeti* every month to the police, the navy and the army, and to the local government.
>
> (Interview, December 2004)

The first *lokalisasi* on Karimun was established at Pelipit in the early 1960s.[21] The largest *lokalisasi* currently operating is called Payalabu. Although the location of

Payalabu has shifted several times since it was established in 1977, it has kept its name.[22] The sex industry underwent a number of changes in the 1990s, which resulted in a diversification of the venues and the increasing presence of karaoke bars and discotheques. By 1997, it had grown considerably, as demonstrated by the establishment of a number of hotels and entertainment premises in the town. The foreigner-dependent sector of the sex industry experienced a massive expansion after the Asian financial crisis of 1997–8, when the purchasing power of Singaporean and Malaysian sex tourists increased by a factor of more than five.[23] As the number of tourists increased, a brothel complex of over 50 shop-houses developed in an area called Puakang in the middle of Tanjung Balai Karimun near the traditional market. Approximately 600 sex workers operated from Puakang, servicing a mixture of local and foreign clients.

In these early post-crisis years, sex came to define Tanjung Balai Karimun. Around the year 2000, Tanjung Balai Karimun experienced a sex-led construction boom, with some 50 new hotels being built. According to a major investor in the industry, hotels were fully booked for months on end, and many tourists had to resort to renting rooms in private homes instead (Confidential Interview, August 2006). Sex workers engaged by foreigners came and went freely in the large hotels, inhabiting not only guest rooms and the smoky corridors but also the public spaces of the lobby, restaurants and bars.[24] These sex workers were clearly distinguishable from other women by both their clothes and demeanour. They would appear in their lingerie in the restaurants at breakfast with wet hair, and in their finery in the lounges and bars in the evenings.[25] In the late afternoon sex workers wearing spaghetti-strap singlet tops and high heels, often smoking cigarettes, would sit on clients' knees, feeding them from their plates, in the open-air night market and on the large open-air promenade of the Hotel Holiday, a multi-storey three-star hotel on the waterfront. As one sex worker in the town described it, 'in people's minds Balai became just a place for sex' (Interview, August 2006).

The community in Tanjung Balai is divided over the presence of the sex industry. Many people recognize the economic benefit that sex tourism has brought not only to those directly involved in the industry, but to the community as a whole. However, interviews with a cross-section of people from Tanjung Balai conducted in 2006 suggest that many are offended by the presence of the sex workers, and the effects the industry has had on their community.[26] After regional autonomy was introduced in 1999, local lobby groups opposed to prostitution, drugs and gambling developed more leverage with elected officials and administrative policy-makers.[27] When the regent was elected at the end of 2001, sections of the community demanded that the problem of the 'sin industries' be addressed. A Tim Operasi Penyakit Masyarakat (Social Ills Operation Team) was formed, and the local government gave brothel operators in the Puakang district an ultimatum to clear their premises by 7 February 2002. In May, shop-houses in the Puakang complex were sealed by the police and the sex workers dispersed. About half of the sex workers relocated to an area known as 'Villa Garden' in an area that had previously housed karaoke businesses. Many others became freelancers, who live in the community and operate from hotels and bars.

The industry began to decline in 2003 as a result of both these and other external pressures. The Singapore economy experienced a downturn in 2002 and there were significant job losses in many industries. The working-class men who frequented the islands for sex found themselves with less disposable income. The SARS epidemic of 2003 also had a significant impact on their mobility into and out of Singapore. There was an even more dramatic downturn in the sex industry in the second half of 2005 after Sutanto, the new Indonesian national Head of Police, issued an edict that gambling was no longer to be tolerated. The sex industry, which had been closely tied to gambling, was badly affected. Around the same time, the local authorities once again increased their surveillance of commercial sex activities outside the limits of the *lokalisasi* and began targeting the *simpanan* (lit. kept women) of foreign men.[28]

As a result of these developments, the number of sex workers active in the town began to shrink. According to NGO data, the number of women residents in Payalabu decreased from 242 in 2003 to fewer than 200 in 2004, and then to just 162 in mid 2006, while another 611 sex workers operated from Villa Garden or as freelancers living in the community.[29] As a consequence, although sex tourism was still a major industry in 2006, it was much less visible than it had been two years earlier. Life has become more difficult for the sex workers as the numbers of sex tourists have decreased. As Ani observed:

> It's not like it used to be. They have to take more clients every day, and they can't afford to pick and choose. When I was working, there were always plenty of clients. My friends tell me now that there are a lot fewer now. But the sex workers, they're stuck here. How can they go home when they've already signed a contract? Sometimes they have to accept locals – even though they only pay a pittance – just to earn enough to put food on the table.

The organization of brothels

In Tanjung Balai Karimun, as in other parts of the Riau Islands, women operate in a range of different situations including brothel-based sex work, bar and hotel-based sex work, and longer-term arrangements with particular clients. There are two main types of sex workers in the town: those who work as freelancers and those who work in brothel complexes. Freelancers live in the community, in a rented room or a share house, or in a shop-house in a commercial district. They run their own businesses, and are not controlled by a madam or a pimp, and therefore pay no commission. They seek clients in the bars and hotel foyers most often frequented by foreigners. They may bring clients back to the premises, but are more likely to accompany them to a hotel room – or in some cases, such as Lia's – to travel to Singapore or elsewhere to meet them.

In contrast, brothel workers are managed by a madam. In Payalabu, the main *lokalisasi* on Karimun, there are two kinds of brothel workers: *anak sewa* (renters) and *anak potong* (profit-sharers). *Anak sewa* pay around Rp. 600,000 per month for a room, but their clients pay them directly and they manage their own costs.[30] In contrast, _anak potong_ pay a relatively low rent, but their fees are collected by their madam, and they buy everything they need from her on credit. Theoretically they are paid the balance at the end of their contract (which ranges from six months to one year), but often they find themselves in debt, and are forced to sign another contract. Women in Payalabu generally work at night, although regular local clients, such as civil servants, mine workers, labourers and motorcycle taxi drivers, tend to come during the day. Most of the women's nocturnal clients are sailors from local and visiting fishing fleets and from foreign cargo vessels.

As many of the women in the _lokalisasi_ live with their families, Payalabu is not very different from other semi-rural neighbourhoods during the day, except for the absence of early-morning bustle. When we visited Payalabu during fieldwork in 2004, we saw women out sweeping their front yards in _dastar_ (smock dresses) just like those worn by women all over Indonesia. The area was tidy and well-maintained, and the only visible clue that the area was a _lokalisasi_ was the local clinic, which displayed posters about reproductive health in its windows, and the illuminated Sutra condom advertisements outside some of the houses. But by 6.00 pm, the sex workers are dressed and waiting in their sitting rooms or on their verandas, hoping to attract customers. At 12 midnight, a local security officer rings a bell, and clients who wish to spend the night must enter a room, having paid Rp. 10,000 to the security officer to guarantee their safety.[31] Sex workers in Payalabu earn between Rp. 50,000 and Rp. 70,000 for anything up to two hours' work. The local term for these short-term bookings is _curi ayam_ (stealing a chicken). For Rp. 150,000 clients can spend the night in the _lokalisasi_, saving the cost of a hotel. Alternatively, clients can pay Rp. 350,000 and take their chosen sex worker to a hotel or other venue, leaving their identity card or licence behind as a guarantee that they will return. There is no fence around Payalabu, and no guards on the entrance during the day. However, the _lokalisasi_ is isolated and it is difficult to find transport to Tanjung Balai Karimun, so the women have difficulty leaving the complex except in the company of a client.

The system is very different at Villa Garden, the successor to Puakang where Ani worked. Villa Garden, home to many relatively newly arrived sex workers, is not recognized as a _lokalisasi_ by the local government. Villa Garden consists of about 50 townhouses crowded together in a walled community with just a single gate, approximately 700 metres from a major road, only 15 minutes from the centre of Tanjung Balai Karimun. It has a much less homely feel than Payalabu, and the movements of the sex workers who live there are considerably more restricted. Villa Garden does not have a collective security system as in Payalabu. Instead, every house has its own security guard, and residents are not permitted to visit their neighbours. There are no facilities for entertaining clients in the Villa Garden complex, so all business between the sex workers and their clients is transacted in hotels outside the complex itself.

The sex workers in Villa Garden are generally much younger than those at Payalabu, and many are brought directly to the complex from other parts of Indonesia. Women who arrive by ship are charged Rp. 500,000, and those who came by plane Rp. 2.5 million, for their transportation. They must work to pay off that debt before they receive any money. The hours of work at Villa Garden are the opposite of those at Payalabu. The sex workers are dressed and ready by 8.00 am, and clients can make a selection any time between then and 4.00 pm, when they must leave the complex. Charges per night vary. Clients pay approximately Rp. 350,000 for a sex worker who has been in Tanjung Balai Karimun for some time. Prices go up sharply to Rp. 1 million for those who have just arrived, and around Rp. 5 million for a virgin.[32] Unlike Payalabu, locals seldom visit Villa Garden, where the clientele consists predominantly of working-class Singaporean men who have come to the islands specifically for sex.

Women's experiences of sex work

In the Indonesian context, an array of terms is used to describe women who get paid for providing sexual services and are primarily employed as sex workers. These include terms with strong (negative) moral overtones such as *wanita tuna susila* or *WTS* (women without morals), and *pelacur* (prostitute). The more neutral terms *pekerja seks komersial* (commercial sex worker, PSK) or *pekerja seks* (sex worker) are used by women's groups and NGOs, and sometimes by the sex workers who access their services.[33] In the Riau Islands, sex workers are commonly referred to as *lontong*, after a dish consisting of rice cakes and vegetable curry (a play on the term *lonte* – a Javanese word for prostitute or 'loose' woman). They are also known as *ayam* (chickens), a term which is commonly used in Indonesia for prostitutes, and is also favoured by Singaporeans visiting the islands. In Tanjung Balai Karimun sex workers are sometimes referred to as *ayam bersepatu* (chickens with shoes), because of the distinctive wedged-heeled sandals that they often wear. The sex workers themselves generally refer to themselves as *ayam* or *anak asuh* (foster child) – with reference to their *mami* (a term for a madam, but also widely used for 'mummy' in middle-class Indonesian families). As noted at the beginning of this chapter, the women we interviewed invariably referred to their paid sexual activity as *pekerjaan*, or work, even when they were bemoaning their lot. In the words of one of our informants, 'I didn't want to do this kind of work [*pekerjaan macam ini*], but then I thought, my children need food, I need a living. What else can I do? Why not? Perhaps it's fate' (Interview, September 2006).

The experiences of sex workers in Tanjung Balai are as varied as the places in which they work, as the stories of two former sex workers show. In 1997, Ani, a 22-year-old Javanese divorcée with one child from Lampung, was tricked into the sex trade by a neighbour who promised her lucrative work in Malaysia. On her arrival in the islands Ani's friend told her she was not going overseas, but was going to work in a local salon instead. When she arrived at the salon, Ani was dismayed to find that although some women were indeed cutting hair, most provided a different kind of service. The salon was located in the Puakang complex described above. According to Ani, most of the madams in the complex were Chinese who had come from Medan. The women working there were mostly Javanese women from around Medan in North Sumatra and Sundanese women from Indramayu. Ani, who describes herself at the time as 'stupid and uneducated, just a naïve

village girl', worked in the sex industry in Tanjung Balai Karimun for two years
before a client bought her out of debt bondage in order to marry her. Her clients
were mostly from Singapore and Malaysia, although occasionally she was asked to
have sex with locals. The Singaporeans usually booked her out for at least a night
and took her to a hotel. Many of her clients would pretend she was their girlfriend,
or 'like a wife, only hired'. Sometimes they would invite her out to eat, or they
would order food up to the room. Ani preferred that, because she did not like to be
seen in public with her clients.

Some of Ani's clients treated her well. For example, there were times when a
client, rather than cancelling his booking when she claimed she had a headache or
was menstruating, would just keep her company and let her get some rest. These
men, however, were relatively rare. In Ani's words, 'the nice ones were nice, but
most of them were bastards':

> Sometimes they weren't satisfied with just one – they'd order two or three girls
> and want to make out like on the VCDs [pornographic video compact discs].
> Or sometimes they'd call their friends after we got to the hotel and I'd have to
> have sex with three or four men. I really didn't like that. And sometimes they
> want anal sex. I've experienced that twice. Once with a Chinese – I was so
> ashamed. I told him that he couldn't treat me like that just because he paid for
> me. I'm a human being, not an animal. I told him I didn't care if my madam got
> angry, I was going to report him to the police.[34] That scared him – he went back
> to Singapore straight away. The other time, [the client] was an Indian.

Lia, the widowed daughter of Javanese transmigrants in Deli Serdang, had a very
different experience of sex work. Unlike Ani, who had been no further than Jakarta
before she was brought to the Riau Islands, Lia had spent a short time in Singapore
as a foreign domestic worker.[35] After returning to her village, a friend suggested
that she come and work in Tanjung Balai Karimun to earn money to support her two
children. At first she was employed by a local Malay woman married to a man from
Flores who ran a small independent brothel. But Lia resented having to share her
takings with the madam, who deducted large amounts of money for food and lodg-
ing on top of her 50 per cent cut, and decided to run away. It was easy enough for
Lia to establish a freelance operation, because she had kept a file containing the
contact details of clients she had liked when working in the brothel. In addition to
meeting clients in hotels in the islands, Lia made herself available for visits to
Singapore. After receiving a phone call from a client she would make the short trip
to Singapore by ferry, and stay for anything from one night to a week. Lia's 'house
visits' were mostly to Chinese and Indian men she had met while working in the
brothel, but she also made new contacts on the ferry. The arrangements were mutually beneficial. All Lia's costs were covered, and she went home with S$200 per
day in hand – four times the going rate for an overnight booking in Tanjung Balai
Karimun at the time. Her clients had the convenience of not having to travel to the
islands and/or to pay for a hotel, and received 24 hours' service for the price of a
short-term visit to a sex worker in Geylang, one of Singapore's red light districts.

Ani's and Lia's day-to-day experiences of sex work were intimately connected to the nationality of their clients as well as the working conditions in a particular brothel/workplace. Most of Lia's and Ani's clients were Singaporeans and Malaysians since local men could not afford the Rp. 250,000 for an overnight booking, let alone the tips the sex workers expected from their overseas clients. Ani claims that she sometimes got tips of up to Rp. 100,000 but commented that not all foreign clients like to tip: 'The tight ones are just that – tight. They never hand over anything. The best thing is to get regular customers. They give the best tips.' Local clients in Tanjung Balai Karimun can generally only afford to pay for a short-term booking or at most one or two days. They seldom take the sex workers off the premises. In contrast, foreign clients, although working-class in their home countries, can afford to pay much more because of the favourable exchange rate.[36] Most foreigners dislike the atmosphere of the *lokalisasi*, and prefer to take sex workers to a hotel. In addition to generally tipping well, they often buy the sex workers good food and clothing.

However, according to Ani and Lia, not all foreigners are the same. On the whole, Ani had the least trouble with her Singaporean Chinese clients, who were clean – not like the local Chinese, she said – and least likely to be violent. Malays were generally okay, but Ani really did not like Indians:[37]

> The Indians are very rough. They think they can do whatever they like because they've paid for us. I hated going with them because I know what they are like. Once I tried to refuse, but my madam got really angry and threatened to fine me a million rupiah, so I had to go.[38] Those Indians are awful. Once I screamed so much the security officer came up to the room. They're bastards you know. They think they can do anything. Then in the morning when it was time to leave, he only gave me 2,000 rupiah to get home. That's not enough even to get an *ojek* (motorcycle taxi)! Even an *ojek* costs 10,000!

Like Ani, Lia's experiences of sex work depended not only on the vagaries of the individual client, but on their ethnicity:

> They have very different characteristics. The Indians are really rough. They drink too much and they're dirty, and they like to have anal sex. They also like to come in groups and all have sex with the same girl. The Chinese are really clean, but they're always complaining. The Malays are a bit naughty – maybe they think that because we're from the same ethnic group they can make lots of demands.[39]

However, both women felt that, despite their ethnic differences, their Singaporean clients had a lot in common, in particular a sense of national superiority in their interactions with Indonesians. Although not personally wealthy, the men felt superior to the women in a way that local and Malaysian clients did not. As Lia put it:

> Singaporeans really look down on Indonesian women. They think that because they have money they can do whatever they like. That's my experience. They

think because they have money they can do whatever takes their fancy. In the middle of the night, when they're drunk, they get angry, and sometimes they hit you. And the Indonesian [sex worker] has no way to escape. She just has to keep her mouth shut and accept it.

As these accounts demonstrate, class, ethnicity and nationality intersect in complex ways to shape the experiences of sex workers in Karimun. Working-class Singaporean men travel to the Riau Islands in search of both sexual gratification and intimacy. In their interactions with Indonesian sex workers they find a space to momentarily escape from their marginalized position in Singapore's developed economy. The favourable exchange rate between the Singapore dollar and Indonesian rupiah means that, as Lia says, 'they have money [so] they can do whatever they like'. But Indonesian women's attractiveness lies not only in their comparative cost; it also lies in the nature of the experience that the client's money can buy. As Ani says, the men can pretend that the women are their girlfriends, 'like a wife, only hired'.

These forms of intimacy can be important to working-class Singaporean men, many of whom have found that their marginal economic position has made it difficult to find marriage partners in Singapore, or, where they are married, that their wives' access to education and paid employment begins to challenge traditional views of women's sex roles (AWARE 2004). According to popular wisdom in Singapore, they come to Karimun to fulfil their fantasies, to 'live like Kings' (Arshad 2003) surrounded by submissive ('traditional') women.[40] Women like Ani and Lia play their part in these fantasies by playing the part of attentive 'girlfriends', while poking fun at the Singaporeans behind their backs.[41] As much as their clients may pretend that they are rich men, Karimun's residents know that it is simply an act; that they only have money to spend because of the favourable exchange rate. In Lia's words, 'there's nothing special about them'. Working-class Singaporean men's power in the political economy of Karimun reflects Indonesia's unequal position in its relationship with Singapore. Ultimately these inequalities are played out on the bodies of Tanjung Balai's sex workers. As Ani and Lia argue, sex workers' experiences with their clients are mediated by ethnicity and the women construct a hierarchy of preferred customers based on ethnic stereotypes, but risks remain regardless of nationality. Apart from violence, the women are also at risk of contracting a range of sexually transmitted diseases. In 2002, Riau Province recorded the fourth highest rate of HIV/AIDS infection after Jakarta, Papua and East Java (Darwin *et al.* 2003: 271).[42] Ani constantly worried about the impact of her work on her physical health: 'Even most of the foreigners don't want to use condoms. They say it's not comfortable. They don't realize the risk they run of getting one of those diseases.'[43]

It would be a mistake, however, to understand Ani and Lia's stories simply in terms of oppression. While not all women are able to exercise the same degree of autonomy as Lia had in running her freelance business, neither are all women placed in extreme conditions of exploitation and coercion. Our research supports Sedyaningsih-Mamahit's (1999) study of the Kramat Tunggak *lokalisasi* in Jakarta which describes four types of women who work in the brothel: (1) women 'forced' into sex work by personal circumstances; (2) women who joined the brothel through friends or sisters; (3) women who were abused or tricked into prostitution; and (4) women who chose sex work as a rational economic business decision. Ani and Lia fit the third and fourth typologies respectively. Women also experience different trajectories after they enter the sex industry. For some women it may be a short-term episode as they move from one stage of life to another. For other women, sex work becomes a way of life. They get stuck in the system through a range of circumstances, including, for example, the need to support local boyfriends with their earnings from sex work. These non-work identities loom large in the stories that many women tell about entering sex work – women are tricked or forced into prostitution by boyfriends, they choose sex work because their husbands/boyfriends cannot find work or have abandoned them; and/or they work to provide for their children (Sedyaningsih-Mamahit 1999). When boyfriends or husbands are also pimps, or when the women fall pregnant to their clients, it becomes even more difficult to separate out the different aspects of their working and non-working lives. For women who live and work within a *lokalisasi*, particularly those whose children live with them, the markers that exist in many other occupations between the 'workplace' and 'home life' are rarely present. This experience is not unique to sex workers,[44] but when it is combined with strong moral sanctions against prostitution that effectively separate sex workers and the 'moral community', this close meshing of work and home is strengthened for women in the *lokalisasi*. However, as is shown in the following section, the work–family divide is significantly stronger for women like Lia and Ani, who lived apart from their children while engaged in sex work.

Moving into the lower middle class

The stories that Ani and Lia tell about their entry into the sex industry and their experiences of sex work are part of a mobility narrative that is shared by all migrants to the Riau Islands. It is a story of young women and men who *merantau*, or travel far away from their villages in order to make their fortune. While many find the reality of life in the islands vastly different to how they imagined it, they end up staying for a variety of reasons. In his study of prostitution in Batam, Johan Lindquist (2004) argues that the experience of *malu* (shame) is a significant force that keeps the migrants from other parts of Indonesia in the islands – the shame of returning home with nothing is stronger than the shame of engaging in illicit or immoral activities. Our research shows, however, that while being 'ashamed' plays an important role in how women like Ani and Lia negotiate the boundaries between their working and non-working lives, they choose to stay in Karimun precisely because it provides them with greater opportunities for social, cultural and physical mobility. Just as the sex industry is 'set apart' from moral society in Indonesia, the Riau Islands are set apart from life 'back home'. The physical distance that separates Karimun's sex workers from their villages and families means that they have less to lose: they are unlikely to meet members of their home communities in

Tanjung Balai and do not fear that they will be 'found out'. At the same time, a strong sense of shame and fear of what their families will think shapes the way they manage the intersection between work and family.

Both Ani and Lia have kept the nature of their employment a secret from their parents. Despite her pragmatic attitude to her involvement in the sex industry, Lia told her parents that she was working in a supermarket: 'How could I have told them? It would have broken their hearts.' She went to great lengths to keep her secret from them:

> I was careful not to start smoking, because it's a difficult habit to break. I also didn't bleach my hair. So when I went to the village, I looked normal – my hair was black, I wore ordinary clothes, and I didn't smoke. I just looked normal. I had a child, and I wanted to protect my parents. There was no way I was going back to the village with bleached hair, smoking! Absolutely no way! So my parents never got suspicious.[45]

Meanwhile, Ani is continually worried that her parents will discover that she has been employed as a sex worker. Ani did not have the opportunity to visit her parents while she was working in the brothel because of her debt bondage to her madam. However, even if she could have travelled, she says she would not have risked returning to the village for fear that her secret would be revealed.

Both women are able to maintain the fiction of their 'good jobs' in the islands because their parents have taken on the responsibility of caring for their children. Through their financial remittances, Ani and Lia are able to present themselves as 'good mothers and dutiful daughters' while at the same time effectively separating their working lives from their family lives. This separation comes at an enormous emotional cost, a cost that Lia reconciles through her ability to support her family.[46] In contrast, not even the ability to provide for her parents and child resolves Ani's feelings about her job as a sex worker. Her overwhelming emotional response is indeed one of shame. She describes how completely mortified she was, as a girl who had never worn a skirt that showed her knees, the first time a client told her to undress:

> If I remember my past, I'm ashamed of myself. If my child ever found out, or my relatives, I'd be even more ashamed. I hate thinking about my past, because when I remember it I feel really sick. That kind of work is shameful. It is disgusting.

Ani's shame was intensified by the reactions of many people in the local community, who made no attempt to hide their own disgust and who would sometimes throw things at passing sex workers.

> That's what made me bitter. They treat sex workers like rubbish. They keep their distance because they think sex workers are disgusting. What they don't know is that sex workers still have a sense of their own worth. They still have feelings, and normal thoughts.

Ani points to the contradictions inherent when sex becomes work. While she acknowledges the sentiments of the wider community and agrees with their assertion that 'this kind of work is disgusting', Ani refuses to allow her job to define her as a person – what she does is not 'who she is'. Even sex workers, she argues, 'have feelings'. But more importantly, they are also women of worth. For Ani and Lia, this worthiness is expressed in their abilities to support their families and provide for their children. Their sense of worth is threatened, however, when work and family intersect and for this reason they ensure that these two parts of their lives are kept far apart.

Ultimately, the most effective means to bring work life and family life into alignment for those sex workers who do not live in a *lokalisasi* is to leave the industry. Marriage to foreign men has provided Lia and Ani with a means to stop working in the sex industry without returning to their former, impoverished, lives. Ani met her husband, a 57-year-old Chinese client – a widower – in 1999. He paid S$2,000 to her madam to release her debt with the brothel, and after marrying her, bought a two-bedroom house in Tanjung Balai where Ani lives with her child.[47] Ani's husband provides her with Rp. 4 million housekeeping money per month, but also pays for other expenses when he visits. Ani's husband used to come once a month when he was still working full time, but now he spends more time in Tanjung Balai. Ani also has the chance to travel abroad to Singapore, Malaysia and Thailand, but more importantly, she feels safe and secure with her husband. Marriage provided her with a break from her old life. She made sure they bought their house a long way from the area where she used to work, and she adjusted her lifestyle to suit the neighbourhood, copying the way her neighbours dressed and talked. Marriage has also allowed her to re-engage with her family and become reunited with her child. Ani says that, although her husband is old and not very good-looking, she would not swap him for the most handsome man in the world, because he loves her, her child and her family. She cannot believe how different he is to her first husband, who beat her and cheated on her when she was pregnant.

Lia, too, married a former client, a Malaysian man who had a wife who could not bear children, who offered to make her his legal second wife – an offer that she accepted after considering her options. Lia's husband sends her 1,500 Malaysian Ringgit per month to cover her living costs.[48] He comes to visit once a month, usually for three to four days, but sometimes up to a week. If her husband is too busy to come to the islands, she sometimes goes to Malaysia, where they meet in a hotel. For Lia, becoming a housewife in the Riau Islands is not about reconstructing an idealized nuclear family with the children from her previous marriage, who have remained with their grandparents in Deli Serdang. Lia's husband's first wife knows he has married again, but the two wives have never met. Lia acknowledges that her position is tenuous. She wants to have a child but worries that her husband might abandon her and the baby. If that were to happen, she matter-of-factly asserts that she would go back to sex work to support her children. Life in Karimun affords her this possibility because she can slip in and out of her life as a sex worker without her family knowing, and thus still maintain her strong sense of herself as a dutiful mother and daughter. As long as she is careful not to bring traces of her work life with her when she visits her family, Lia is able to maintain the fiction that even supermarket checkout operators can attain the dream of middle-class domesticity in the Riau Islands.[49]

Sex workers in the Riau Islands have opportunities for social and economic mobility not available to prostitutes in most other parts of Indonesia. The heterogeneity of the community and the rapidity with which migrants come and go mean that it is relatively easy for women to reinvent themselves after leaving the sex industry. Interviews with residents in middle-class neighbourhoods where 'Batam wives' like Lia and Ani set up house in Tanjung Balai Karimun and Tanjung Pinang suggest that communities are not eager to embrace ex-sex workers who cling on to their former lives. However, the relatively diffuse social structures of these communities mean that women can reinvent themselves and avoid the stigma of their past. Ani has successfully made that transition. She 'made a point' of buying a house a long way from where she lived before, and no longer associates with her former friends. Reflecting on these decisions, she observed:

> I wanted a different way of life. I wanted to be like ... like ... I don't know – the sort of people whose way of life you aspire to. You know, they're respectable. I learnt that from them. I learnt a lot from those kinds of people. The way they dress, they way they talk – I followed their example.

Lia has used similar strategies, also with great success. She has started wearing a *jilbab*, or Islamic headscarf, in an attempt to further distance herself from her past. For Ani and Lia, at least, the social fluidity of Tanjung Balai Karimun, combined with their new-found economic resources, has allowed them to move from sex work into the lower middle class.

Conclusion

We do not want to suggest that all women working in Tanjung Balai's sex industry can exercise the same degree of autonomy as Ani and Lia. Not all women have the same opportunities, whether because of personal circumstances, the nature of the workplace or their conditions of work. Similarly, not all women are able to take advantage of opportunities to leave the sex industry, although many in the islands do make this shift. Ani and Lia's stories remind us that to understand the meaning of sex as work we need to pay particular attention not only to the specificities of women's lives but also to the culturally embedded meanings associated with sex work, sex roles and family. Sex work in the Riau Islands is not a morally neutral occupation. As elsewhere in Indonesia sex workers are subject to a pathologizing discourse that sets them apart from the 'moral community'. This discourse is expressed in the language used to describe women who provide paid sexual services (immoral or wanton women) and in the assertion that women who enter the sex industry are duped and/or depraved. Karimun's sex workers acknowledge that 'this kind of work' (*pekerjaan macam ini*) is heavily laden with moral proscriptions not found in many other jobs; it is shameful work and thus sets them apart. For Ani and

Lia, it is the discursive construction of sex workers as *wanita tuna susila* that constrains and structures their lives. Morality, rather than whether their entry into sex work was voluntary or coerced, is perhaps the most significant factor in their management of work life, home life and family.

Our informants assert that, regardless of how they ended up in the brothel-based sex industry, what they do is 'work'. They do not pretend that sex work is not difficult work fraught with risks of violence and ill-health, and neither professes to have enjoyed their time as a sex worker. Indeed, Ani's response to it was one of overwhelming shame and disgust. At the same time, however, they claim that it has provided them with opportunities not available in the other types of dangerous and dirty jobs that poor, uneducated Indonesian women typically perform. For Lia, who worked for a short time as a domestic worker in Singapore, freelance sex work was not only less physically demanding, but also allowed her to exercise greater personal autonomy. Most importantly, it has given both women a chance to support their parents and children. For this reason, despite negative community attitudes, both women assert that sex work in fact allows them to be 'worthy women', 'good mothers' and 'dutiful daughters'.

In their claim that what they do is not who they are, Ani and Lia argue for a separation between their sense of self and their work. They acknowledge that such a separation is difficult to achieve and for this reason they spend considerable time policing the boundaries between their working and family lives. In many ways, the story of Lia and Ani is also the story of the Riau Islands. Ani's and Lia's experiences of sex work and their ability to keep work and family separate are the product of the particular spatiality of the sex industry in the islands. The geographical distance between their home villages and Karimun facilitates this boundary maintenance in ways that would not be possible if they worked closer to home. Located far away from their families and friends, they are able to manage the personal shame of sex work by portraying themselves as migrants who have 'made good'. Moreover, Karimun's geographical proximity to Singapore and Malaysia not only provides the conditions for a large sex industry to emerge but also presents the conditions for women like Ani and Lia to leave their jobs as sex workers. Marriage to foreigners has offered both women the chance to become 'respectable housewives' and overcome the self-imposed separation between their family lives and their lived experiences in the Riau Islands.

Notes

1 This figure is based on the population of the Districts of Karimun, Meral and Tebing as of May 2002 (Kabupaten Karimun 2002). The fieldwork on which this chapter is based was funded by an Australian Research Council (ARC) Discovery Project grant 'In the Shadow of Singapore: the limits of transnationalism in Insular Riau' (DP0557368) – see project website at http://www.uow.edu.au/arts/research/intheshadow/. Research for this chapter began during initial visits to Karimun, Batam and Bintan in 2004; repeat visits were made in 2005 and 2006. Interviews were conducted in Indonesian and translated by the first author, who has been travelling to the Riau Islands since 1993. Thanks to Nick Long and Lyn Parker for providing helpful comments on an early draft of this chapter.

2 Before the Special Economic Zone (SEZ) was announced, the three islands were part of the Indonesia–Malaysia–Singapore Growth Triangle (IMS–GT), which was established in 1990. The underpinning philosophy of the IMS–GT was economic complementarity in which Singaporean capital would be combined with Indonesian and Malaysian labour and land to facilitate cross-border regional growth (Sparke *et al.* 2004). In recent years, the promise of the IMS–GT has not been realized and the new SEZ is an effort to reinvigorate economic development in the islands. The history of economic interaction between Karimun and Singapore is much longer than the life of the Special Economic Zone, or the growth triangle that preceded it (see Ford and Lyons 2006).

3 Unlike destinations like Bali, the islands are not a recognized destination for female sex tourists. Male homosexual sex work represents a relatively small segment of the industry. Researchers working on this area have confirmed the presence of homosexual sex tourism in the islands, but note its underground nature (Personal communication with Dede Oetomo, March 2007).

4 Pseudonyms are used throughout this chapter at the request of informants, except in the case of NGO activists. The stories of Ani and Lia are based on in-depth interviews conducted in August 2006, which were taped and transcribed.

5 For accounts of other sex workers in the Islands see Lindquist (2002, 2004).

6 The terms 'Batam wife', 'Bintan wife', 'weekend wife' or 'mistress', are widely used to describe an Indonesian woman in a medium- to long-term relationship with a foreign man in the Riau Islands.

7 The sex industry in Indonesia, as elsewhere, is extremely diverse. Our study focuses primarily on brothel-based sex work. For a brief overview of other types of sex work see Surtees (2003).

8 According to statistics supplied by the NGO Kaseh Puan, in September 2005 the brothel at Payalabu near Tanjung Balai Karimun employed 156 sex workers, of whom 10 were from the Greater Jakarta Area, 115 from West Java, 19 from Central and East Java, 10 from mainland Sumatra and 2 from Sulawesi. According to sources within the industry and NGO activists, some local girls go to the discotheques and 'sleep around', but they hardly ever engage in sex for money.

9 In addition to the different forms of sex work, many women who receive money or gifts in exchange for sex acts may not consider what they do to constitute work and/or prostitution.

10 These two areas have a long history of supplying young women for Indonesia's sex industry. This practice is said to have begun in the pre-colonial period. Extreme poverty and low education levels mean the practice continues today and it has resulted in chain migration within entire families with mothers, sisters and daughters all working in the sex industry. For further discussion see Sulistyaningsih (2002).

11 These observations have been corroborated by men and women working in the industry.

12 In 2004 one newspaper reporter claimed that approximately 600 Singaporean men visited the island of Batam every Saturday (Tan 2004). This figure is extremely difficult to verify and we have not seen any comparable figures for Karimun. However, interviews with sex workers and NGO workers in Tanjung Balai support the findings of the Batam survey.

13 In September 2006, S$10 was worth US$6.30.

14 Although Singaporeans also clearly come for gambling and other activities as well as sex, this sentiment has been routinely reflected in the more than 80 general interviews conducted in the islands for our broader ARC project.

15 Rebecca Surtees (2004: 2) notes that the draft criminal code then being circulated criminalized sex work only in the case of solicitation in public spaces (Article 434); and included articles about intermediaries who facilitate and profit from sex work (Article 432) and the trade in women for sex work (Article 460). According to a representative of Komnas Perempuan (Indonesia's National Commission on Violence Against Women), the draft was due to enter parliament for discussion in 2007 (Personal Communication, 31 October 2006).

16 While Islam and Christianity both contain strong moral sanctions against sexual relations outside marriage, attitudes towards pre-marital sex vary throughout different parts of Indonesia. Some Indonesians are more tolerant of sex outside marriage than many others, and these differences are not always the result of religious beliefs. However, since *Reformasi* the sex sector has been targeted by Islamic leaders, who have succeeded in shutting down the operation of numerous nightclubs, massage parlours and brothel complexes in Indonesia, most notably Kramat Tunggak in Jakarta. Some local governments have also implemented new, stricter measures. For example the local government of Tangerang, in Greater Jakarta, has passed local bylaws that permit the 'the arrest of any person who displays the "qualities" of a prostitute' (see Warburton 2006: 42).

17 Kamala Kempadoo (1999: 12) notes that similar official brothel complexes were established by the colonial government in the Dutch Caribbean.

18 *Lokalisasi* were expanded during the Japanese Occupation (1941–5), primarily to serve Japanese soldiers (Jones *et al.* 1995) and this may be the origin of the use of the term *mamasan* to describe brothel madams.

19 The term *lokalisasi* fell out of official favour during the Abdurrahman Wahid presidency (1999–2001) because it was seen as legitimating prostitution. However, it remains the most commonly used term for areas from which sex workers can operate on a long-term basis in relative safety.

20 *Halal* and *haram* are Islamic terms for 'that which is permitted' and 'that which is forbidden'.

21 Our thanks to Rina Dwi Lestari of the NGO Kaseh Puan for providing information on the history of the sex industry in Tanjung Balai Karimun.

22 Others in the regency include Batu Tujuh, which was established around the same time as the original Payalabu, and another on nearby Moro Island. There is also a small *lokalisasi*, comprised of just a few brothels, at Bukit Jepang.

23 The cash rate for rupiah fell from Rp. 1779 for S$1 at the beginning of August 1997 to a low of Rp. 9958 in mid June 1998, before stabilizing at around Rp. 5,000 in late 1998.

24 These observations are based on a fieldwork trip to Tanjung Balai Karimun in December 2004.

25 As Muslims are required to bathe and wash their hair after having sex, wet hair – particularly in the morning – is often taken to suggest recent sexual activity.

26 Concerns most often cited included the effects of the visual presence of sex workers on children and public morality in general, and not wanting sex workers or former sex workers living in residential areas.

27 This is true for Batam and Bintan as well, but regional autonomy has been particularly influential for Karimun. Until 1999, Karimun was a *kecamatan* (district), the second tier of local government under the *Kabupaten* (regency) of Kepulauan Riau, the administrative centre of which was located almost five hours away by boat in Tanjung Pinang on the island of Bintan. When the regional autonomy laws were introduced in 1999, Tanjung Balai became the administrative centre of a new *kabupaten* called Karimun with its own *bupati* (regent) and a local parliament (*Dewan Perwakilan Rakyat Daerah*, DPRD).

28 This was not the first time there has been a centrally initiated government crackdown. Every year the sex and gambling industries are subject to intense scrutiny around the Muslim fasting month of Ramadhan, when local governments force entertainment venues to close. In the past, sex workers would return and the gambling establishments would re-open not long after the Idul Fitri celebrations were over. In contrast, Sutanto's edict continued to be enforced.

29 The sex industry continues to reinvent itself. From the middle of 2005, massage parlours offering the services of sex workers began to emerge in the Kota Kapling and Padi Mas areas.

30 In September 2006, the value of Rp. 1 million was US$110.

31 The sex workers themselves pay Rp. 35,000 per month to the security officers.

32 Prices quoted here are for 2006.

33 Jones *et al.* (1995: 18) note that the latter term is rejected by the government, 'particularly those involved in the collection of labour force statistics, on the grounds that it implies the acceptance of prostitution as a valid category of employment, an option they would like to avoid'.

34 There is a strong cultural objection to heterosexual anal intercourse in Indonesia. In November 2006 a Swedish national was arrested in Batam for demanding anal sex from a prostitute (TVRI National News, 14 November 2006).

35 Lia worked for a wealthy Chinese family in the Hua Guan district. She decided to break her contract and come home once her six-month bonded period was up because she could not stand the work and was not allowed to leave the house.

36 In 2006 the going rates for locals were between Rp. 50,000 (short-term) to Rp. 350,000 (all-night booking), and for foreigners between Rp. 150,000 (short-term) and Rp. 1 million ('deluxe' all-night booking).

37 The terms 'Chinese', 'Malay' and 'Indian' refer here to the ethnicity of the clients, not their nationality. The majority of foreigners who travel to Karimun for sex are from Singapore and Malaysia. Both countries classify their populations into official 'racial' categories based on historical country of origin, and thus the term 'Indian' here may refer to Singaporean or Malaysian men of South Asian ethnicity. A significant number of South Asian seamen who are docked in Singapore also visit the Riau Islands, so it is also possible that some of the men Ani and Lia describe are Indian nationals; however, most seamen use the *lokalisasi* at Payalabu rather than the urban brothel complexes.

38 At that time Ani earned Rp. 125,000 per night – half of what the client was charged.

39 Although both Ani and Lia are Javanese rather than Malay, they identify broadly with Malays (as opposed to Chinese and Indians), and would be perceived by their customers as Malay. Ali, the former karaoke operator from Tanjung Pinang, has his own theories about the ethnic differences amongst Singaporeans. He claims that Malay men are simply looking for pretty girls with whom they can have lots of sex. In contrast, Indians and Chinese don't care if the girl is pretty – they're more interested in 'quality of service'. Chinese men like to get massages, while Indian men want girls who will get drunk and 'play the fool'. He says:

> They [Indians] like girls who are funny – pretty girls won't do things like go swimming when they're drunk, so they prefer the plainer ones. The difference between the Chinese and the Indians is that the Indians are arrogant ... downright rude. They see a girl and just grab her – they don't ask whether she is interested or not. The Chinese are different. They sit down with a girl first and ask her if she wants to go with them, and don't take offence if she isn't interested.

40 This expression is commonly used in the islands to describe Singaporean men's objectives in coming to the islands.

41 During fieldwork, on a number of occasions we witnessed women sitting with foreign clients, fulfilling their every whim, while simultaneously engaging in a desultory running commentary with their friends. While some foreigners speak enough Malay/Indonesian to transact sex services they clearly had no idea what the women were saying about them.

42 Since reporting began, 272 full-blown AIDS cases have been reported in Mainland and Insular Riau, 162 of which were in the Riau Islands. In the second quarter of 2006 alone, 16 AIDS cases in the Riau Islands were reported to the Ministry of Health (2006).

43 Since the mid 1990s there has been an increasing interest among public health scholars in examining the link between prostitution and the spread of HIV/AIDS and other sexually transmitted diseases in Indonesia. This has given rise to a number of studies of *lokalisasi* in Jakarta and Surabaya, looking at condom use by sex workers and their clients (see Ford *et al.* 2000; Jones *et al.* 1995; Sedyaningsih-Mamahit 1999; Sulistyaningsih 2002; Thorpe *et al.* 1997; Wolffers *et al.* 1999). These studies show that condom use by sex workers is very low, and that this reflects general social attitudes towards condom use.

44 Many home-based workers face the same issue, as do foreign domestic workers who live in their employers' homes and are expected to be available 24 hours, 7 days a week.
45 In his study of sex workers in Batam, Lindquist (2004: 499) also notes that the process of returning home involves a transformation in which the identity of the prostitute is masked and the process of becoming a moral person (particularly through dress, non-smoking, etc.) is emphasized.
46 The emotional cost of separation from children is a problem faced by migrant workers in many cultures (see Constable 1997), including Indonesia. However, there is a significant tradition of Indonesian women leaving their children for work (or sometimes, in the case of middle-class women, for study) that appears much more established than in modern Western societies. This may at least partly explain why, although Ani's son now lives with her, Lia has not attempted to bring her children to Tanjung Balai Karimun since leaving the sex industry.
47 In 1999, the value of S$2,000 was approximately US$1,135.
48 In September 2006, the value of MY$1,000 was US$274.
49 Ani and Lia's marriage choices also point to the difficulties in drawing clear boundaries between sex work and 'normal' marital sex, and highlight the ways in which material exchanges underwrite other forms of sexual relations (Red Thread Women's Development Programme 1999: 273). For further discussion of marriage between foreigners and sex workers in the Riau Islands see Lyons and Ford (2006).

References

Agustinanto, F. (2003) 'Riau', in R. Rosenberg (ed.) *Trafficking of Women and Children in Indonesia*, Jakarta: International Catholic Migration Commission and the American Center for International Labor Solidarity.

Arshad, A. (2003) 'Weekend husbands are hot property in Bintan', *The Straits Times*, 9 March.

AWARE (2004) *Beyond Babies: national duty or personal choice?*, July, Singapore: Association of Women for Action and Research.

Barry, K. (1996) *The Prostitution of Sexuality*, New York: New York University Press.

Bourdieu, P. (1977) *Outline of a Theory of Practice*, trans. R. Nice. Cambridge: Cambridge University Press.

Constable, N. (1997) *Maid to Order in Hong Kong: stories of Filipina workers*, Ithaca, NY: Cornell University Press.

Darwin, M., Wattie, A. M., Dzuhayatin, S. R. and Yuarsi, S. E. (2003) 'Trafficking and sexuality in Indonesia–Malaysia cross-border migration', in M. Darwin, A. M. Wattie and S. E. Yuarsi (eds) *Living on the Edges: cross-border mobility and sexual exploitation in the greater Southeast Asia sub-region*, Yogyakarta: Center for Population and Policy Studies, Gadjah Mada University.

Ford, K., Wirawan, D. N., Reed, B. D., Muliawan, P. and Sutarga, M. (2000) 'AIDS and STD knowledge, condom use and HIV/STD infection among female sex workers in Bali, Indonesia', *AIDS Care*, 12 (5): 523–34.

Ford, M. and Lyons, L. (2006) 'The borders within: mobility and enclosure in the Riau Islands', *Asia Pacific Viewpoint*, 47 (2): 257–71.

Jones, G. W., Sulistyaningsih, E. and Hull, T. H. (1995) *Prostitution in Indonesia*, Working Papers in Demography No. 52, Canberra: Research School of Social Sciences, Australian National University.

Kabupaten Karimun (2002) *Data Penduduk Menurut Jenis Kelamin Kabupaten Karimun Sampai Dengan Bulan Mei 2002*. Online: http://www.kab-karimun.go.id/id/ statistics1. asp (accessed 30 October 2006).

Kempadoo, K. (1999) 'Continuities and change: five centuries of prostitution in the Caribbean', in K. Kempadoo (ed.) *Sun, Sex, and Gold: tourism and sex work in the Caribbean*, Lanham, MD: Rowman and Littlefield.

Law, L. (2000) *Sex Work in Southeast Asia: the place of desire in a time of AIDS*, London: Routledge.

Lindquist, J. (2002) 'The anxieties of mobility: development, migration, and tourism in the Indonesian borderlands', unpublished PhD thesis, Stockholm University.

Lindquist, J. (2004) 'Veils and ecstasy: negotiating shame in the Indonesian borderlands', *Ethnos*, 69 (4): 487–508.

Lyons, L. and Ford, M. (2006) 'Love, sex and the spaces in-between: Riau wives and their Singaporean husbands', paper presented at Conference on International Marriage, Rights and the State in Southeast and East Asia, Asia Research Institute, National University of Singapore, 21–22 September.

Ministry of Health (2006) *Cases of HIV/AIDS in Indonesia Thru' June 2006*. Online: http://www.lp3y.org/content/AIDS/sti.pdf (accessed 30 October 2006).

Murray, A. J. (1991) *No Money, No Honey: a study of street traders and prostitutes in Jakarta*, Singapore: Oxford University Press.

Red Thread Women's Development Programme (1999) ' "Givin' lil' bit fuh lil' bit": women and sex work in Guyana', in K. Kempadoo (ed.) *Sun, Sex, and Gold: tourism and sex work in the Caribbean*, Lanham, MD: Rowman and Littlefield.

Schotten, C. H. (2005) 'Men, masculinity, and male domination: reframing feminist analyses of sex work', *Politics and Gender*, 1 (2): 211–40.

Sedyaningsih-Mamahit, E. R. (1999) 'Female commercial sex workers in Kramat Tunggak, Jakarta, Indonesia', *Social Science & Medicine*, 49 (8): 1101–14.

Sparke, M., Sidaway, J., Bunnell, T. and Grundy-Warr, C. (2004) 'Triangulating the borderless world: geographies of power in the Indonesia–Malaysia–Singapore growth triangle', *Transactions of the Institute of British Geographers*, 29: 485–98.

Sulistyaningsih, E. (2002) *Sex Workers in Indonesia: where should they go?* Jakarta, Indonesia: Manpower Research and Development Center, Ministry of Manpower and Transmigration.

Sullivan, B. (2003) 'Trafficking in women: feminism and new international law', *International Feminist Journal of Politics*, 5 (1): 67–91.

Surtees, R. (2003) 'Commercial sex work', in R. Rosenberg (ed.), *Trafficking of Women and Children in Indonesia*, Jakarta: International Catholic Migration Commission and the American Center for International Labor Solidarity.

Surtees, R. (2004) 'Traditional and emergent sex work in urban Indonesia', *Intersections: Gender, History and Culture in the Asian Context*, 10. Online: http://wwwsshe. murdoch.edu.au/intersections/issue10/surtees.html (accessed 26 September 2006).

Tan, T. (2004) 'It's Saturday – 600 S'pore men hit Batam for sex', *The Straits Times*, 22 March.

The Straits Times (2004) 'Client – 68-year-old security guard, girlfriend – 17-year-old Indonesian', 22 March.

Thorpe, L., Ford, K., Fajans, P. and Wirawan, D. N. (1997) 'Correlates of condom use among female prostitutes and tourist clients in Bali, Indonesia', *AIDS Care*, 9 (2): 181–97.

Warburton, E. (2006) 'Private choice or public obligation? An examination of institutional and social regimes of veiling in contemporary Indonesia', unpublished honours thesis, Department of Indonesian Studies, University of Sydney.

Wolffers, I., Triyoga, R. S., Basuki, E., Yudhi, D., Deville, W. and Hargono, R. (1999) '*Pacar* and *tamu*: Indonesian women sex workers' relationships with men', *Culture, Health and Sexuality*, 1 (1): 39–53.

10 Straddling worlds

Indonesian migrant domestic workers in Singapore

Rosslyn von der Borch

Labour migration can be a catalyst for many changes in a migrant domestic worker's sense of herself and of what she seeks in her life. In this chapter, I explore four themes that emerge, among many others, in an exploration of the process of identity formation among 'successful' Indonesian migrant domestic workers in Singapore. These themes are personal change, loss, ambivalence about returning home and transfer of gains. Successful migrant domestic workers involve themselves in a range of Sunday social activities, vocational courses, religious organizations, sports clubs, welfare groups and micro-businesses.[1] For women from rural areas, especially those who are very young when they arrive, the activities and opportunities that are available to them in the global city of Singapore have a profound impact on their identity formation.

Before continuing, however, it is necessary to clearly state that while there are many 'successful' migrant domestic workers, the experiences of the women who appear in this chapter are not representative of those of Indonesian migrant domestic workers generally. Indonesian domestic workers are among the lowest paid migrant workers in Singapore, and the most likely to be poorly treated.[2] Additionally, the recognition that some women are 'successful' in migration does not exonerate employers, host communities, agents, and sending and receiving governments from the responsibility of better protecting all women in migration, or of improving their access to the means of consolidating the gains they make.[3] Even the most 'successful' migrant domestic worker is employed under conditions that are unregulated, unpredictable and largely beyond her control. Her success is heavily dependent upon having a 'good' employer.[4] Without the protection of legal minimum employment standards, each new employment contract brings with it the risk of reduced freedom of mobility and exploitative employer demands.

This chapter draws upon research carried out over a period of six and a half years, during which time I resided in Singapore. My principal research method was daily social interaction with, and participant observation among, both migrant domestic workers and employers. This was supplemented with a series of in-depth interviews with 18 migrant domestic workers and 13 expatriate women who employed live-in migrant domestic workers. With four exceptions, my interviewees were not women from among my daily social circles, although some were introduced to me by women I knew.

Personal change

Women who leave their villages and their community of family and friends in Indonesia in order to work in Singapore are challenged to make many adjustments. As labour migrants they straddle three 'worlds': that of their family and community of origin, the world of Singapore within which they play the role of migrant domestic worker, and the middle-class world that they dream of inhabiting in the future. The more 'successful' they are in migration, the more complex the relationship between these worlds may become. Some of the changes that migrant domestic workers experience may be sought and welcomed, but the development of ambivalence about returning home, or of a fractured sense of self, may be unsought and unforeseen, and difficult to navigate. The change experienced by migrant domestic workers impacts upon their lives (whether positively or negatively) well beyond the period of their migration.

I began reflecting on the issue of how migrant domestic workers straddle their worlds after meeting Nina, the eldest of a family of nine children. Her parents were farm labourers. Her father supplemented their income during times when farm work was not available by working as a carpenter. Nina grew up in Gunung Kidul. I knew Gunung Kidul to be a dry, mountainous district in Central Java, with one of the lowest per capita incomes in Java. Water is in short supply there for much of the year, so when their own wells dry up people must walk long distances to draw brackish water from other, still viable wells, for drinking, cooking and washing.

On the day of the interview, I had already begun to wonder how Nina, who sat beside me fashionably dressed, wearing high heels and carefully made up, coiffed and manicured, experienced the changes in her life. Several months later I met Nina again at a party organized by Halima to celebrate her *de facto* partner's birthday and the release of Risa's boyfriend (a Bangladeshi foreign worker, who had been arrested for illegally working in his employer's restaurant) from jail. The party was held at the popular East Coast Park. During the afternoon, some of the group decided to hire a tandem bicycle. Everyone took turns on the tandem, amid much laughter and teasing. At one point I was struck by the sight of Nina riding off behind a friend, wearing only her bathers and a large filmy scarf wrapped loosely around her and tied at the neck.[5] Her mobile phone had rung just as her turn came to ride the tandem, and for a moment she could not work out where to put it so that she could both talk on the phone and have her turn on the bike. Eventually she tucked the phone between her breasts, put her 'hands-free' attachment in her ear, climbed onto the rear seat of the tandem and rode off along the sea-front path, laughing and talking, past the restaurants, the roller bladers, the joggers, and all the other people enjoying their Sunday at the park. It seemed a long, long way from life in Gunung Kidul, and I wondered again about her experience of straddling the worlds she inhabited.

Constable suggests that migrant workers, like the exiles about whom Said has written, 'develop a plural vision that allows – perhaps requires – them to create a new place' in both their host country and their country of origin. As many who live between two or more cultures can attest, plural vision can be 'both alienating and inspiring, a source of awareness and dissatisfaction, and a source of pleasure and apprehension' (Constable 2004: 124, citing Said). One of the consequences of having plural vision and of straddling (or living between) worlds, is identity change. Whether it is sought or unsought, each woman will negotiate this process idiosyncratically, working with the pieces of her own life and self. Constable has argued that for many women one of the outcomes of the migratory sojourn is the fragmentation of their sense of self into 'home' and 'away' pieces (2004: 114). Some degree of fragmentation of self can be the experience of anyone who lives between cultures, but what may be truer of the experience of migrant domestic workers than is the case for others whose experiences are in some ways comparable, is the manner in which *structural* disempowerment and limitations impact on their capacity to craft coherent selves and cohesive lives out of their range of experiences.

While agreeing with Constable (2004: 114, citing Kondo) that 'coherent, bounded and whole' selves are ultimately an illusion, I suggest that many migrant domestic workers (particularly 'successful' long-term migrants) experience incoherence, unboundedness and fragmentation in very high degree as they straddle the worlds in which they live. The liminality that is a part of migrant domestic workers' experience is one of the central challenges that these women must negotiate in migration (Aguilar 1999). Yeoh and Huang propose that one of the catalysts for the initial fragmentation of the migrant domestic worker's sense of self is her realization of how she is perceived by the host community. Not only is she removed from the familiarity of her home context, she experiences a 'rapid reduction of "self" to immigrant (as well as ethnic, classed and gendered) "other" in the host nation' (2000: 424). Similarly, Margold (2004: 49) draws attention to the 'cultural reframings of self' that some women will undertake as a result of seeing themselves 'refracted in their host's eyes' and realizing the extent to which they and their country of origin are 'disregarded and devalued' by the host community. What Pinches (1992) might call 'the contemptuous eye of the host society' is relentlessly trained upon these women as they go about their work and their lives in Singapore, increasing their vulnerability, and undermining their gains.

Not all migrant domestic workers are comfortable with acknowledging the changed identity that results from their migration. For some, continuing to represent themselves as the same women who left home (sometimes many years before) is a way of keeping their connections with home alive, especially if their absence has been prolonged. Assertions of being 'still the same' may also serve to cover ambivalence about returning home, or guilt about a prolonged separation from children. This would appear to have been the case with Dian. When I asked Dian if she felt that she had changed in any way as a result of living in Singapore, she replied, 'When I go home my neighbours say I am different. But I say, "What's different? I'm still me."' Her neighbours insist, however, that she has changed:

They say, 'But you are different. You still look young.' [Dian dresses very stylishly]. When I go out walking with my sons and daughter, my neighbours say, 'Oooh, you don't look like their mother! You look like their friend.'

When I commented that she dressed like a young woman Dian was pleased, and revealed her pleasure in attending to her appearance:

Yes. This makes me happy. I work hard, I've made sacrifices; I've been successful. I don't want to just work myself into the ground, give money out all the time, but not take care of myself, not take care of my hair ... [gestures at her well-groomed hair] not take an interest in my clothes ... [gestures at her clothes] then I'd look older than I really am. I don't want that.

Despite appearances to the contrary, Dian did not wish to represent herself as changed by her years in Singapore. Part of the reason for this may be attributed to the fact that she enjoyed a greatly expanded sense of power and autonomy in Singapore that she could not, at that point (or perhaps ever) replicate in Indonesia. In confronting the tensions inherent in the question of whether or not to return home, her strategy was to normalize the contradictions in her life by denying them.

Some other women, however, revel in their stories of transformation. One day, after I had known Halima for nearly four years, she showed me, laughing, the photos in both the original passport she had used when she came to Singapore and her current one. They were a study in identity change. Halima's original passport photo (which had been taken about six years before) showed a diffident, simply dressed and presented young rural woman, staring blankly at the camera. Her new passport photo showed Halima confident, with fashionable clothes and hairstyle, and engaged with the camera. Halima had been employed in a Western expatriate household in Jakarta for some years before coming to Singapore, and had experienced significant personal change during that time. But it was her migration to Singapore that enabled her to embody the possibility of a future enhanced social status, and to work towards it. Through her increased income and the access to a variety of social and educational opportunities that migration allowed her, Halima gained a level of empowerment and an expanded personal vision that were not available to her at home.

Susie also revelled in the changes in herself that labour migration had enabled. She described a series of significant changes in her sense of self that had occurred while working for her first expatriate employer: the opportunity to feed her hunger for more learning and her pride in her 'increased' intelligence; her sense of upward mobility; the empowerment that accrued to her as her employer's personal ally and representative at her employer's children's school; her growth in assertiveness; and her pleasure in 'passing' as middle class (comparing herself with the Malay wives of some of the 'European' fathers at the American School). She spoke in particular about having learned a new, assertive way of speaking. I asked her whether she carried over her new way of speaking when she went home to Indonesia for holidays, or if she had to change back to her 'old' way:

I have to change back. Sometimes it gets me into trouble, because sometimes when I'm talking to my family I say [speaks loudly and abruptly]: 'What?' And my sister says, 'Why are you speaking like that? Don't speak like that. You must be being influenced by bad people.' That's what she says. And I say, 'Okay.' Then I talk softly again. [...] Yes, I have definitely changed. [Voice very animated] Very definitely changed. I wasn't like this before. I was definitely not like this before. People who see me now say, 'Is this really *you*?' Sometimes my sister says, 'Is this *you*??' ... I'm very happy to have worked for those people, because they taught me how to be strong. How to fight back if people try to take advantage of me. I'm very grateful to that madam [her employer].

One of the more complex areas in which migrant domestic workers are challenged to explore their self-definition is that of sexuality. Because of their distance from the constraints of family and home community values, and for a variety of other reasons (adaptation to new cultural frameworks, youth, loneliness), many migrant domestic workers enter sexual relationships while in Singapore (generally with male migrant workers, or their domestic worker peers) although they may be married, or have had little or no sexual experience when they arrived. Heterosexual relationships, in particular, occur in treacherous terrain in which the public sexualization of migrant domestic workers is prevalent, their sexual availability is assumed, and the exchange of money for sex may be common. In the host-community imagination, domestic work and the even more stigmatized sexual work are closely linked. The debasement of migrant domestic workers places them, by inference, one short step away from being those most debased of women: prostitutes. Nurjannah described the continual sexual harassment that is part of her life in Singapore:

Everywhere you go, everywhere you turn your – I mean everywhere you go. Every corner you go. Everywhere. There's a man around. Ah ... yeah ... there's a man around. [...] Wherever I go, even though I wear the outfit, men will come to me and approach me and follow me around. Then I have to shut them off.[6]

This environment makes the healthy, free and private expression of their sexuality almost impossible for migrant domestic workers. The intense awareness of themselves as (hetero)sexualized women in the host community elicits a variety of responses among them. Many choose either to present themselves in a self-consciously chaste manner, or to exaggerate their sexuality (see Chang and Groves 2000). Nurjannah is in the former group. She is highly involved in religious activities, and regards the individual woman's self-control as the key to avoiding immoral behaviour in migration.

It's how we can control our minds, right? If [a woman] doesn't want to do bad things, she won't. [...] If we cannot control ourself [sic] – that's number one, controlling our minds. If we cannot do that, that's it.

Nonetheless, she recognizes that there is a tension between the desire to 'do the right thing' and the need for intimacy:

> But sometimes people just want to have a little bit of happiness. [...] Some people are looking for – like – love – for a little while. Some people are just looking for money. Maybe they are right. But I don't know. Maybe too, people come here just 18 or 20 years old, they've never been in love, never had a boyfriend, and here they meet someone like that [the men to whom she referred to above] and maybe they think 'Oh, he loves me so much.'

For some women, sexual relationships with men are actively sought as a means to both short-term financial gain and a hoped-for long-term upward mobility (through striking it lucky, and finding a 'rich' man to marry) while in Singapore. Other domestic workers choose to eschew sexual relationships with men while in migration, seeking sexual relationships with their domestic worker peers instead. Further research is required for us to understand the processes at work in this choice, but both scholars and migrant domestic workers have noted that lesbian relationships are common in migrant domestic worker communities (see Sampang 2005; Widyawati 2005).[7]

Not all migrant women's experiences of being sexually active while in Singapore are cause for concern of course. Dian, who had a Singaporean boyfriend, told me that while she'd had no idea about how to make love when she married (at 17) she was 'an *expert*' at it now (at 42), and expressed a genuine ease with her sexual identity in Singapore. But she entered migration a divorcee and the mother of three children, and she was in a steady relationship with a Singaporean man. Halima, too, was experienced and in charge of her sexuality.

Overall, however, I believe that given the widespread sexualization of migrant domestic workers, the censure of their sexuality, their predation by men, their lack of knowledge about sexual and reproductive health, and the sudden rupture with the boundaries and values of their home communities that migration entails, there is reason for concern about the way being sexually active in Singapore affects these women's identities. If they feel 'wrong', '*tidak bener*', then this is a serious issue. Sri wept as she told me that she would go to hell because of not being able to say her daily prayers because she had to care for her employer's dog. She had grown up in a village close to a *pesantren* (Islamic religious school), she said, and she could recite the Koran, thus her punishment would be greater than that meted out to some of her peers who did not share her knowledge of religion. I was slightly bemused by the stated reason for her distress, as I knew that many domestic workers cared for dogs, yet still said their daily prayers. Almost immediately, however, Sri began to tell me about her boyfriend and the relationship she had had with him for several years. She told me that she never took her best friend (who was sitting with us) with her when she went out to meet her boyfriend, as she did not want to involve her in 'bad things'.

During an interview in which Halima talked to me about sexuality issues, she stopped short in the middle of regaling me with stories about what goes on in the bars and discos on Orchard Road on Sundays, laughed ruefully, and said in an (uncharacteristically) quiet and sombre tone:

> That's why sometimes I have to laugh. These Javanese, where did they learn to drink beer? [giggles awkwardly] That's what gets me. Who did I ask? I asked Rahayu: 'Yu, how did these Javanese get so good at drinking beer? Where did they learn how to do it?' [addresses me] Who knows, let's hope Rahayu does-n't also drink beer.... What I know for sure is she smokes a lot [squeals with awkward laughter]. It's confusing. I know for sure that she smokes. She smokes a lot. Dita is crazy. Yeni drinks a lot. And smokes *a lot*.[8]

Unlike Widyawati's (2005) reflections on the off-day behaviour of her compa-triots in Hong Kong, Halima conveyed no sense of moral censure through these words. Rather, she communicated a sense of loss at the rupture with the traditional values of her community, and perplexity about the moral vacuum that replaced them. But however sexuality is expressed among migrant domestic workers in Singapore, it bears the marks of these women's exclusion from the mainstream community, and of their struggle to define their identities in the worlds they straddle.

The personal change experienced by migrant workers is brought into sharp focus when viewed in terms of their changing role in and relationship to, their home com-munities. Migrant domestic workers become family providers on an unprecedented scale, in a manner that challenges the ideal gender role of feminine domesticity that has been assigned to women in Indonesia since the New Order period. One of the outcomes of this changing role may be the development of tensions in the relation-ship between migrant domestic workers and their home communities. These ten-sions may gather around the issue of engaging with their families as the 'new' people they have become as a result of migration (as in the case of Susie above). Frequently they arise because community or family members suspect that the migrant domestic worker is in fact working as a prostitute, or because families demand increasingly large remittances, and develop unrealistic perceptions about the level of affluence and luxury in which the domestic worker lives while abroad – perceptions which the domestic worker herself is sometimes loath to dispel.

The migrant domestic worker is also affected by her family's process of negotiating the challenges posed by the 'active impacts' of her migration – the newly acquired money, goods, ideas, attitudes, behaviour and innovations (Hugo 1995: 290–91) that she transmits to family members as her own means and identity change. Nina explained that her parents are so awed by the things she buys for them that they will not use them. Ani said that her parents, too, view their new relative prosperity with a certain disbelief. Nonetheless they are immensely proud to be living now in a house made of bricks and concrete rather than the traditional wood or bamboo. Nurjannah described the way in which members of home com-munities, while welcoming certain material changes, may resist accepting others. In particular, reactions to changes in a woman's way of being may meet with disapproval:

I don't think it's ah ... what's the word? – welcome – if you go home behaving the way we do here, wearing nice clothes, speaking – ah, I don't know how to explain it – speaking like: oh, I was so confident when I was in Singapore so I have to speak like this in the village. No. We can't do that. I can't do that in my village, because the people in my village are so ... ah ... behind. I mean, they're not educated people.... If we go back to the village, we have to speak our language. But some people might say, 'Oh, I don't understand what you're talking about.' Because we get used to speaking English here. Or people who come back from Saudi have got used to speaking Arabic. So when they go back to their villages, they don't know what to say. Even though they intend to speak Javanese, English comes out, or Arabic. So the old people don't like them, you see? And sometimes we behave strangely. [...] [So they say] 'Oh she's disgusting' or something like that. 'Why does she have to behave like that? Why has she come back with this attitude? Why does she have to speak like that? Why does she no longer like the food she used to eat before she went?' That sort of thing.

Nurjannah's words resonate with those of Susie regarding her sister's reaction to her new way of speaking. But despite some negative reactions from members of their communities, most of my interviewees' comments on their experience of financing their families indicate that they have benefited both socially and psychologically through the increased power that attaches to them as providers. Susie, for example, took immense pleasure in using an unexpected financial windfall to make a grand gesture when she returned to Indonesia after finishing her contract with the American woman she referred to above. She had left Indonesia to escape conflict with her parents-in-law, whom she believed looked down on her because of her poor background:

The most interesting trip home for me was last year. Last year I got a big bonus from my American boss. So I went shopping in Takashimaya [an exclusive department store in Singapore], and I bought a few dozen shirts, and I gave them out to the people in the village. All of them. I bought a few dozen men's shirts. People were saying, 'Wow, it's great to work in Singapore. Look at that. So wonderful! She's brought lots of money home!' That sort of thing. When in fact the money was from my boss [...]

They gave me a bonus of about S$3,000. That's a good bonus. So when I changed it into rupiah I had a lot of money in my hands. I had this much [holds her hands apart, indicating a huge wad of notes]. When I went back I gave it to people like this [demonstrates tossing notes out in all directions]. My husband was going like this: [demonstrates his look of shock]. I said, 'Husband, this is not my money.[9] I was given it, let me do as I like with it.' My husband said, 'Okay, whatever you like.' I went home taking those shirts that I bought at Takashimaya. I said to the salesman, 'Give me a dozen of these, and a dozen of these.' He packed them for me and I went home.

While this gesture may have served to deepen local misperceptions about their migrant members' work and life abroad, being a 'one day millionaire' (Constable

2004: 114) on returning to her village was a moment of fantastic power for Susie, and she relished telling me this story. The desire to effect grand gestures upon their homecoming is common among migrant domestic workers. Many women like to return home (whether for holidays or permanently) with a 'bang' if they can, showing off their new material wealth and increased social status. Some may borrow money from their fellow migrants to make this possible. Aguilar (1996: 128) argues that through conspicuous displays of material consumption, migrant domestic workers not only place themselves above others in the community, they also challenge the position of subordination within which their home communities are situated at the national level, demonstrating their village communities' upward mobility. Homecomings, then, are complex events in which, despite the presence of jealousy and disapproval, the whole community takes pride.

Loss

While successful migrant domestic workers make substantial gains in migration, many also describe a deep sense of loss. For those who are mothers, the loss of their direct mothering role is particularly deeply felt. While not all women might choose or desire marriage and motherhood, many do. Yet most migrant domestic workers are young women, abroad during the years in which they would otherwise be taking on these roles at home. Santi, for instance, who had been working in Singapore since 1992, talked about how she had originally come to Singapore as a result of a decision she made with her husband to secure a better future for themselves and their child. However, upon her return two years later, she found – as have so many of her peers – that her husband had taken up with another woman. She said that she felt that all her efforts during those two years had been a waste. Not wanting to remain in her village, she decided to leave her child in the care of her mother, and return to Singapore, where she has worked ever since. Anita, a confident and stylishly dressed woman, unexpectedly began to sob when I asked her why she had originally come to Singapore. She tried to say that she had come here to 'find a better future' for her children. Her children were now adults, and her husband long gone. Her friend Mulyani tried to comfort her:

> Don't remember what's past. Look to your children's future. They're both lucky really. They have a house. Myself, 15 years ago I didn't have a house. My mother didn't have a house. I'm being honest here.... We all went to live with my grandmother. I went to Saudi [Arabia] for two years to support the family. So, well it really is painful to remember the past. But there's no need to recall it. Well, we do need to remember it, but just the lovely times we spent with our husbands. [Those memories are] like a whip driving us forward into the future. Especially our children's future. It's probably too late to think of our own future [laughs wryly] isn't it? ... [all laugh].

The prolonged separation of mother and children that accompanies labour migration is a major source of both loss and gain for many migrant mothers, and one of the more emotionally complex terrains these women must negotiate. Many migrant mothers suffer intense feelings of loss and guilt as a result of not being physically present during their children's childhoods. Many have told me that they must not stay too long when they go home, as it makes the re-separation between mother and children too difficult. Parrenas (2001) has documented the thinking and feelings of migrant domestic workers' children. She notes that many experience psychological stress, particularly in their younger years, and that many have said they would have preferred their mother's presence over the consumer items they were able to have as a result of her work abroad. The children of migrant domestic workers, Constable (2004: 113) writes, may be 'hostile and angry' towards their mother when she returns for holidays. Women who leave babies or toddlers at home find that their children do not recognize them on their return, and do not regard them as their mother.

Parrenas (2001: 125) found that many of her informants 'spoke in a detached manner when directly asked about their thoughts and feelings over family separation' and emphasized 'the material gains that the family now enjoys, plus their ability to communicate from a distance'. My own conversations with migrant mothers support this finding. In talking to me about leaving her children in the care of her parents and her prolonged migration in Singapore, Dian said:

> All my children live with my parents. So perhaps without their help my children wouldn't have made it this far. I just had to leave them, entrust them to my parents. But even that is stressful. Why? Because when I married I didn't want to burden my parents. Do you see? That's why. And I wanted to have a good husband. But it didn't turn out that way. So as it's turned out this way, this is my fate. I had to think ahead, before it all got worse. I came to Singapore. Perhaps I could have just stayed there, but I couldn't have earned as much compared to here in Singapore. How can we pay for education if we haven't got anything?
>
> I am thankful. I'm happy to see them now. Because although it's been hard for me, I've been able to put them through school. [One of my husband's relatives even sent me a letter saying] 'How is it possible ... that you've been able to put your children through high school?' Because most Indonesians don't aim for [senior] high school, just to finish junior high is hard enough. You know? And sometimes kids without a father don't want to go to school at all. So I've proved I can do it. My in-laws ask, 'Are your children all at school?' And I say that thankfully my children have all gone on to high school. And they haven't just gone to village schools. They go to schools in the city – in Semarang – expensive ones. In the past I had thought that only a husband and wife who were both earning could afford those schools. But because I work in Singapore – I don't care about money, I just support my children.

Dian feels that her prolonged migration is justified by the realization of her ambitions for her children. We also see her investment in other motivations for choosing migrant domestic work – her pride in having 'outdone' her ex-husband's family, and in having been able to do more (in a material sense) for her children than would ever usually be possible for a working class single mother in Indonesia. Like Parrenas' (2001) Filipina respondents in Los Angeles and Rome, Dian stressed that she has been able to maintain intimate relationships with her children through letters and phone calls. Susie also emphasized this:

> I call often. Sometimes I ring my husband three times in one day. Early in the morning when I wake up, 'Papa, how are you?' 'Okay, okay,' he says. Noon, 'Papa? Are you home yet?' The same with my children. My son is now 8 years old. And the eldest, my daughter, is 18. She'll be going to university soon, God willing. I want my daughter to be a doctor, that's what I want. Hopefully. She's in the top 5 per cent at school. I call my daughter all the time, because I bought her a mobile phone. I bought it for her. Sometimes my mobile phone bill is S$200 for one month. Because I talk to my family a lot. Sometimes three times a day. At the minimum, three times a week. I talk to my husband any time, any time. Sometimes I talk to my son before school. I say, 'Hello, are you okay baby? Have you had breakfast?' 'Yes Mum, I've had breakfast.' 'Okay then, I'll ring you again tomorrow morning. I'll wake you up. Bye bye.' Just to say that costs $2. $2 $3 $2 $3 but it all adds up. By the end of the month – blagggh! – but at least I'm happy. My children are close to their Mama. I'm always asking them, 'How are you? What are you doing? What's going on?' I know everything that's going on in the household. That's more important [than money] for me I think.

Neither Dian nor Susie made any reference to their children suffering due to their prolonged absences, although Dian's words, above, suggest the 'urge to overcompensate for their absence with material goods' that Parrenas (2001: 123) noted among her informants. This suggests some level of discomfort about her prolonged absence from her family. There is also a correlation with Parrenas' observation (2001: 125) that migrant mothers 'consciously underplay' the emotional gaps caused by separation from their children and stress the positive impacts of their migration upon their children and the fact that they can maintain intimacy with them.

Ambivalence about returning home

Despite their love of their families and their assertions of intimacy with their children, neither Dian nor Susie was eager to return home. Both said that their families had repeatedly asked them to come home, but neither, at the time of the interview, was planning to do this. Dian was emphatic as she explained her response to her family's requests, 'My children say, "You're old now Mum, you should come home and rest." And I say, "Are you ready to feed me? I don't want to ask you for food until you've really *made it*."' Susie said that she had told her family she wouldn't stay away longer than seven years, and that she was now approaching the end of this time limit. However, she then became very animated and said, 'But if I want to, then I'll stay on here.' Dian and Susie are not alone in their ambivalence about returning home. Nina, for instance, spoke very sentimentally about her home and family in Gunung Kidul, but when I asked her about her plans for returning to Indonesia her tone of voice changed markedly. She sounded evasive and disinterested at first:

> Ummm ... possibly ... [speaks quickly and abruptly] but I haven't worked out where I'll live. Maybe I'll start a business. But maybe not in my village, because my village is quite ... quite.... Actually it's okay in Jakarta. But from a financial point of view – maybe I can't. [Brighter tone] Maybe I'll do it in my village. Maybe I will set up a hairdressing and beauty salon. I will improve my skills before I go back. While I'm in Singapore I'll do some more courses. I'll make sure that I know more, become expert – an expert. So then I'll be able to teach my sister or relatives when I return.

As Constable observes, 'once the process of transnational labor is in place, new reasons to continue [working abroad] and new rationales for staying [abroad] may be set in motion' (2004: 122). Sometimes women stay away for much longer than they initially envisaged because of increasing consumer demands and rising expectations in their families (see Constable 2004: 106; Yeoh and Huang 2000: 425). More often, however, it is due to personal ambivalence about the return home. The reasons for this ambivalence may be idiosyncratically defined in large part (cf. Constable 2004); however some common factors can be identified. My general observation is that while in Singapore many of my interviewees dress fashionably, eat well, take courses, assume peer leadership roles, patronize discotheques, bars and cinemas on their days off, and generally make the most of life in this fast-paced city, within the constraints of their employment situations. To return home would require sacrificing many, if not all, of these things. Many of the gains (particularly material) made by migrant domestic workers become unsustainable when their migration ceases. As Nurjannah explained:

> [When you go back] you have to adapt. Don't – ah ... how to say ...? Lots of people still have money when they arrive home. So if they want to go somewhere, they can pay for the transport. They still have money for shopping, they still wear their pretty clothes. But by the time they've been home a month or two – even the water in the village is different, right? So their clothes have already started to ... well, they don't look like they did in the city. So they can't keep being all pretty. Their skin definitely changes. Why? They can't keep maintaining it, can they? So of course it changes – looks change, clothes change. [...] Once her money is already spent, and she doesn't have enough, then she'll have to go back to the same old thing as before. [...] Once she can no longer support her new lifestyle, she has to go back to the ordinary one. [...] She feels very sad: Why can't I keep what I had in the city? Now I don't have any money, so whether I want to or not, I have to go back to the city and earn more money so I can keep up my city lifestyle.[10]

There is a high level of dissonance between these women's roots in their rural communities of origin, their lives in Singapore, and their urgent (and vulnerable) aspirations to membership of the middle class, which is not readily resolved. My interviewees negotiated this dissonance in varying ways. Where Susie and Nina talked sentimentally of the 'simplicity' of home, and used terms such as 'my culture' in the self-conscious manner of one newly looking in from the outside, Dian attempted to normalize the dissonance between her life in Singapore and her home community through denying difference. When I asked her if she had had any difficulties in adjusting to living with and working for a Western family, her quick and insistent reply seemed to be an attempt to reframe her origins in terms that were more congruent with her current status and ambitions:

> I was used to it. I married into circumstances the same as this. I was used to mixing with Europeans. I was used to it. Because I married my husband, who was in engineering. We were used to people from other countries. I was used to it. And when I was little I also lived with people who lived like this. Because my father was employed in a company. In the plantation section. Coffee, rubber. It was a big company. We were used to it. From when we were little we were already used to living like this. So I wasn't shocked.

Dian was anxious to establish that she was at ease with middle-class lifestyles and Westerners. She used ambiguous language in describing the work of her father when she was growing up, and of her ex-husband, perhaps because she wished to represent herself as part of the middle class. But earlier she had told me that her ex-husband's sister had been surprised that all her children had gone through high school. High school education, while beyond the reach of many in Indonesia, is not beyond the reach of members of the middle class. In saying that her ex-husband was in '*lingkungan engineering*' (in the engineering field) Dian may have been reframing the fact that he worked in some capacity on construction sites. As '*staff di company, bagian perkebunan*' (staff in a company, the plantation section) her father may have been a coffee picker, or a rubber tapper.

Looking to the future

Some migrant domestic workers, my interviewees among them, make significant gains while in Singapore, both in financial and material terms and in areas such as personal development and the acquisition of skills and knowledge. Aguilar (1996: 128) argues that through these gains, labour migrants challenge the 'hierarchies of class and status' that dominate in their homelands, and that through labour migration they 'execute their own levelling mechanisms on … transnationalised but class-divided nation[s]'. He comments on the 'confidence and cosmopolitanism' that migrants bring with them upon their return home, no longer 'awed' by their national elites. My own research supports Aguilar's suggestions in a general sense, while raising questions as to the extent to which the gains made by these women are sustainable once their time in migration ceases. For a variety of reasons (because they are content to return to life in their village, or out of pragmatism, for instance) not all women seek to maintain the changes they experienced in migration after their return home. Some go abroad with just one particular goal in mind – improving their house, for instance, or putting family members through school. Once this goal is achieved they are content to return home and to resume a life similar to the one they led prior to migration. Even women whose experiences in Singapore are harsh state that they experience an overall sense of gain from their migration so long as they are paid for their work. As the accumulation of capital is a primary motivation for most women who enter labour migration, their sense of success and satisfaction with the outcome of their migration is ultimately measured against whether or not they return home with money at its end.

But what of those who *do* seek to transfer the gains they make in Singapore to their home countries? What is possible? With Constable (2004: 124), I note that while labour migration may provide domestic workers with new experiences, desires, options and visions, it does not provide the means for successfully transplanting them. Thus the consolidation of any gains made while in migration, whether concrete (material and financial) or intangible (personal development, lifestyle changes, empowerment), is one of the more difficult challenges faced by the migrant domestic worker. While Aguilar asserts that the successful completion of the labour migration 'pilgrimage' is measured, primarily, in terms of the migrant's return home at the end of a contract, 'loaded with presents and an amount of savings' (1999: 115), many women – my interviewees among them – are not content to return home simply as 'one day millionaires' (Constable 2004: 113–14). They seek enduring change, but find this is not easily realizable.

Among the factors that contribute to the difficulty of the transferral and consolidation of gains made while in migration, structural impediments rate highly in both Singapore and Indonesia. For instance, in addition to financing the education of family members at home, some women invest in educational and training opportunities for themselves while in Singapore, with a view to increasing their skills base. A variety of migrant worker centres and private institutions provide courses on Sundays that can be taken by migrant domestic workers. This kind of opportunity would simply not be available to these women in their home countries. However, migrant domestic workers are not permitted to use these skills in an income-generating capacity while in Singapore, and some of their skills therefore become redundant. Nina had spent a lot of time and money learning new skills, but as she explained to me, it was more difficult than she had thought to leave behind the life of the 'poor person':

> So far I've done a computer course. That's finished. And I've done a hairdressing course. But you know, even if you finish a course and you get that certificate, if you don't practise, it can end up meaning nothing. So I've done some courses.... I think my sewing has improved a bit now. But I have to keep practising. Actually I would like to learn make-up, because those two things connect. A joint business offering those two things would be good. Maybe when I go back I'll work with someone else before going out on my own. Actually in

Singapore the courses are quite good, but if you don't practise it's nothing. Nothing.

I do courses every Sunday. At the training centre you can enrol whether you've got an employment pass [i.e. you are a foreign worker] or you're Singaporean. The centre is quite nice. I got my dressmaking certificate there. But now I have to improve my drafting, because if you don't know how to draft.... So maybe I need to take drafting classes next. [...] To get my dream I need to improve on what I've done, like my courses and things. Actually I'd have more money if I didn't do the courses, but money doesn't mean much to me if my brain doesn't get something. But without money I can't open a business. So maybe from now on I need to just save my money so I can open a business. [...]

I never thought, back then, that I'd be in Singapore now. I just thought I'd be at home, having fun or something. But finally I had this on my mind, because my sister said, 'Come. You need to change your life.' And so on and so forth. 'Okay?' So now I actually dream something, but I can't get it. Because I thought that by coming to work in Singapore I'd get a better life, with everything better than before. But so far I still feel it's the same: standard life, as a poor person, with nothing to do, and no wealth or anything.

Nina draws our attention to one of the conundrums domestic workers face where the consolidation of their gains is concerned. They are excluded from the means to put their education and training to work while in Singapore (where they must stay if they are to maintain their financial gains) yet it will be difficult for them to put them to work in rural areas of Indonesia without first having amassed some capital with which to establish a small business. Nurjannah talked about the kinds of obstacles that can stand in the way of a returned migrant successfully establishing a small business upon her return home:

Maybe someone dreams of, say, 'When I've saved up so much money, I'll open a restaurant when I go back home, or a provisions shop, or a small business.' She can do that. If she's got the skills. But it won't be as she imagined it. Because she's imagined it will be like here in Singapore. The way they run a business here. But when she gets to the village, she has to do things as they're done in the village. So the outcome will be different, you know? Money's not worth much there, you know? Here we use dollars, which go a lot further. In one day there you only make a little bit and it's not worth much.

Despite the odds being against the successful transferral of the migrant woman's gains made in migration, many women are relatively upbeat about their plans for the future. Reflecting their new level of participation in and status in their home community, some women envisage using the gains they make while in Singapore to the benefit of others when they return home. Nina, earlier, spoke of her intention to pass on skills she has gained in Singapore to her sister or other family members upon returning to Indonesia. Dian and Halima also stated that part of their intention in returning to Indonesia was to help others there. Dian, with her customary confidence and positive outlook, explained that:

> It's all up to us. For example I have a hobby: I like to cook. I really would like to have my own restaurant. Also, because I'm skilled with my hands, you know, I'd like to have a bridal salon you know, doing make-up and stuff. I enjoy that too. I really enjoy doing business. When I go back to Indonesia I'd like to start a business. My family are already saying I needn't work in Singapore any longer, but I say when I've got enough money, and my children are all independent, already successful, perhaps my life will be happier, because I want to have a workshop where I'll employ orphans. I'm a philanthropist. I want to help people, although I also don't have it easy.

Halima had already employed an uncle to drive a taxi that she had bought with her Singapore earnings:

> I imagine that if I have my own business later, I can help my family or my friends from the past. For now I've bought one car. Later I'll buy another one. [These cars are then driven as taxis.] Maybe I can go on expanding. I'll buy two cars, three cars, right? I can then help several people. If one person uses the car in the daytime, and another at night, two shifts, you know. Then I can help people.

Nurjannah hoped to move to Batam, and to bring her family to live there with her. I asked her why she wanted to move there:[11]

> The thing is, there's no water in my village if it doesn't rain. If it doesn't rain there for a week or two, the wells dry up, and we have to get water from other places ... like out in the rice fields or somewhere. We have to walk, or sometimes these days people use motorbikes. We take drums [to fill up]. It takes about half an hour to go there and back. Yes, it's a long way. So in my village there's not much water, and life is hard. So I thought that if I move to Batam, perhaps there'll be lots of opportunities for us there. I can bring my brothers and sisters or my family over. That's what I'm thinking. That's what I want to do, but I don't know if I'll be able to or not.

Nurjannah is being realistic about her plans for the future. She knows that migrant domestic work in Singapore may not, in fact, prove to be a 'bridging occupation' (Yeoh and Huang 2000: 422) for herself, or most of her friends. Halima expressed this view more poignantly. During one of our interviews, while ranting about friends and acquaintances frittering away their money on alcohol, cigarettes, and huge mobile phone bills, she suddenly stopped mid-sentence and her voice changed, becoming thoughtful and quiet. Where she was usually definite in everything she said, she was suddenly searching for the words to explain what she wanted to say:

They really – I don't want to – like – it's always – what do you call it? How do you – how to say it, Rossi? Like – they don't want to *change*, you know? For myself, you know, there are things I want. I've got dreams, right? I don't want to end up with nothing when I stop working here. Have to go to work in the rice fields again. I absolutely can't work in the rice fields, Rossi. I can't. Get it? I don't want to. That's why I say: I can't work in the rice fields, I never learned to work in the rice fields, so how could I work in the rice fields? But these others, like they work here, and build a house in Java – okay, so there's a house in Java, then. But then they've got no money left. You know? I know they're all like that in Java. They've got no money after that. No money, so they have to go to the rice fields again – I don't want to do that! *I* say: Okay, there's a house, that's a start, you know? Then I'll do something like open a shop. I don't want to go to the rice fields. If I've got my own shop then that'll take care of what I need for everyday expenses, right?

Halima knew, however, that even after seven years of domestic service in Singapore, earning substantially more than most domestic workers for much of that time, it was far from certain that she would achieve her goal.

Conclusion

While the migrant domestic worker employed in a 'good' situation in the global city of Singapore has access to income, opportunities and experiences otherwise not available to poor Third World women, her access is nonetheless subject to multiple limitations. Her free time is severely limited, she does not have the option of using her new skills to move out of domestic service while in migration, and she may not accumulate sufficient capital while in migration to put her new skills to use upon her return home. She does not have migration mobility (except to seek employment in another country as a migrant domestic worker), nor the option of permanent migration, nor does she have financial security. What these women do have, and can control (while in migration) is their money. Whether they save it, remit it, or spend it with great intensity of purpose on alcohol, phone bills, or grand homecoming gestures, it is their possession of money, and the possibility of consumption, that provides 'the balm' (Aguilar 1999: 119) that tames the indignities, frustrations and injustices these women experience in migration.

Through the straddling of worlds that labour migration entails, many migrant domestic workers experience substantial changes in their sense of self, and in what they seek from their lives. Yet numerous social and structural impediments prevent them from consolidating and transferring the gains they make while in migration to their home countries. To consider the nature of the gains and losses made by women in labour migration is to constantly come up against contradictions and tensions. The woman who, through labour migration, increases in status in the eyes of her home community simultaneously loses status upon arrival in her host community. The woman who finds new and satisfying means of self-expression or a new identity in migration finds that she can no longer consider her return home without ambivalence. The woman who takes pleasure in learning new skills in migration might find that her skills become redundant over time, as she is prohibited from putting them to work. The woman who begins to dream of a life in which she uses the intelligence or leadership skills she developed in migration finds herself unable to gain the kind of work in which she can apply them. The woman who, distanced from the patriarchal constraints of her home community, seeks a sexual relationship of her choice, finds herself sexualized to such an extent in her host community that the navigation of sexual relationships is unusually treacherous, and may result in damage to both her reproductive health and her sense of self. These women are vulnerable in terms of their migration status, their lack of legal protection, the power of their employers to set terms not only for their work but also their private lives, and often also in terms of their position as providers for families with increasing needs. All their gains can be said to be fragile.

It can be argued that the means to the gains made by migrant domestic workers is, in many ways, merely 'loaned' to them anyway; they have no right to be in Singapore, they can be repatriated literally at a moment's notice, and are not allowed to make Singapore (or most other receiving countries – Canada being a notable exception) their permanent home. Nonetheless, the women whose voices are heard in this chapter, and thousands of other women who regard themselves as 'successful' labour migrants, do experience an overall sense of gain and self-empowerment in migration. Despite the losses they experience and the tensions that migration introduces into their lives, they view their migrations as gambles that have paid off – albeit in ways they did not foresee as well as in the ways they imagined when beginning their migration.

Notes

1 I am using the term 'successful' very broadly here – in the way that I understand the women themselves use it. 'Successful' means above all that their migrations result in financial gain, but also that they have an employer who allows them a regular day off (weekly, fortnightly, monthly) during which they involve themselves in the migrant domestic worker subculture that thrives on Sundays, and avail themselves of some of the educational or peer leadership opportunities that are open to them while in Singapore. I use 'successful' in inverted commas to alert the reader to the fact that parameters of these women's 'success' are severely constrained, as will be described in the body of the chapter.
2 For instance, the majority of Indonesian domestic workers receive no days off at all while working in Singapore (see Yeoh and Huang 1999: 1159). They are also among the lowest-paid migrant domestic workers in Singapore. Wages for Indonesian domestic workers in 2007 started at around S$240 a month, while Filipina domestic workers could expect to earn at least S$360 a month. See reports such as FOKER (2005) and Human Rights Watch (2005) for information about the poor treatment of many Indonesian domestic workers in Singapore.
3 Nevertheless, there are many reasons why it is important to document and to engage with the experiences of women who are 'successful' in labour migration. First, this enables recognition of the ways in which these women, who live in the margins of global cities, and who work in the service of middle- and upper-class households, extract the greatest possible gain from the limiting conditions under which they live and work. It is also important that government policy-makers, non-governmental organizations and advocacy groups understand the experiences of these women in order to support their efforts

to claim legal, political and economic space – not only in their host country, but perhaps even more importantly, in their home countries when they return to them. Researchers such as Aguilar (1999) and Constable (2004) have written about some of the issues surrounding 'success' in migration in the context of Filipino labour migration.

4 Employers who are judged 'good' by migrant domestic workers must, at a minimum, pay the domestic worker on time, and allow her a regular day off.

5 Her attire that day contrasted strongly with the very modest clothing worn by Javanese women in Indonesia when outside of their own homes.

6 By 'the outfit' Nurjannah means the Islamic dress adopted by many Indonesian domestic workers on their days off: a long-sleeved, ankle-length dress or skirt and blouse and a head-scarf.

7 Sampang (2005: 76) also states that some lesbian Filipinas choose to migrate together, seeking to live their sexuality more freely away from the constraints of the family and community at home.

8 Indonesians, being Muslim, generally do not drink alcohol. Alcohol is not generally served at parties or in homes, and bars are commonly considered to be places of ill-repute. It is also considered inappropriate for women to smoke in Indonesia.

9 She meant that she did not 'earn' that money as such, it was a gift to her from her employer.

10 Awareness that their husbands or families might expect that they will reassume their previous gender role in the family upon return may also contribute to (or be a major factor in) ambivalence about return – although some research has shown that within their home communities the gender status of migrant domestic workers improves, with husbands demonstrating increased respect for their migrant wives, and taking a greater role in child-rearing (Hugo 2002: 169, citing research by Indonesian NGO Yayasan Pengembangan Pedesaan).

11 Batam is part of the Riau Islands Special Economic Zone in Indonesia. It is experiencing rapid development as an industrial off-shoot of land-scarce Singapore (see Ford and Lyons ch. 9 this volume).

References

Aguilar, F. V. Jr (1996) 'The dialectics of transnational shame and national identity', *Philippine Sociological Review*, 44 (1–4): 101–36.

—— (1999) 'Ritual passage and the reconstruction of selfhood in international labour migration', *Sojourn*, 14 (1): 98–139.

Chang, K. A. and Groves, J. M. (2000) 'Neither "saints" nor "prostitutes": sexual discourse in the Filipina domestic worker community in Hong Kong', *Women's Studies International Forum*, 23 (1): 73–87.

Constable, N. (2004) 'Changing Filipina identities and ambivalent returns', in L. D. Long and E. Oxfeld (eds) *Coming Home? Refugees, migrants, and those who stayed behind*, Philadelphia: University of Pennsylvania Press.

FOKER (2005) *Problems Faced by Indonesian Migrant Domestic Workers in Singapore: data and facts*, prepared by A. S. Wisnuwardani, A. B. Buntoro, Mulyadi and S. Palupi, Jakarta: Working Forum for the Justice of Migrant Domestic Workers and Institute for Ecosoc Rights.

Hugo, G. (1995) 'International labor migration and the family: some observations from Indonesia', *Asian and Pacific Migration Journal*, 4 (2–3): 273–304.

—— (2002) 'Women's international labour migration', in K. Robinson and S. Bessell (eds) *Women in Indonesia: gender, equity and development*, Singapore: Institute of Southeast Asian Studies.

214   *Rosslyn von der Borch*

Human Rights Watch (2005) *Maid to Order: ending abuses against migrant domestic workers in Singapore*, Report No. 17, New York: Human Rights Watch.

Margold, J. A. (2004) 'Filipina depictions of migrant life for their kin at home', in L. D. Long and E. Oxfeld (eds) *Coming Home? Refugees, migrants, and those who stayed behind*, Philadelphia: University of Pennsylvania Press.

Parrenas, R. S. (2001) *Servants of Globalization: women, migration, and domestic work*, Stanford, CA: Stanford University Press.

Pinches, M. (1992) 'The working class experience of shame, inequality and people power in Tatalon, Manila', in B. Kerkvliet and R. B. Mojares (eds) *From Marcos to Aquino: local perspectives on political transition*, Honolulu: University of Hawaii Press.

Sampang, C. (2005) *Maid in Singapore*, Singapore: Marshall Cavendish.

Widyawati, R. (2005) *Catatan Harian Seorang Pramuwisma*, Surabaya: Jawa Pos Books.

Yeoh, B. and Huang, S. (1999) 'Spaces at the margins: migrant domestic workers and the development of civil society in Singapore', *Environment and Planning A*, 31 (7): 1149–67.

—— and —— (2000) 'Home and away: foreign domestic workers and the negotiations of diasporic identity in Singapore', *Women's Studies International Forum*, 23 (4): 413–29.

Index

Printed in the United States
by Baker & Taylor Publisher Services